A Sustainable Future

12 Key Areas of Global Concern

Edited by Klaus Wiegandt

'Our future is not predetermined. We ourselves shape it through our action.'

Klaus Wiegandt

First published in Great Britain in 2017 by
Haus Publishing Limited
70 Cadogan Place
London SW1X 9AH

Published in agreement with the Stiftung Forum für Verantwortung

First published in Germany in 2016 by S. Fischer Verlag as
Mut zur Nachhaltigkeit: 12 Wege in die Zukunft

ISBN 978-1-910376-73-7
eISBN 978-1-910376-74-4

Printed in the Czech Republic via Akcent Media Limited

Typeset in Garamond by MacGuru Ltd

www.hauspublishing.com

Dedicated to our grandchildren Livia, Timm, and Theo, representative of all children throughout the world.

Contents

Foreword

Klaus Wiegandt

As a former executive of a major corporation, I turned my attention to sustainability late in life, and my commitment has less to do with a key moment. Instead, in the mid-1990s my intellect and my gut feeling signalled to me: this insatiable resource and energy consumption with its consequences for the environment on a planet with limited resources is irresponsible with a view to future generations. So when I retired, I began to delve into the scientific literature on important questions concerning sustainability, and I came to the decision to devote myself to these topics, mostly through my foundation Forum für Verantwortung (Forum for Responsibility), which I established in the year 2000.[1]

I was further encouraged by the then largest and most comprehensive stocktaking effort on sustainability: the Millennium Ecosystem Assessment, published by the UN in 2005. Over a period of five years, more than 1,000 scientists had compiled the state of knowledge on various areas of sustainability. The findings could not have been more shocking. All the important developments on the globe were going in the wrong direction: the global population, resource and energy consumption, rising greenhouse gas emissions, the state of the oceans, and – both between states and within individual countries – an increasing gap between rich and poor.

I was very sceptical about the prospects for scientists, environmental activists, and NGOs to successfully induce the political

---

1   www.forum-fuer-verantwortung.de

community to put in place the necessary underlying conditions for a change of direction through environmental summits and resolutions within the UN framework. For example, internalisation of costs or artificial increases of energy prices would have resulted in the responsible politicians quickly being voted out of office. In democracies, one cannot and must not expect that politicians will be willing to accept that consequence in return for taking action. In addition, a change of direction would have required, and still does require, every individual to contribute in his/her role both as a consumer and as a citizen. To this day broad strata of the population have little understanding and insight about necessary steps toward society becoming sustainable.

So I decided to set the course for my small foundation to make a contribution toward a scientifically conducted discourse about sustainability with and in civil society. The goal is to empower individuals to make their contributions toward sustainable development both as consumers and as citizens.

I knew from my own experience that there was a plethora of literature on sustainability topics, but it was written by scientists for scientists and not for interested citizens. In a first step, I published twelve books on sustainability in which scientists laid out the current state of research in their fields, as well as options for action in a style comprehensible to a general reader. The book series was released in German by Fischer Taschenbuch Verlag in 2007. One year later, it was published in the United Kingdom in English translation. Some of the books were also translated into Japanese, Chinese, Korean, and Arabic.

In a second important step, I joined forces with the ASKO EUROPA-STIFTUNG and the European Academy of Otzenhausen to establish the educational initiative Encouraging Sustainability. Its goal is to make knowledge about sustainability's complex interdependencies accessible to broad circles of civil society and the business community, beyond those studying it scientifically. On this basis, it hopes to encourage people to deal responsibly with the resources supporting our lives.

We commissioned the Wuppertal Institute for Climate, Environment and Energy to develop didactic modules on the topics 'sustainable development', 'resources/energy', 'consumption', 'climate/oceans', 'water/food/population', and 'the economic system/the new world order' on the basis of the book series. The modules are designed to support teachers and disseminators imparting knowledge about sustainability to participants in various training and continuing educational situations, especially in seminars and workshops. In combination with the books, this created a scientific and comprehensible foundation for seminars, workshops, two audiobooks, and a large number of lectures and articles in newspapers and magazines.

Fixed features in our foundation's annual calendar of events have included the colloquium for early-career scholars 'Pathways out of growth-driven society' in Otzenhausen since 2011 and the 'ZEIT WISSEN Award Encouraging Sustainability' conference in Hamburg since 2012. The award honours initiatives from the business and scientific communities that make outstanding contributions to the future of our society in the field of sustainable development by generating and applying new, exemplary concepts.[2]

Even though some of the volumes have been revised for new editions, our twelve-volume book series on the future of the Earth no longer reflects the most current scientific knowledge; the purpose of the present volume is to provide an update describing the developments of the past ten years.

The contributions are intended both to introduce new readers to the topics in question and to update readers who are already

---

2   For more information about the foundation's activities, see: Forum für Verantwortung, 15 years. *From evolution to sustainability 2000–2015*. Seeheim-Jugenheim, 2015.

well informed. Since, in the final analysis, this is about what each of us has to do, I conclude this book with a wake-up call to mobilise civil society.

Last, but not least, I would like to document the following for our grandchildren Livia, Timm, and Theo, as representatives of the roughly 2.5 billion people under 20 today, for later historical scholarship: in the future, no present-day policy maker will be in a position to justify their actions by asserting that the extent and severity of the consequences of unchecked climate change were unknown.

Policy makers are failing to do justice to their responsibility for climate mitigation today because they have only a superficial understanding of the complex subject matter and because they understandably fear being voted out of office in the next democratic elections if they put the decisive underlying conditions in place.

However, politicians have also done little in the past decades to inform about the essential changes to our economy's wasteful production processes. Though millions of citizens are working in the most varied areas towards a sustainable world of tomorrow and are a reason for hope, they are not networked at national or international levels, and they are still a minority which politicians can ignore without fear.

These progressive forces must network nationally and internationally under the umbrella of climate mitigation. Their activities must clearly focus on mobilising millions more citizens for climate mitigation. Only if efforts are successful to set a constantly growing mass protest movement in motion will it become possible to set the course over the next 15 years toward slowing down climate change.

In my opinion, this is the most promising way to enable our grandchildren and their descendants to live tolerable lives in dignity on this planet.

Acknowledgements

I owe a great debt of gratitude to all the authors who immediately agreed to collaborate on this volume despite the tight time frame I proposed.

I would like to include in these thanks all staff members of the foundation, especially Dr. Hannes Petrischak and Annette Maas, who contributed to planning this volume and making it a reality. We reached the decision not to update the entire series, but to add this volume after stimulating and constructive discussions with Wolfram Huncke, who has always supported me as an excellent adviser. And in this context, I would also like to thank my two colleagues Arno Krause and Klaus-Peter Beck, without whose support, especially financial, the initiative Encouraging Sustainability would never have attained such a large sphere of engagement. Thanks are likewise due my foundation's Association of Friends, for it would be impossible to realise such ambitious book projects in the absence of unreserved, and not only financial, encouragement from its members.

Last, but not least, many thanks to our experienced editor Ulrike Holler, who has been involved in all our book projects from the beginning and without whose drive and gracious perseverance it would not have been possible to produce this volume.

Klaus Wiegandt
Seeheim-Jugenheim, June 2016

Our planet: how much more can Earth take?

Jill Jäger, Ines Omann, Fritz Hinterberger

Introduction

In 2007, we wrote the book *Our Planet: How Much More Can Earth Take?* because the situation on our planet was much more serious than many people believed. We also wanted to point out good options for action. Here, we would mainly like to present new questions, insights, challenges, and ideas that have become more important in the past ten years. In the introduction, we answer a number of questions that show what we believe is key, as we did in the 2007 book.

1. What does global change hold in store?
The term 'global change' describes the profound changes in the environment that have been observed in the past years and decades: climate change, desertification, species extinction, etc. The transformation of the environment, but also of society, accelerated dramatically in the second half of the twentieth century. In recent years, scientists have been able to show that some changes are already so serious that they may pose a significant risk for the development of society (see section 'Global transformation').

2. Is the situation really so dramatic, or do we still have time to act?
The situation is dramatic for three reasons in particular: most factors relevant to environmental changes (such as economic development, consumption in industrialised countries, the size of the global population, resource and energy consumption) are

still seeing unchecked growth. The governments of the world have agreed to both climate goals and sustainability goals in recent years. It is urgently necessary to take the implementation of measures seriously in order to reach these goals (see section 'Global transformation').

3. What are the driving forces for environmental changes?
Human activities are the strongest forces driving global change. Consumption of natural resources is affected by agriculture, food production, industry, energy supply, urbanisation, transportation, tourism, and international trade. These activities alter the composition of the atmosphere, the characteristics of the Earth's surface, biodiversity, the global climate, and the ocean currents (see section 'Global transformation').

4. By how much do we have to reduce resource consumption?
It is true that in the past 30 years, many countries have achieved relative improvements in efficient use of raw materials. Globally speaking, humankind creates approximately 40% more economic value from one ton of raw material than just 30 years ago. Yet these improvements have not been able to balance out the increase in the amount of resources consumed. The global economy is growing, and therefore we are also producing and consuming more and more. That is why efficiency gains are more than compensated for by economic growth. Human activities consume natural capital 1.5 times as quickly as nature can renew it. In 2013, approximately 85 billion tons of material, including biomass, were extracted and used globally. In addition, 50 billion tons were extracted, but not used. In other words, a total of 135 billion tons. Recent studies show that material extraction should not exceed 45 billion tons if we are to remain within the boundaries of a safe operating space for humanity. At the global level, this would mean a total reduction of material consumption by more than 60% (see section 'Resource consumption').

5. What kind of transformation do we need?

We are in a situation of multiple crises, accompanied by profound transformation processes that are occurring more quickly and more intensively than ever before. That is why humankind is confronted with major challenges. How can we meet these challenges? By negating them and continuing as before, or by acknowledging them and the transformation dynamics they entail? If we opt to acknowledge them, there are again two options: either we let this transformation just happen, risking a 'change by disaster', or we decide to shape the transformation: 'change by design'. Can the current situation of multiple crises be seen and used as an opportunity for a holistically designed transformation? In this respect, implementing the guiding principle of 'sustainability' also involves a fundamental transformation of our present-day consumption, production, and decision-making patterns (see section 'What type of transformation do we need?').

6. What can we do?

The transformation to a more sustainable world can be achieved only by a radical change in thinking in the political and business communities as well as in society in general. It will have to be accompanied by organised and moderated processes, whereby all actors (the political, business, and scientific communities and civil society) jointly develop visions of a sustainable world, jointly decide how their vision can be reached, and jointly develop, implement, and evaluate transformation paths. Transformation requires experimentation and learning processes. Even today, we can learn a lot from successful small-scale experiments and begin to shape a happy and resource-efficient world.

Global transformation

The Earth as a system – biophysical boundaries

In 2009, Johan Rockström, Director of the Stockholm Resilience Centre, and a large group of renowned scientists published a study clearly presenting the extent to which human activities have changed the Earth system. Rockström and his colleagues defined 'planetary boundaries'. Overstepping these boundaries has uncertain consequences and potentially causes greater and dramatic changes for humans and the environment. Boundaries for the following parts of the Earth system were determined on the basis of scientific work:

> climate change, ocean acidification, stratospheric ozone depletion, changes to the nitrogen and phosphorus cycles, global freshwater consumption, land-system changes, loss of biodiversity, atmospheric aerosol loading, and chemical pollution.

With the exception of the last two areas, for which it was not possible at the time to quantify the boundaries, the researchers determined those boundaries and examined whether or not they had been exceeded. They found that three boundaries had already been overstepped: climate change, loss of biodiversity, and changes to the nitrogen cycle. The authors emphasised that gaps in knowledge still existed and also that the boundaries were partly linked to other boundaries. In other words, if one boundary is exceeded, that might impact other boundaries. But nonetheless, this study shows that human development is in danger if these biophysical boundaries in the Earth system are ignored.

A new version of this study of the planetary boundaries was published in 2015. Will Steffen and his colleagues scrutinised the same processes in the Earth system, two of which have been renamed: 'loss of biodiversity' is now 'loss of biosphere integrity' to

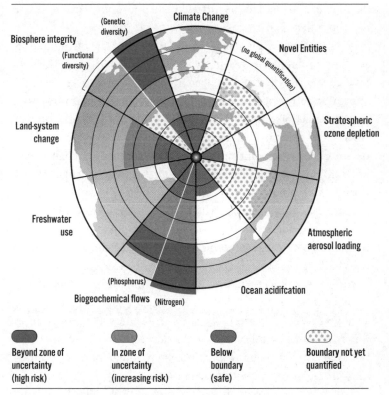

Fig. 1: Planetary boundaries. Source: Steffen et al. (2015a)

underline the influence of human activities on the entire function of ecosystems. 'Chemical pollution' was changed to 'introduction of novel entities' to reflect the fact that new technologies can have many different impacts.

The results of this study are summarised in Figure 1. Two boundaries have still not been quantified. The study also shows where uncertainties remain. Four boundaries have already been exceeded: climate change, loss of biosphere integrity, land-system change, and changes to the nitrogen and phosphorus cycles. These four boundaries are discussed below.

The analysis of planetary boundaries is based on numerous studies conducted in recent years. It is founded upon the fact that the Earth system has been relatively stable over the past approximately 11,700 years, the Holocene period, permitting the development of agriculture, urbanisation, and complex human societies. If human activities destabilise this balance of the Holocene, then irreversible and sudden environmental changes are possible that cannot be predicted and that pose a danger to the future development for all creatures populating the planet.

Kate Rayworth (Rayworth, 2012) complemented these biophysical boundaries, which define a safe operating space for humanity, with socioeconomic aspects. This combination reflects the challenges of sustainable development more cohesively: it is necessary to respect the biophysical boundaries and simultaneously fight poverty and achieve a good quality of life for all. Figure 2 shows this combination. The socioeconomic aspects provide an inner boundary, while the biophysical processes show the outer boundary. In between is a space in which humankind can flourish in a safe environment with social justice.

Is it possible to remain within the ring? Would eliminating poverty not necessarily entail overstepping the biophysical boundaries? Rayworth answers these questions with a clear 'No!' For instance, she shows that the additional calories required for the 13% of the global population suffering hunger today account for just 1% of current global food supply. Electricity supply for the 19% of the population who have no electricity today would increase global CO_2 emissions by only 1%, according to Rayworth. The greatest stress for the planetary boundaries today is the consumption by the richest 10% of society and the production patterns it entails. Roughly half of CO_2 emissions are produced by just 1% of the global population. 33% of the global sustainable nitrogen

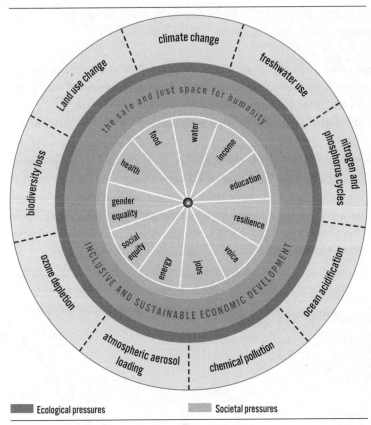

Fig. 2: The combination of planetary and socioeconomic boundaries.
Source: Rayworth (2012)

budget is used for meat production in Europe – and Europe accounts for just 7% of the global population.

The four planetary boundaries which have already been exceeded

Climate

As described in detail in our 2007 book, climate change is considered the most important environmental problem of the future by far. Since 2007, the state of knowledge and climate policy have developed further (see the contribution by Mojib Latif in this volume).

The year 2015 was the warmest since 1880 (Fig. 3). Temperature data from NASA showed that the global average surface temperature in February 2016 was 1.35°C higher than the average temperature for that month in the period 1951–1980. Up till then, there had never been a 1.35°C increase from one year to the next. The previous record (1.15°C) was achieved in January 2016.

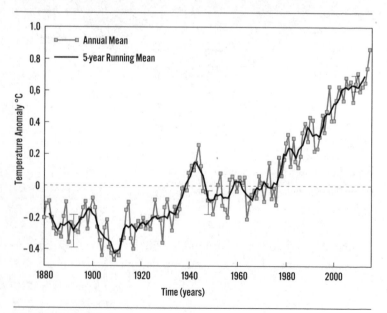

Fig. 3: NASA's Global Land-Ocean Temperature Index (1880–2015). Source: http://data.giss.nasa.gov/gistemp/graphs_v3/

In 2013 and 2014, the Intergovernmental Panel on Climate Change (IPCC) published its Fifth Assessment Report. It was reported that the warming of the Earth can be seen distinctly and that it is 'extremely likely' that human activities are the main cause of the observed warming since the mid-twentieth century. Changes of the global water cycle, melting of snow and ice, rise of the average global sea level, and some changes in extreme weather and climate events have already been observed.

The IPCC Assessment Report underlines that the climate changes of recent decades have had significant consequences for the environment and human beings. Sensitive ecosystems such as coral reefs or the Arctic are already manifesting the consequences of climate change. Wheat and corn yields, important food staples, are suffering overwhelmingly negative impacts, and water resources in many regions are being harmed.

What form could future developments take? New climate and socioeconomic scenarios were constructed to answer this question. There are a large number of possible scenarios because both socioeconomic development and future climate policy measures can impact greenhouse gas emissions. Accordingly, these scenarios show that the average global surface temperature will rise by 0.9°C to 5.4°C by the end of the century compared with pre-industrial levels. These values are of course subject to some uncertainties.

In the discussion about future climate change, one very important question concerns the maximum amount of greenhouse gases that can still be emitted in line with the goal of seeking to prevent dangerous global warming. The IPCC states that cumulative CO_2 emissions, that is, the total emissions since the beginning of industrialisation, largely determine the average global warming of the Earth's surface in this century. If average global warming must be limited to less than 2°C with a probability of more than 66%, then cumulative CO_2 emissions since 1870 must be limited to approximately 2,900 Gt CO_2. Roughly two-thirds of this amount had already been emitted by 2001. So if warming is to be kept below 2°C, we can only emit about another 1,000 Gt of CO_2.

Climate change therefore remains a major challenge. The risks and costs are increasing. It will hardly be possible to increase greenhouse gas emissions in the future without major consequences for society and the environment.

In December 2009, the 15th Conference of the Parties to the United Nations Framework Convention on Climate Change (UNFCCC) took place in Copenhagen. The goal was for the signatories to agree to a new set of rules for climate mitigation after the expiration of the Kyoto Protocol in 2012. But it proved impossible to adopt a treaty in Copenhagen. Only three years later, at the 18th UNFCCC conference in Doha in 2012, was it decided to continue Kyoto II for the period 2013 to 2020. After that, further negotiations focused on the period after 2020. At the 21st UNFCCC conference in Paris in December 2015, the goal was to adopt a treaty for the period after 2020. After intensive preparation and, at times, tough negotiations, the Paris Agreement was accepted by 195 member states.

The Agreement asserts that global warming should not exceed 2°C compared with the pre-industrial period, and efforts are to be made to limit it to not more than 1.5°C. Another goal is to reach a balance between greenhouse gas emissions caused by human activities and CO_2 sequestration. CO_2 sequestration occurs through natural or technological processes. In advance of the conference in Paris, 186 states submitted voluntary national climate goals. But these voluntary objectives will not be enough to limit the temperature increase to less than 2°C. From 2023 on, the goals will be reviewed and potentially enhanced every five years. However, some scientists think that reviewing and enhancing the goals in the second half of the next decade will be much too late if the 2°C target is to be reached.

Many hailed the Paris Agreement as a success and as a signal that the climate problem is being taken seriously, and that it was possible to reach an international agreement. But others are not so happy. In the case of voluntary commitments, there are no sanctions if a country does not reach the goal it set for itself. The words 'fossil fuels' are not even mentioned in the Agreement. Some scientists doubt that it is even still possible to limit warming to not more than 1.5°C and emphasise that reaching this goal requires rapid and sweeping changes in the economic system with major societal impacts.

The integrity of the biosphere
The destruction of ecosystems reduces nature's ability to support human societies. Ecosystems provide a number of services such as pollinating fruit trees, cleaning water, and providing culturally important landscapes.

In 2001, the European Union set itself the ambitious goal of halting biodiversity losses by 2010. Biodiversity encompasses the diversity within species (genetic variation), the wealth of species, and the diversity of ecosystems. When, after 2010, the European Environment Agency showed clearly that the target had been missed, a new vision and a new goal were prepared.

The vision:
In the European Union, biological diversity and ecosystem services provided by it will be protected, valued, and restored in an appropriate way by 2050. Biodiversity furnishes a necessary contribution to human beings' quality of life and economic well-being. Catastrophic changes caused by the loss of biodiversity must be prevented.

The goal:
The loss of biodiversity and the destruction of ecosystem services will be halted in the European Union by 2020; biodiversity and

ecosystem services will be restored to the maximum extent possible, while the EU's contribution to preventing global losses of biodiversity will be increased.

As the European Environment Agency showed in 2015, this goal is again very ambitious and remains an enormous challenge. In 2015, 60% of the evaluations of species and 77% of the evaluations of habitats in Europe had non-satisfactory results.

As explained in more detail in the chapter by Josef H. Reichholf in this volume, biodiversity is under threat owing to multiple factors: the spreading of invasive alien species, climate change, pollution, over-fertilisation, and changes of habitats. This is a result of numerous indirect factors such as demographic changes, economic interests, and societal patterns of consumption. According to the OECD (Organisation for Economic Co-operation and Development), these direct and indirect threats to biodiversity will continue

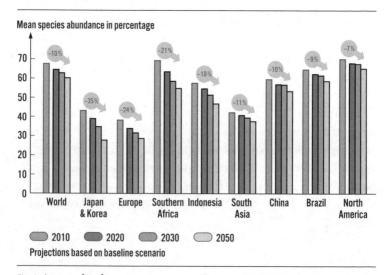

Fig. 4: Average biodiversity, 2010–2050. Source: OECD Environmental Outlook to 2050

to exert pressure on biodiversity. Figure 4 shows the results of an OECD study illustrating that biodiversity will continue to be lost in all regions through to 2050 if countermeasures are not taken.

The boundary concerning the integrity of the biosphere has already been overstepped. How could the loss of biodiversity and the destruction of ecosystems be reversed? One proposal came from an international study in 2010 (TEEB 2010): we must measure and pay for the contribution of biodiversity and ecosystem services to human beings' quality of life. In other words, it is about the value of nature and how we valuate it! The advantages of protecting ecosystems and their services are often much greater than the costs, but the market system rarely considers the entirety of the social and economic values provided by ecosystem services.

Changes to the nitrogen and phosphorus cycles

Human activities have drastically impacted the nitrogen and phosphorus cycles. The main causes are the production and application of fertilisers. Human activities are transforming more atmospheric nitrogen into forms of reactive nitrogen than all terrestrial processes combined. This reactive nitrogen is usually emitted into the atmosphere and is not taken up by plants. If it is washed out by rain, it pollutes rivers, lakes, and coastal waters, or it accumulates in the biosphere. Large amounts of phosphorus are also not taken up by plants and accumulate in water bodies, resulting in frequent algae blooms that use up the oxygen in the water.

The planetary boundary for phosphorus was set by Rockström and colleagues so that a large-scale loss of oxygen ('anoxic event') in the ocean can be prevented. The flow of phosphorus into the oceans is to be less than 11 Tg P per year. Steffen and colleagues calculate that more than 14 Tg P per year are applied to agricultural land as fertiliser. The boundary for nitrogen is based on detailed scientific studies and was set at 62 Tg N per year. This boundary is exceeded by agriculture in North America, Europe, India, and East Asia.

Risk to forested land

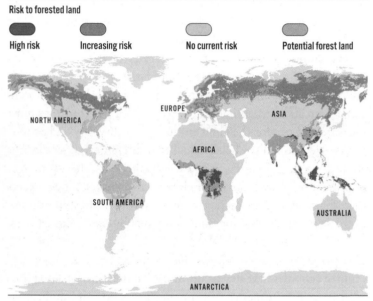

High risk   Increasing risk   No current risk   Potential forest land

Fig. 5: Changes in forest area. Source: Steffen et al. (2015a)

Land-system changes

The land surface has been and is being changed in many parts of the Earth. Forests, pastureland, and wet meadows are converted for agriculture or urban development. The changes have major consequences for other biophysical boundaries such as the integrity of the biosphere or the water cycle. Steffen and colleagues developed a new method to assess land-system changes. Whereas Rockström and colleagues used agricultural land, the new studies analysed the remaining forest area. It was argued that forest area is much more important in the interaction between land surface and climate. So the planetary boundary is reached when the forest area in the tropical and boreal latitudes is less than 85% of the potential area, and the boundary in the mid-latitudes is 50% of the potential area. The forests in the mid-latitudes have less impact on the global climate. Figure 5 shows where this planetary boundary has already been overstepped and where the greatest risks lie. According to Figure 5, the boundary has been exceeded in the tropical forests of Africa and Southeast Asia, while the risk of overstepping the boundary is increasing in the boreal forests of the Northern Hemisphere.

The causes of global change

In the 2007 book, we described the causes in detail and emphasised the impacts of human economic activities, which have been increasing constantly since the Industrial Revolution. We used charts to show how human activities have accelerated extremely quickly, especially since 1950. These trends have now been described for a further ten years. W. Steffen and colleagues show that the 'great acceleration' is continuing. The trends for global regions are interesting. For instance, the global population is continuing to grow, but most of the growth is taking place in non-OECD countries. This is contrasted by the fact that the growth of the global economy (GDP) and thus of consumption is taking place mostly in OECD countries. Some indicators of the state of the Earth system were found to be growing more slowly (atmospheric methane concentration) or have stabilised (stratospheric ozone concentration).

Since the economic crisis of 2009, global economic growth has been significantly weaker than before, and there is no reason to assume that this will change in the coming decades. Although this diminishes the annual intensification of pressure on the environment, it does not reduce the pressure itself, which is continuing to grow – albeit less strongly.

Europe reduced its greenhouse gas emissions by approximately 23% between 1990 and 2014. Global emissions from fossil fuels and industry increased by 0.6% in 2014, but projections showed a reduction in 2015. The strong upward trend with growth rates of 2.4% between 2005 and 2015 seems to have been broken. The main reason for this is that China is using less coal and significantly more renewables.

The global population is continuing to grow, and the projections are updated regularly. The number of people on Earth has more than doubled since the 1960s to more than 7 billion in 2013. The United Nations projections show that population growth is slowing and that the mean value for the year 2050 is 9.6 billion. This number will continue to be highly dependent on which measures are implemented. If investments are made in education and health and in strengthening the role of women, the birth rate will decline. Population growth is taking place mostly in developing countries; in contrast, in some regions, the population is decreasing, e.g., in the Caribbean, Japan, Russia, and Latin America.

As we described in the 2007 book, the Millennium Development Goals (MDG) were adopted at the Millennium Session of the United Nations in New York in 2000 and were to be reached by 2015. Goal 2 was to achieve universal primary education: '... children everywhere, boys and girls alike, will be able to complete a full course of primary schooling.' This goal is very important for reducing the birth rate in the future. In 2015, the United Nations published the MDG results. In 2000, 83% of children in developing countries were enrolled in primary school; in 2015, 91%. The number of children of school age who do not go to school was cut by almost half during that period. There were significant improvements in sub-Saharan Africa: school enrollment was up by 20% from 2000 to 2015, compared with an 8% increase between 1990 and 2000. Also highly relevant for curbing population growth: the literacy rate of young people between 15 and 24 years of age rose from 83% to 91% between 1990 and 2015, and the gap between men and women decreased.

Sustainability goals

The series of UN conferences on sustainable development continued in 2012. After the United Nations Conference on Environment and Development in Rio de Janeiro in 1992 and the subsequent conference in Johannesburg in 2002, the Rio+20 Conference took place in Rio de Janeiro in 2012.

The outcome document of the Rio+20 Conference, 'The Future We Want', includes many policy statements and reflects on the results of the previous conferences. It recognises that progress since the first conference in 1992 has been uneven. For this reason, it is necessary to do more to implement earlier commitments. The differences between industrialised and developing countries must also be reduced further. Three important goals in the Rio+20 outcome document are: poverty eradication; recognition and reaffirmation of the Rio principles agreed at the 1992 conference; and development of an economic system based on sustainable development and poverty eradication ('the green economy') in already existing environmental/sustainability strategies. Although the Rio+20 Conference made some steps in the right direction, for example strengthening the United Nations Environment Programme, many participants and observers were disappointed, thinking that the results were weak in light of the great challenges.

The Rio+20 Conference also underlined how important and useful sustainability goals are and culminated in a decision to establish a process in which governments as well as all other stakeholders would develop global sustainability goals. An Open Working Group on Sustainable Development Goals (OWG) was founded following the conference. After meeting many times, this group presented its proposal for 17 goals and 169 targets in July 2014. They were adopted by the United Nations as the global Sustainable Development Goals in September 2015 and are included in the 2030 Agenda for Sustainable Development.

The first seven goals correspond to the Millennium Development Goals: to end poverty (goal 1) and hunger (goal 2); and to achieve health (goal 3), education (goal 4), gender equality (goal 5), availability of water and sanitation (goal 6), and sustainable energy supply (goal 7). The primary economic goals formulated are to promote sustainable economic growth and decent work (goal 8) as well as resilient infrastructure and sustainable industrialisation (goal 9). The other goals are to: reduce inequality within and among countries (goal 10); create sustainable settlements (goal 11), sustainable consumption and production patterns (goal 12); combat climate change (goal 13); conserve the oceans (goal 14) and ecosystems and biodiversity (goal 15); as well as to guarantee peaceful and inclusive societies, access to justice, and effective institutions (goal 16). Goal 17, finally, is to strengthen the means of implementation and revitalise the Global Partnership for Sustainable Development.

What are the next steps after adoption of the goals and targets? How is implementation to be monitored? The United Nations appointed a 'high-level political forum' for this purpose. The signatories have committed to reaching the goals and submitting to periodic monitoring, but it has been emphasised time and again that implementation of the goals is a national matter. The high-level political forum will meet annually, but national reports on implementation of the goals are voluntary. Much work still remains to quantify the targets. In the absence of quantified goals, it is hardly possible to measure whether a goal has been reached or not.

From knowledge to action

In recent years, science has been able to specify the risks of global environmental changes. The necessity of a sustainable and climate-compatible future is increasingly recognised. At the same time, it is becoming clearer that this future can succeed only if the economic system and society are restructured. As the German Advisory Council on Global Change (WBGU) writes in its 2011 report, this restructuring amounts to a 'great transformation'. According to the WBGU, this means that production, consumption patterns, and lifestyles are changed in such a way that global greenhouse gas emissions can be reduced to an absolute minimum in the coming decades and climate-compatible societies can develop.

The WBGU concludes that this great transformation can succeed only with a new social contract. Humanity must take on collective responsibility to prevent dangerous climate change and other planetary risks. The new social contract is an agreement to change: it requires a culture of mindfulness (arising from ecological responsibility) combined with a culture of participation (as a democratic responsibility) as well as a culture of responsibility towards future generations (responsibility for the future). Both the state and society must act. We add more detail to the topic of transformation in the section 'What kind of transformation do we need?'

Resource consumption

Resource consumption and the planetary boundaries

Although a scientific depiction of the planetary boundaries is important and relevant, it is quite difficult to derive concrete recommendations for action and political measures from it that ensure that these boundaries are *not* overstepped. For this reason, work has been underway for several years to develop concrete indicators and to formulate goals for resource consumption as well as for individual economic activities. For it is always production and consumption that result in exceeding planetary resource consumption.

Rockström and colleagues themselves state that the 'knowledge gaps are disturbing' concerning the ability to identify concrete limit values for planetary boundaries. Scientific knowledge of many environmental impacts is not yet sufficient to permit us to formulate concrete targets or limit values, as was done for the climate change boundary (2°C goal), for example. Yet it is urgently necessary to formulate limit values, analyse risks and uncertainties, and identify planetary boundaries using the precautionary principle.

It is helpful to consider that all activities that bring us closer to overstepping the planetary boundaries have something to do with global resource consumption. For this reason, much work has been undertaken in recent years to propose goals for global resource consumption and to gather data that describe its development in relation to individual activities on the part of consumers and producers.

It builds on Rockström's and Steffen's concept of a 'safe operating space for humanity'. This concept sets out a framework within which our socioeconomic activities must take place so that the functioning of the Earth system and its ecological and societal subsystems are not harmed or even damaged irreparably.

That is why the following questions are key for operationalising the 'safe operating space' in the sense described above:

- What are the maximum amounts of materials than can be used to restore or maintain the equilibrium between ecological carrying capacity and human activities without damaging the functioning of the Earth system (irreparably)?
- When was the point in time (or the period of time) when the Earth system was still in equilibrium (before any boundaries had been exceeded, or when the ecological equilibrium was not yet in danger)?

By how much do we have to reduce?

In order to propose reduction factors and goals for the extraction, use (including production), and consumption of material resources, we must first calculate those amounts of materials that can be used *without* causing serious environmental impacts at the global level. Only in this way will it be possible to restore the Earth system to a condition that can still be called a 'safe' operating space.

The international community, national governments, and civil society became aware of the imbalance between the human need for resources and the ability of the ecosystem to regenerate as early as the start of the 1970s. From today's perspective, it is interesting to see that the relationship between human demand for natural resources and the ability of the ecosystem to produce biotic materials and to absorb wastes, but also to guarantee the ecosystem services provided by water and land, became disrupted just at that time. It is for this reason the year 1970 has been proposed as the latest point in time for determining those amounts of biotic and abiotic materials that can be extracted and consumed in the future without endangering the safe operating space for humanity.

In addition to all the resources used today for production and consumption, all the resources extracted, but not used, must also be taken into account. Why are they, too, relevant for global change? In the end, it is irrelevant to nature which benefits we humans derive from the enormous upheavals we cause in nature.

Both mining and harvesting renewable resources always also cause extractions of resources that ultimately remain unused, but that impact the ecological balances just like those used by human beings. This is also true of food production and for cultivation of energy crops and plants used as raw materials. It is true that renewable resources regenerate, but on a finite planet, they too are finite, and cultivating and harvesting them means intervening in nature (see section 'The integrity of the biosphere'). Nature cannot absorb such interventions if they are too intensive, which results in irreversible processes and ultimately in overstepping the planetary boundaries.

Every production process causes wastes. This ultimately means that resources that were extracted or harvested are not included in the final product. That is why we speak of (invisible) ecological rucksacks that every instance of production and consumption entails. Taking everything together, we speak of total material consumption (TMC).

TMC provides a more comprehensive image of the upstream materials streams as it also takes into account the unused fractions associated with imported products and the secondary materials used. (The latter permit inferences about the impacts of re-use, substitution of materials, or increased material efficiency.) As Krausmann and colleagues illustrated (2009), the environmental impact of extraction and use of construction minerals, for example, is usually indirect, and therefore still difficult to quantify, which is why cross-category goals are necessary as a first step. Even if no direct connection between the use of aggregates and environmental destruction has been scientifically confirmed, at least the size of the material flows and the composition of the materials can serve as proxy indicators for environmental pressure.

An estimated 40 to 60% unused material extraction must be added to these figures, since the relationship of unused to used material extraction will continue to worsen through to 2050 despite improved technologies. This is due mostly to the increasingly difficult access to the material deposits and the decreasing concentrations of metals, rare earths, etc. in the crude ores.

With this assumption and using 1970 as a reference year, this results in a limit of about 45 billion tons TMC. Global material extraction should not exceed roughly this figure if we are to remain within the boundaries of the safe operating space for humanity. At the global level, this would mean a total reduction of material consumption by about 65%, compared with the year 2008. Assuming a global population of approximately nine billion people in 2050, we can derive a relative goal of 5 tons TMC per person.

Similar goals can be derived for the resources water and land, for which planetary boundaries have also been discussed. Besides these overarching goals, the various geographical, socioeconomic, and climatic realities in the different countries and continents must be studied, and the differentiations already described must be translated into targets.

In 2013, the amount of material, including biomass, extracted and used globally was already up to approximately 85 billion tons.[1] Another 50 billion tons of material extracted, but not used, must be added, amounting to 60%, resulting in 135 billion tons as the total amount of material extracted by humans. In other words: 135,000,000,000,000 kilograms. That amounts to 18 tons per person per year or 50 kilograms per day of resource consumption caused by one dweller on planet Earth. The regional differences are enormous, ranging from 2.5 tons in Yemen or Rwanda to 12

---

1   www.materialflows.net

to 15 tons in Austria and Germany, and up to 21 tons in the US or 44 tons in Australia. These figures do not even include material extracted but not used, for which another 60% must be added to the figures given to estimate the total impact of our lifestyle.

If the global economy were to continue to grow at this rate (the 'business-as-usual' scenario) and emerging markets and threshold countries were to reach the same consumption levels as the rich countries, total global material consumption (including unused resources) would increase to 250–300 billion tons in 2050.

As early as 2011, the European Commission named in its 'Resource Efficiency Roadmap' materials, land, water, and greenhouse gases as those resources and environmental categories with which progress toward sustainability was to be measured.

The goal is to cover the main environmental categories so as to be able to derive directionally reliable quantitative statements for the most important ecological impacts of production and consumption. The main environmental categories (biotic and abiotic resources, water, land area, and air) determined by the OECD are taken into account. Inclusion of all these categories helps observers to perceive when environmental problems are merely shifted and to orient measures towards an accordingly comprehensive sustainability approach.

Five indicators can be derived from the five main environmental categories (see Fig. 6).

MAIN ENVIRONMENTAL CATEGORIES	Greenhouse gas emissions	Water	Land	Non-renewable resources	Renewable resources
INDICATORS	CO_2 footprint	Water rucksack	Real land use	Abiotic material rucksack	Biotic material rucksack

Fig. 6: Main environmental categories and indicators derived from them for formulating goals for global environmental consumption. Source: SERI

Schmidt-Bleek (see his contribution in this volume) and others proposed this magnitude, namely a 'factor 10', for the industrialised countries as the reduction of resource consumption necessary for global ecological equilibrium. This corresponds to a 90% reduction to one-tenth and also to the goal of 5 tons TMC per person per year formulated above. What matters is the absolute amount of resource consumption, not its relation to economic performance (measured as GDP) or per capita. It is irrelevant to nature how much utility we human beings gain from one kilogram or one ton of resources.

How should a reduction be realised?

Only when the order of magnitude of resource consumption and a goal (factor X) have been determined does the question arise how that reduction can be achieved. This goal already requires significant changes in all countries' economic activities, mostly however in the EU, the US, China, India, and Brazil.

Resource efficiency as called for by European and also national policies in many countries means producing more with a given amount of resources, or requiring a smaller amount of resources for a given amount of production. If we relate a country's resource consumption to its economic performance, i.e., its gross domestic product, this yields material or resource productivity. For example, if Germany's resource consumption is to be reduced to one-fifth by 2050 and its economic performance is to be doubled at the same time (which corresponds to 2% economic growth), each unit of gross domestic product must be generated with only one-tenth of today's resource consumption in 2050. In other words: it must entail a significant increase of material productivity. This is also called (relative) decoupling of resource consumption from economic performance, an important economic indicator. In other words, economic growth eats up efficiency gains.

That is why there have been many discussions in recent years whether an increase in the efficiency of economic production is sufficient for the environmental protection required or whether a significant amount of sufficiency is also needed. 'Sufficiency' means that an increase in the quality of life may entail not only lower resource consumption, but also lower per capita income. Many studies show that economic growth in the rich parts of Earth, for example in Western Europe, the US, or Japan, results in hardly any increases of quality of life and that the low growth that is still possible is concentrated among the top few per cent of the wealthy. The most recent studies (see the contribution by Bernd Meyer in this volume) also provide evidence for the fact that jobs tend to be created when individuals work less and gainful employment can be distributed among a larger number of people. This also corresponds to many people's wishes for more free time instead of higher pay; in Austria, the 'free time option' is already reflected in some collective bargaining agreements.

In light of the extent of the changes necessary for effectively preventing overstepping of the planetary boundaries, it quickly becomes clear that both efficiency *and* sufficiency are required.

Who has to do what?
In a complex society, we should not expect that simple solutions exist for reducing resource consumption. Instead, all societal actors are called on and able to contribute something to improve the situation described above: the business community, the political community, and each and every individual.

Entrepreneurs can contribute to making businesses and products more environmentally friendly (i.e., by using a smaller amount of resources) throughout their life cycles.

Citizens can question our consumption patterns and point out steps toward sustainability, and thereby animate other people to act sustainably. Politicians and voters can create the legal framework for sustainable production and consumption patterns and act sustainably to provide a good example. Scientists can give qualified, comprehensive answers to the major questions posed by consumers, entrepreneurs, and the political community, and highlight opportunities for sustainable development. Awareness-raising measures can take on a key role to reach resource goals – for each and every citizen, but also in the realm of business. In order to reduce the ecological rucksacks, it is necessary to consider the entire value-added chain: from extraction or harvest of resources, to production and transport, to use and later disposal or recycling of the products.

And a third criterion besides efficiency and sufficiency is (again) becoming more important, namely 'consistency'. Consistency is the qualitative compatibility of the remaining (reduced) material flows with the natural cycles. The materials used are to be produced in a way that is entirely nontoxic for humans and the environment, and they are to be used in a way that does not cause any irreversible changes of biological processes or health. This applies especially to many chemicals, hormones, medications, and microparticles.

The following 'hot spots' can be detected in the individual sections of these value-added chains:

- The material used should have a small 'rucksack', be lightweight, separable, renewable, recyclable, and biodegradable.
- In their use phase, products are to be durable, robust, adaptable, and multipurpose.
- This also places special demands on their design (functional, timeless, adaptable, modular, original).
- It should be possible (technically and from an organisational and economic point of view) to repair and upgrade technology.

- Regions play important roles in this context when it comes to closing cycles of materials, products, and services.
- Finally, new markets for first-, second- (and third- and fourth-) hand products and services are needed, and they are emerging today in many places.

In terms of actors, the following options can be identified:

- Mining/cultivation: more efficient extraction/harvesting
- Manufacturers of upstream products: recycling, bio-economy
- Producers: re-manufacturing, reference to needs
- Service providers: re-use, cascades
- Users/consumers: repairs, cascades

The globalised world economy is characterised by increasing differences in per capita resource consumption. Rising emerging economies such as China or Brazil with their strong growth dynamics are approaching the consistently high consumption levels of the rich industrialised nations.

Many scientists are also expressing considerable doubts whether all countries of the world will be able to achieve 'green' growth as discussed in the concept of the 'Green Economy', for our current economic system is still too highly dependent on inputs of natural resources. It is true, however, that many countries have achieved relative improvements in efficient use of raw materials over the past 30 years. Globally speaking, humankind creates approximately 40% more economic value from one ton of raw material than just 30 years ago.

Yet these improvements have not been able to balance out the increase in the amount of resources consumed. The global economy is growing, and therefore we are also producing and consuming more and more. Efficiency gains are more than compensated by economic growth. This burgeoning hunger for resources brings

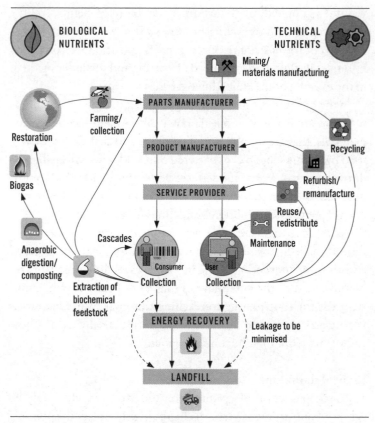

BIOLOGICAL NUTRIENTS

TECHNICAL NUTRIENTS

Mining/ materials manufacturing

PARTS MANUFACTURER

Farming/ collection

Restoration

PRODUCT MANUFACTURER

Recycling

Biogas

SERVICE PROVIDER

Refurbish/ remanufacture

Reuse/ redistribute

Anaerobic digestion/ composting

Cascades

Maintenance

Extraction of biochemical feedstock

Consumer

Collection

User

Collection

ENERGY RECOVERY

Leakage to be minimised

LANDFILL

Fig. 7: The circular economy – an industrial system that is restorative by design. Source: The Ellen MacArthur Foundation (2013). *Towards the circular economy: Economic and business rationale for an accelerated transition*

about social and ecological conflicts, especially when the true costs of the rising demand for increasingly scarce resources are 'exported' to other countries and regions of the world.

That is why resources that have been 'acquired' and are thus already available should be used in a more rational and sustainable way, for example through investments in more efficient recycling, downcycling, and upcycling processes. This would make it possible to cut the costs of resource imports and also to keep needed resources in closed cycles instead of wasting and squandering them at the expense of the exporting countries.

In the future, our economy must specialise in high-quality products that are made of domestic raw materials and secondary raw materials, that are durable and repairable, and that can be shared, used by multiple people, or bartered or resold. This will enable the development of a new, modern service sector in addition to production. The concept of the 'circular economy', which the EU has taken up, provides important guidelines for this process.

All these changes are necessary, but by no means sufficient conditions for reducing resource consumption to the extent required and thus for preventing humanity from exceeding the planetary boundaries. But the good news is that a multitude of opportunities exist for contributing to reaching this goal. What matters is that efforts go beyond small steps; we must radically rethink how to live and work together on our planet.

Radical rethinking
A drastic reduction of resource consumption can ultimately be achieved only through a radical change in thinking in the political and business communities and in society in general. Long-term political targets for the development of the global community in the coming decades are needed; processes such as 'A resource-efficient Europe – Flagship initiative under the Europe 2020 Strategy' initiated by the European Union are already working on determining such target values. Waste management and the circular economy can make important contributions here, but must be viewed in a larger context. Resource consumption must be reduced dramatically in absolute numbers if we are to avoid overstepping the planetary boundaries.

What kind of transformation do we need?

Introduction

The change or transformation we are already beginning to experience today is often called 'great'. The term 'great transformation' goes back to Karl Polanyi's *Great Transformation* (1944), a work published following the end of two world wars and a long economic crisis. Polanyi describes two parallel transformations: one is the consequences of the long economic crisis and bloody war as well as the emergence of a social market economy and welfare capitalism. The other is the transition from an agrarian to an industrial society, which he sees as a great transformation in which economic growth and technological progress increase substantially.[2]

The current-day transformation could be one from a neoliberal 'fossil society' to a post-fossil or sustainable society which no longer centres around economic growth, or rather: which must not centre around economic growth any longer.[3] This transformation requires fundamental changes from the individual level (lifestyles) to forms of work, economic activity, and production, to a transformation of institutions and values. Representatives of the various schools of transformation characterise it as a radical systemic change. As shown in the section 'Global transformation', we can now detect features of a crisis. The financial and banking crisis of 2008 gave us an indication of what is to come. Unfortunately, it seems we did not learn much from that experience; the opportunity for radical change was not taken, in financial market regulation, in a restructuring of the tax system, or in a redefinition of work.

And yet: old structures are breaking open, and new ones are not yet to be seen, or only in a few places. Major uncertainties exist in civil society, but also among those politically responsible.

2   Novy (2015)
3   WBGU (2011)

The dominance of the West and the view of it as an ideal are increasingly being challenged, not least because our lifestyle is not transferable to the whole world; the resources (materials, energy, land, and water) are simply not available, and the side effects would be catastrophic not only for future generations, but would be perceptible even by today's generation, at least in disadvantaged regions (extreme events, poverty ...).

This raises the question: Can the current situation of multiple crises be seen and used as an opportunity for a holistic transformation?

In this section, we point out some approaches on the basis of research and practical experience. Before we do so, we would like to examine where this journey should take us and what the goal of this transformation is; it has already begun, and we would like to be involved in shaping it.

In the Brundtlandian sense, 'sustainable development' means development that permits all people alive today to satisfy their needs and thus enjoy a high level of well-being within the planetary boundaries, so that future generations can also satisfy their needs with a certain freedom of choice. In other words, it means enabling a good life for all, whereby the objective conditions for a high quality of life are given, thus laying the foundation for subjective well-being. All people should be given the same opportunities to shape their lives as they like and to flourish on this basis (Sen). However, this cannot occur in unfettered freedom, but must take place within the planetary boundaries so that cross-generational justice can be guaranteed.

Of course, happiness cannot be regulated by law. Instead, the goal must be to create political, cultural, and economic underlying conditions that enable people to develop and to live out their individual happiness.

As Andreas Novy (2013) says, the good life for all can drive a European development model for the twenty-first century if the goal is to transform the European welfare model in an ecologically and socially sensitive way. Ultimately, it should be a model for the whole world.

Various politically legitimated commissions have recently committed to the goal of a good life for all, including the Stiglitz-Sen-Fitoussi Commission (Commission on the Measurement of Economic Performance and Social Progress) appointed by Sarkozy in France in 2008, the Advisory Council on Global Change (WBGU) and the Bundestag Committee of Inquiry 'Growth, Prosperity, Quality of Life' (late 2010 through to April 2013) in Germany, or the Beyond GDP debate initiated by the European Commission in 2009.

The Stiglitz-Sen-Fitoussi Commission was formed to examine how national prosperity and social progress can be measured without relying on GDP as an indicator. Twelve recommendations centring around the topics of classic measurement of domestic product, quality of life, and sustainability were made, such as paying more attention to the distribution of income, wealth, and consumption. Health, political voice, and social connections and relationships as well as opportunities for all to develop human capabilities are considered to be relevant dimensions for quality of life besides the material standard of living.

The Committee of Inquiry 'Growth, Prosperity, Quality of Life' focused on the question: 'How can societal prosperity, individual well-being, and sustainable development be defined and modelled appropriately in a society in light of the fact that focusing on growth of gross domestic product (GDP) is no longer sufficient?' In other words, its remit was also to develop a new, holistic indicator to replace GDP as the target dimension in the long term. The result was 10 guiding indicators in three areas: material prosperity, social affairs and participation, and ecology.

Additional important questions included: Do limits to growth exist, and how will Germany handle potentially lower growth rates in the coming decades? Concrete options for action were also to be defined. The parties reached the consensus that resource consumption must be reduced and that technical innovations were insufficient to guarantee a high quality of life for all. But they did not agree about the question of whether economic growth was the solution; commission members even said that this question and the question about drivers of economic growth were sidestepped, and that there was neither a clarification of an up-to-date concept of prosperity nor sufficient discussion about social policy. For example, following the Beyond GDP initiative launched jointly by the OECD, the EU Commission, the Club of Rome, and other organisations, the OECD developed the Better Life Index, which describes the quality of life in all of its member states very comprehensively.

All these movements originated from the conviction that contentment and a high quality of life can no longer be generated (solely) through economic growth, but that other criteria focusing on the good life for all are necessary.

Transformation and research

The last ten to twenty years have seen the development of various schools of transformation research that attempt to understand the transformation holistically and also to promote it. Two of them have become established in the German-speaking countries: the Vienna School, represented above all by the Institute of Social Ecology, and the Frankfurt School of the ISOE (Institute for Social-Ecological Research).

The Vienna School of Social-Ecological Research (main proponents: Fischer-Kowalski, Haberl) focuses on the explanation and (historical) analysis of socio-metabolic transitions across long time scales. The object of research is the socio-metabolic system, which interacts with its natural environment and co-evolves with it, in other words, which is dependent on it for its development. A great transition is necessary which moves from one dynamic state to another via a non-linear incremental path for society to reach a sustainable state. These changes encompass not only a change in the use of energy and resources, but also include the establishment of entirely new forms of societies.

The next great transition is necessary because our resources are finite, and it will presumably be messy. It is the energy system that is decisive for our society's socio-metabolism; that is why it must be changed, presumably from a fossil system to one combining solar with other renewable energy sources. This transition must entail major changes in our lifestyles, forms of working, and the economic system, and would involve the end of opportunities that capitalist economic growth has been offering. However, the current global transition is moving toward non-sustainability (two-thirds of all humans are undergoing a transition from the agrarian to the industrial system). In comparison, the sustainability transition in the global North that we are discussing is insignificant. As long as fossil resources can be burned, this will occur within the existing regimen. So this school has a more pessimistic view and gives little reason to hope for an imminent transition to a post-fossil, sustainable era.

The Frankfurt School of Social-Ecological Research (important proponents: Becker, Jahn) has more normative aspirations and focuses on the regulation of societal relationships with nature toward more sustainability. Such regulation can be more or less successful in terms of sustainability. The success of these societal relationships with nature is indispensable for the development and reproduction of individuals and society and thus also for a high quality of life. They involve human and social needs, such as availability of food, water, energy, housing, mobility, health, and education, and for this reason they should be regulated in a manner that enables individuals and societies to satisfy their needs. This reflects the idea of sustainable development. Regulation refers to satisfying needs at the individual level, but also at the meso level (institutions; organisations providing water, energy, and food; or the infrastructure necessary to do so, for example) and the macro level of societal structures and processes (ownership, production, gender relations). Social-ecological transformation means changing the forms and patterns of the regulation of the societal relationships with nature across time and space. These transformations can be evolutionary, or coordinated and intentional (change by design), but they often elude social control (change by disaster).

While these schools primarily work at the macro level and emphasise the societal, institutional, and political components, the focus of the Dutch transition management (TM) approach lies in understanding how transitions emerge and also how they can be supported and guided (managed).

This approach emerged in the area of technical-social innovations in certain sectors (energy, mobility) and was gradually expanded and adapted for regions and municipalities. Before explaining it in more detail, we will discuss the understanding of transition as applied in this approach.

A transition is defined as the radical, structural transformation of a societal system as the consequence of a co-evolution of economic, cultural, technological, ecological, and institutional developments at different levels.[4] For a transition to a new 'mainstream' to happen, a fundamental transformation of structures, cultures, routines, and conventions must take place. Material infrastructures as well as economic and institutional ones can be changed. Collective and individual actors are relevant. The transitions take place at multiple levels: the niche, the regime, and the landscape. That is why the approach taken is referred to as being from a multi-level perspective.

Niches are characterised by individual actors, often called pioneers of transformation or frontrunners, who already live out new

---

4   Rotmans and Loorbach (2010), p. 108

practices, behaviours, or routines and have put them into practice. They included, for example, organic farmers in Austria in the 1980s. Despite many warnings, they switched to organic farming without being able to take advantage of financial or other support. On the contrary, they were belittled, but they believed in their idea. Even though new ideas and practices often come into being simultaneously in different places, since their time is ripe, the actors are still on their own and not yet networked with one another at this stage. Niches are usually supported by overarching visions. The actors are often called visionaries, or (negatively) oddballs.

If enough niches develop with respect to the same topic, then the regime can also become part of this transition. This succeeds if there are windows of opportunity and the stability of the old regime is no longer a given; this constellation permits the breakthrough of the new regime. Regimes are the currently prevailing systems with the dominant structures, cultures, routines, and conventions. Their actors are those who hold power and represent the existing dominance, and who generally oppose changes. In terms of our example of organic farming, it is conventional, intensive agriculture, which is backed by existing support systems, laws, rules, and consumer behaviours. Its political lobbying is strong and still stable. But if niches grow stronger, if there are an increasing number of pioneers, and if society responds to them by demanding more organic products, the regime begins to falter and is ready for a breakthrough. New support for organic farming, the development of Bio Austria (an organic farmers' association), supermarkets carrying organic products, and Austrians' increasing awareness concerning a wholesome and environmentally friendly diet ultimately helped organic farming achieve a breakthrough. The new becomes mainstream, a custom, routine.

If this also happens at the third level, the landscape, then the transition has succeeded. Of the three levels, the landscape is the most difficult to influence. It reflects global trends, such as urbanisation or individualisation, and it includes exogenous factors such as climate change or the growing inequalities between rich and poor. It provides the underlying conditions for transformation at the other levels. The development of the climate, scarcer resources, and the trend in the industrialised countries toward more mindful ways of life played into the hands of organic farming.

Based on a multi-level perspective, this approach serves to understand the dynamics between these levels. They are not independent of one another; ideally, synergies and mutually reinforcing processes can emerge, and individual actors can take advantage of them. Now, on which of these levels does the transformation begin?

Usually it will be in the niches. However, a trend development at the level of the landscape may emerge in parallel, which benefits and thus strengthens the actors in the niches. If one would like to strengthen a transition, then it is necessary to work at all levels and be cognisant of the fact that it is difficult to influence the landscape level.

The transition management (TM) approach, which was, in particular, developed at the Dutch Research Institute for Transitions and is constantly being developed further, attempts to develop methods and instruments to support and accelerate the transition toward a sustainable society and to influence its direction. Trust in the self-organisation of systems and the capabilities of actors are defining features of this approach. It unifies various methods that invite relevant actors to learn, experiment, and change in protected spaces, be they within businesses, organisations, municipalities, or regions.

A European research project developed and applied the TM approach in three pilot communities at the municipal level. The process in one of the pilot communities is presented in the following box.[5]

---

5   Further information available at www.incontext-fp7.eu

The community arena process in Finkenstein, Austria

The goal of the 1.5-year process was to support pioneers on the ground in transformation arenas, to strengthen their visions, to find development paths and solutions, to experiment, and finally to implement innovations, thereby strengthening niches and influencing the regime.

Preparation phase: Approximately 60 interviews were conducted with residents to identify pioneers of transformation. Ultimately, 15 were selected and invited to participate in the following process, the community arena meetings. The process was also organised in terms of topics to be discussed, methods of collaboration to be applied, etc., and a system analysis of the municipality was prepared. The transition team came together, consisting of local politicians and representatives of the business community.

Phase of structuring the problem and envisioning the future: Three arena meetings took place in which the current challenges faced by Finkenstein on the path to becoming a sustainable municipality were discussed and structured and a common vision based on the participants' needs was developed. Its title was: 'We shape Finkenstein to the benefit of all.'

Phase of developing the backcasting scenarios: Paths leading to the vision for 2030 were developed during an arena meeting. A total of 7 working groups were formed (for example, energy, mobility, social affairs, business, culture), which then carried out small projects, measures, and activities with the broader population.

In the next phase, the initial activities were carried out in the form of experiments. The ones that worked were continued even after the end of the project.

The final phase served to evaluate the process and the results and to elect a team that was to support the municipality in realising the common vision following the end of the research project.

During the process, there were three meetings of the researchers and the transition team in which people reported on the steps and results of the arena process and fed ideas and questions from the transition team back into the process.

Three public networking evenings were held to disseminate the results of the community arena process and to integrate the broader population. Here it was important to hear other people's opinions and to take them up in the subsequent work.

Exchange between the actors made it possible for social learning to take place; the pioneers were empowered to champion community development and the well-being of the community members and to network with one another, thereby strengthening the social capital. In this way, governance became an open process of learning and shaping that was reflected at all levels of society.

Actors of a successful transformation

Following our description of the need for a great transformation, its goals, and research approaches, we now turn to how the transformation can succeed, which examples already exist, and what could be done.

As in the transition management approach, changes at multiple levels are needed: by individuals, civil society as a collective, the business community, and the (local to global) political community. We first look at the individual level.

Transformation to a good life for all is a transformation at various levels and by/with various actors.

It is based on the dynamic of interconnected changes, not only in terms of patterns of political action and decision-making. Such a dynamic is also founded on interrelated changes in the areas of technology, the economic system, institutions, behaviours, culture, value systems, and underlying ecological conditions.

The implementation of the guiding principle of 'sustainability' is a fundamental transformation of our present-day consumption, production, and decision-making patterns.

We are subject to a great deal of hype about 'the good life' and happiness. Lifestyle magazines, television and radio programmes, features pages in newspapers all deliver content about how to live and be happy. The topic seems to touch many people – for one thing, because striving for happiness seems to be innate to human beings, and for another, because more and more people in rich societies realise that their current consumption and lifestyle do not make them happy. On the contrary: the multiple stresses and strains we are exposed to, as well as individualisation, result in overextension, which may even bring about depression, feelings of being devoid of meaning, and emptiness. Broader and broader groups of society and fractions of capital sense the difficulty of maintaining lifestyles to which we have become accustomed (Jaeggi, 2014).

In addition, our (Western) lifestyle is not sustainable; it consumes too many resources so that too little remains for the global South and future generations.

Many people realise that a good life means more than buying new cars, trips, clothes, or consumer electronics again and again. Instead, they seek relationships, relaxation, enjoyment, and leisure. All these goods require material production, too – but not as their most important precondition.

Material consumption is increasingly framed as an addiction that can only superficially compensate for shortcomings in 'internal values', the desire for self-realisation, good relationships, and a life in harmony with nature.

At the same time, a change in values can be detected in a part of humanity: cultural creatives, who make up 20–25% of the American and European population. Their attitudes, values, and lifestyles grant the environment, relationships, peace, and justice more importance than do those of the majority populations in these countries. Their problem: they know too little about each other and thus also too little about their actual societal relevance. In any case, 20 to 25% of the population are a factor that can no longer be considered negligible in political or economic terms.

Even though the trend toward individualisation is not decreasing, especially in cities (which will continue to grow), the yearning for community is becoming stronger and stronger. If being embedded in an extended family or a village community previously satisfied needs for participation, community, and emotional security, other forms of community, such as co-housing, energy cooperatives, or urban gardening groups fulfil these functions today. Increasing one's possessions may still be the motto of the masses, but local exchange trading systems, borrowing shops, or groups rescuing food are springing up everywhere. Sharing instead of owning could become a new maxim of our time. The value of quantity is increasingly being replaced by the value of quality.

People buy one T-shirt made of organic cotton or hemp produced under fair working conditions instead of 10 cheap ones from H&M. Organic food is booming and replacing much cheaper products that do not deserve to be called food. Food co-ops and organic markets are welcoming crowds of customers. Social philosopher Hartmut Rosa of the University of Jena, Germany, speaks of people's desire to overcome the objectification of life, or, in Erich Fromm's words, to return from having to being. We wish to return to a condition where we resonate with ourselves, other people, and nature. This ability to resonate, Rosa says, is a precondition for feeling at ease and being happy.

This change of values involves a strengthening of intrinsic values (such as self-acceptance, community, belonging, spirituality) and a weakening of extrinsic ones (prestige, image, success). Researchers such as Tim Kasser and Tom Crompton show that people with higher intrinsic motivations are happier and use smaller amounts of resources than people with higher extrinsic motivations.

These are just a few examples bearing witness to an already ongoing change of values. It is already prompting some people – but not enough – to action. Why? Psychologists speak of the knowledge/intention behaviour gap. We know that our way of life does not do others or ourselves good; we know about the consequences of our actions for ourselves and the coming generations as well as for nature; our values speak against consumerism and overly busy schedules, and yet we do not change anything. Sometimes we intend to take action, but are hindered by our insufficient abilities or a lack of opportunities. Why?

Humans are creatures of habit, and giving up old habits and patterns takes a lot of energy. We typically make such changes during or following crises such as illnesses, losses of people or jobs, separations, or other serious upheavals. Such situations often throw us back to the essence of what we are and what life means to us. But since it would not bring us closer to our goal if people first had to overcome a personal crisis in order to lead a 'good' life, we need other options. The global crisis situation that we are all subjected to should actually be sufficient. A second way to bridge this gap between knowledge and action lies in experience. If we can feel what it is like to lead our lives in a different way for a while, not eating meat, not flying, but instead sharing cars and other equipment, consuming less, perhaps even working less and having more time for the really important things, and if our experiences are positive, then a sustainable transformation would be possible.

These thoughts are based on the hypothesis that a (more) sustainable lifestyle can increase our quality of life. The basis for a high quality of life is formed by objective underlying conditions as well as experiencing subjective well-being.

Definition of subjective well-being

Subjective well-being sets in when I can live life in accordance with my own ideas, when I can satisfy my needs and feel good doing so. It is often equated with happiness or life satisfaction. Specifically in the context of sustainability, it makes sense to differentiate between hedonistic and eudaimonic well-being. Hedonistic well-being results from enjoyment, fun, and joyful events, and often involves consumption.

The second concept harks back to Aristotle, for whom the realisation of virtues was essential for a good and meaningful life. Eudaimonic well-being arises from factors such as self-acceptance, personal development, purpose in life and meaning of life, ecological sensitivity, social contribution, autonomy, and positive relationships with others (Ryff, 1989; Ryff and Keyes, 1995). High eudaimonic well-being permits an enduring feeling of happiness, that is, flow or flow of life (cf. Csikszentmihalyi, 1990).

Needs are the most fundamental component of human flourishing. They also form the basis of our actions – a basis that needs no other reasoning. Needs are universal and neutral, i.e., they themselves are value-free and not more or less sustainable. They cannot be created or repressed from the outside. When advertising or the media talk about creating new needs, it is usually about strategies for satisfying needs. Many approaches to and lists of needs exist, e.g., by Maslow, Nussbaum, Rosenberg, or Max-Neef, but they are fundamentally very similar.[6] The latter generated a list of ten human needs from empirical work in Latin America, Asia, and Europe. They can be identified in all human beings, with varying importance:

- Subsistence
- Protection
- Belonging and love
- Understanding
- Participation
- Creativity
- Leisure
- Identity
- Freedom
- Spirituality

Strategies serve to satisfy needs, and they involve concrete actions. They are concrete, negotiable, and more or less sustainable. For example: I can satisfy my need for freedom by climbing to the peak of a mountain, by expressing my opinion in public, or by speeding along the motorway at 125 miles per hour. While the first example uses more or less resources, the second is immaterial, and the third involves a large amount of material and energy. There are many possible strategies for satisfying any particular need. And immaterial strategies or ones consuming a small amount of resources can be selected for almost every need. This means that a high quality of life is possible with low resource consumption if I am aware of alternative strategies and if they are available. The decision which strategy to choose is basically up to each and every

---

6   Alkire (2002), pp. 181–205

person, and it depends on values, socialisation, culture, habits, and beliefs. Yet we are usually not aware of this freedom of decision, and we apply strategies out of habit because we learned them at some point or are copying our friends' behaviour. Gaining clarity here requires awareness in thinking about and especially in sensing one's own needs, as well as reflection on strategies for satisfying them. This could be supported by providing suitable conditions, for example other forms of schooling or cooperation. The business community and the state each bear responsibility for offering alternative strategies.

The material satisfaction of needs generally results in (short-term) hedonistic well-being that rarely lasts long. We are in the aspiration treadmill, that is, we quickly get used to new things and then feel we need the next one. Eudaimonic well-being may be linked to hedonistic well-being, but not necessarily. If something is meaningful, it can even reduce happiness in the short term, but increase well-being in the long term. Giving up habits such as smoking may not be pleasant short-term, and at times it may even be painful, but it does us good in the long term. This well-being is closely connected to sustainable lifestyles. A lifestyle of sufficiency is closely tied to eudaimonia. It can also be considered a lifestyle of moderation. People who seek such a lifestyle do so voluntarily and think carefully about what they really do or do not need for a good life, and pursue alternative, immaterial strategies. LOVOS (lifestyle of voluntary simplicity) has emerged in recent years: people voluntarily choose a lifestyle free of excess. They are convinced that this lifestyle serves not only the coming generations, people living in poverty today, and nature, but that it also increases their (eudaimonic) well-being.

Time and again, the argument against large-scale voluntary simplicity, namely that more material prosperity leads to more well-being, is put forward. But this is true only as long as a person remains below a certain income level and basic needs are not satisfied.

Trends of income and happiness do not correlate with each other long term, and this is true both in rich and in poor countries.

Above an annual income of approximately 20,000 US dollars, there is hardly any link between income and life satisfaction. Economist Richard Easterlin confirmed this in empirical studies, first in 1974 and again in 2010.

We spoke above about pioneers of change who are essential for a transition to sustainability. It is they who, convinced by their ideas, create niches by developing and trying out alternatives to the traditional lifestyles and forms of economic activity. Interestingly, such niches often come about in different places at the same time. We would like to present a few examples of such niches and pioneers in the following:[7]

- Co-housing or residential projects consist of private houses or apartments with extensive community facilities that are planned, managed, and maintained communally. http://www.cohousing.org
- Energy cooperatives are cooperatives supported by citizens, usually at the municipal or regional level, and pursuing the goal of decentralised, environmentally friendly energy generation independent of corporations. They also offer opportunities for investment in local and regional energy projects. Climate and energy model regions are distinguished by various projects, usually including this type of cooperative. http://www.klimaundenergiemodellregionen.at
- Food coops are cooperatives of individuals and households that source organically produced products directly from local farms, honey farms, etc. http://foodcoops.at/

---

7   Source: Mock, M. *Graswurzelbewegungen: Hie gesellschaftlicher Wandel sprießen und gedeihen kann* (*Grass roots: How social change can thrive and prosper*), pp. 42–45)

- Hospitality networks such as Couchsurfing, which has 10 million members, link travellers with local hosts offering accommodation (usually for free). https://www.couch-surfing.com/
- Ifixit is a global community of people helping each other repair things by networking through an online platform accessible free of charge. www.ifixit.com/
- Makerspaces, fablabs, and open workshops make modern production technologies (e.g., 3D printers) and traditional workshops available to everyone. http://empty-ice-3260.herokuapp.com/en//
- Repair cafés are meetings organised on a volunteer basis where broken objects are repaired. The first repair café opened its doors in Amsterdam; today there are more than 1,000. http://repaircafe.org/en/
- Community-supported agriculture (CSA) is a direct partnership between consumers and producers for one season at a time. There are currently 23 CSAs in Austria. http://urgenci.net/index.php?lang=en and http://www.foodsovereignty.org/
- One of the most common forms of urban gardening, gardening in the city, is community gardens where local residents grow vegetables and make new contacts. https://gartenpolylog.org/en/home
- Time banks are a form of organised neighbourly help and serve to exchange services. The largest Austrian exchange system is the 'Talentetauschkreis Vorarlberg'. Other examples include http://www.transaction.net/money/lets/ and http://www.timebanking.org/.

Of course, a single individual cannot bring about the transformation alone. But individuals organising in groups can develop clout and push the system to a tipping point, or they can motivate or force policy makers to employ governance mechanisms to change underlying conditions in order to benefit the transformation.

We present a few examples of civil-society movements committed to the transition to sustainability in the following:

Eco-villages: People get together to live in eco-villages, which are often organised as cooperatives. They seek to live and broaden a sustainable and globalisable lifestyle that combines a high quality of life with sustainability, thus providing an example of how people can strengthen social cohesion in society and find their place in the Earth's ecological system again. Besides these 'global' goals, eco-villages offer people an opportunity to develop their personalities in a social setting with emotional security. Decisions are usually made democratically, not hierarchically; the eco-village's internal organisation plays a major role; and eco-villages strive to achieve self-sufficiency. Many such communities currently exist and more are being established all around the world. The European Network for Community-led Initiatives on Climate Change and Sustainability is a common Europe-wide agenda and platform for collective action. (http://www.ecolise.eu/)

Transition towns: Transition towns are local coalitions of citizens and innovative municipalities aiming to shape the transition to a post-fossil, regional economy. The first Transition Town was established by Rob Hopkins, the founder of the movement, in Totnes in 2005. The goal is to reduce the carbon footprint through a holistic, participatory approach and to strengthen resilience against global environmental impacts. The spectrum of activities and measures is very broad, reaching from alternative currencies to local exchange trading systems, renewable energy projects, and repair cafés and community gardening. Courses are offered to train people to become transition town trainers, and there is a Transition Network with members in many countries around the world. (https://transitionnetwork.org/)

The **Degrowth** movement, which has become increasingly important in recent years, also deserves mention here. This movement began in France and Spain and is based on the ideas of intellectuals such as social philosopher André Gorz and mathematician and economist Nicholas Georgescu-Roegen. Its nature is both activist and academic (see www.degrowth.org). Degrowth is defined as follows: 'Sustainable degrowth is a downscaling of production and consumption that increases human well-being and enhances ecological conditions and equity on the planet. It calls for a future where societies live within their ecological means, with open, localised economies and resources more equally distributed through new forms of democratic institutions. Such societies will no longer have to "grow or die". Material accumulation will no longer hold a prime position in the population's cultural imaginary. The primacy of efficiency will be substituted by a focus on sufficiency, and innovation will no longer focus on technology for technology's sake but will concentrate on new social and technical arrangements that will enable us to live convivially and frugally. Degrowth does not only challenge the centrality of GDP as an overarching policy objective but proposes a framework for transformation to a lower and sustainable level of production and consumption, a shrinking of the economic system to leave more space for human cooperation and ecosystems.'[8] In concrete terms, this means that a good life for all includes prosperity in terms of time and conviviality as well as a reduction of resource consumption in the global North combined with an orientation toward the concept of sufficiency and a regionally anchored circular economy, enabling self-determination for people in the global South in shaping their societies, the expansion of participatory formats for decision-making, and political participation.

Besides the most varied courses where people can learn skills and competencies for a life without growth, various events take

---

8   http://degrowth.org/definition-2/

place on a regular basis. The major ones include the European conferences, such as the one in Leipzig, Germany, in 2014, with 3,000
attendees. The next conference will take place in 2018; information is available at degrowth.org.

Paths to sustainability

We have shown in this chapter that the challenge of preventing
environmental destruction or reversing it, while simultaneously
combating social injustice and poverty, is very complex. It requires
a change in thinking, and there are examples where people experiment with successful approaches. Paths to sustainability will
always need such experiments, for it is impossible to predict precisely what measures may cause particular impacts because the
various systems are complex and interdependent. The following
points are important for paths to sustainability:

1. All actors (governments, the business community, the scientific community, civil society, and even individuals) bear
   responsibility for a transformation toward sustainability.
2. Participation by all societal actors is a precondition for the
   transformation. This requires dialogues seeking solutions
   iteratively and then putting them into practice, evaluating
   them, and communicating about them.
3. New alliances must put alternatives into real-life practice
   to set an example and experiment with new ideas, but
   simultaneously change institutions, rules, and underlying conditions in such a way that the new can become a
   matter of course.
4. We always need a vision of the future that we want, for us
   and for future generations. In the absence of such a vision,
   we have no goal for the great transformation.

5. Education and information are doubtless cornerstones of the transformation. An educational reform is essential; all aspects of sustainability must be on the curriculum. Education increases the human capital needed to master the major challenges.

6. Cooperation in place of competition supports finding and implementing solutions communally.

7. Integrated policy at all levels (global, regional, national, local) in which sustainability plays an important role in all decisions is vital.

Bibliography

Alkire, S. (2002), Dimensions of Human Development. World Development. Vol. 30, No. 2, pp. 181–205

Crompton, T., Kasser, T. (2010), Common Cause. The Case for Working with Our Cultural Values. Report WWF UK.

Csikszentmihalyi, M. (2004), Flow. Stuttgart: Klett-Cotta.

Easterlin, R. (1974), Does Economic Growth Improve the Human Lot? Some Empirical Evidence. Nations and households in economic growth 89, 89–125.

Easterlin, R., McVey, L., Switek, M., Sawangfa, O., Smith Zweig, J. (2010), The happiness-income paradox revisited, PNAS 107/52, 22463–22468.2010.

Ellen MacArthur Foundation, The (2013), Towards the circular economy: Economic and business rationale for an accelerated transition.

Jaeggi, R. (2014), Kritik von Lebensformen. Berlin: Suhrkamp.

Kraussmann, F., Gingrich, S., Eisenmenger, N., Erb, K.-H., Haberl, H., Fischer-Kowalski, M. (2009), Growth in global materials use, GDP and population during the 20th century. Ecological Economics. 68(10), 2696–2705. doi:10.1016/j.ecolecon.2009.05.007.

Novy, A. (2013), Ein gutes Leben für alle. Ein europäisches Entwicklungsmodell. In: Journal für Entwicklungspolitik XXIX (3), 77–103.

Novy, A. (2015), Die gegenwärtige Krise. WU SRE Discussion Paper 2015/02.

OECD (2008), Measuring material flows and resource productivity. The OECD guide. ENV/EPOC/SE(2006)1/REV3, Environment Directorate. Paris: Organisation for Economic Co-Operation and Development.

Polanyi, K. (1944), The Great Transformation. New York: Farrar & Rinehart.

Polanyi, K. (1978), The Great Transformation. Politische und ökonomische Ursprünge von Gesellschaften und Wirtschaftssystemen. Frankfurt am Main: Suhrkamp.

Rayworth, K. (2012), A safe and just space for humanity. Oxfam Discussion Papers. https://www.oxfam.org/sites/www.oxfam.org/files/file_attachments/dp-a-safe-and-just-space-for-humanity-130212-en_5.pdf.

Rockström, J., Steffen, W., Noone, K., Persson, A., Chapin, F.S. 3rd., Lambin, E.F. (2009), A safe operating space for humanity. Nature 461: 472–475.

Rotmans J., Loorbach D. (2010), Towards a better understanding of transitions and their governance. A systematic and reflexive approach. In: Grin J., Rotmans J., Schot J. (Hrsg.), Transitions to sustainable development – new directions in the study of long term transformation change. Routledge: New York, S. 105–220. In: Schneidewind, U., Scheck, H. (2012). Zur Transformation des Energiesektors- ein Blick aus der Perspektive der Transition-Forschung. In: Servatius H.-G. et al. (Hrsg.), Smart Energy, doi 10.1007/978-3-642-21820-0_2, © Springer_Verlag, Berlin- Heidelberg 2012. S. 45–61.

Ryff, C.D. (1989), Happiness is everything, or is it? Explorations on the meaning of psychological well-being. Journal of Personality and Social Psychology, 57: 1069–1081.

Ryff, C.D., Keyes, C.L.M. (1995), The structure of psychological well-being revisited. Journal of Personality and Social Psychology 69, 719–727.

Steffen, W., Richardson, K., Rockstrom, J., Cornell, S.E., Fetzer, I., Bennett, E.M. (2015), Planetary Boundaries: Guiding human development on a changing planet. Science Vol. 347, no. 6223.

Steffen, W., Broadgate W., Deutsch, L., Gaffney, O., Ludwig, C. (2015b), The trajectory of the Anthropocene: The Great Acceleration. http://anr.sagepub.com/content/early/2015/01/08/2053019614564785.abstract.

TEEB (2010), The Economics of Ecosystems and Biodiversity: Mainstreaming the Economics of Nature: A Synthesis of the Approach, Conclusions and Recommendations of TEEB.

Vereinte Nationen (2012), The Future we want. https//sustainabledevelopment.un.org/futurewewant.html.

Vereinte Nationen (2015), The Millennium Goals Report 2015. http://www.un.org/millenniumgoals/2015_MDG_Report/pdf/MDG%202015%20rev%20(July%201).pdf.

WBGU (2011), Hauptgutachten. Welt im Wandel: Gesellschaftsvertrag für eine Große Transformation. Berlin: WBGU (Wissenschaftlicher Beirat der Bundesregierung Globale Umweltveränderungen).

Climate Change: the point of no return

Mojib Latif

Background and prognoses

When geochemist Roger Revelle wrote more than half a century ago that '[h]uman beings are now carrying out a large scale geophysical experiment', he was describing the gargantuan dimension of human influence on the climate.[1] Paul Crutzen, Nobel Laureate in Chemistry, introduced the term Anthropocene to describe the beginning of a new geologic era in which the influence of human beings on the environment is comparable to that of natural factors. It is not yet too late to prevent 'dangerous'[2] climate change as laid down in the United Nations Framework Convention on Climate Change[3] adopted in Rio de Janeiro in 1992. At the 21st Conference of the Parties in Paris in 2015, countries agreed to limit global warming to 'well below 2°C above pre-industrial levels.'[4] It is hoped that this will make it possible to prevent irreversible processes such as irreparable melting of major land ice masses causing sea levels to rise by many metres or excessive acidification of the world's oceans.

1   New York Times, 1957
2   https://www.ipcc.ch/publications_and_data/ar4/wg3/en/ch1s1-2-2.html
3   http://newsroom.unfccc.int
4   http://unfccc.int/files/meetings/paris_nov_2015/application/pdf/paris_
    agreement_english_.pdf

The climate and the climate system

There are fundamental differences between weather and climate. 'Weather' designates the current condition of the lower atmosphere in a particular place. In contrast, 'climate' refers to longer periods of time. The World Meteorological Organisation (WMO) defines climate as the statistics of the weather over a period that is long enough to allow these statistical properties to be determined. A period of 30 years is generally used as the reference period for describing a particular climate. If we apply this definition of climate to development since the middle of the twentieth century and compare, for example, the average global near-surface air temperatures of the period 1951–1980 with those of the period 1981–2010, then there is a statistically significant temperature increase found of just under 0.5°C. There is no longer any doubt today that humankind has been the main cause of global warming during recent decades by emitting enormous amounts of greenhouse gases into the atmosphere.

Weather research is concerned with the generation, movement, and prediction of individual weather elements, such as a certain low-pressure area or a hurricane. Climate research is interested in the entirety of low-pressure areas and hurricanes, and addresses such questions as whether there will be more or fewer low-pressure areas or hurricanes in a particular region next year, or whether they will become more frequent or severe in the coming decades as a consequence of global warming. When it comes to climate, we are always interested in certain macroscopic characteristics of the atmosphere, not in the microscopic ones. If we seek examples from other areas of knowledge, then throwing dice comes to mind immediately. Climate researchers are not interested in every individual number, but only in the probability of it coming up when the die is cast. Now, the probability is the same for every number, namely one in six. We know that all numbers come up with the same frequency if we cast the die often enough. But we cannot predict the order of the numbers. It remains random. The case is similar if the die is loaded. For example, we may know that six will come up more often than the other numbers. But we don't know which number will come up at the next throw. The individual throw can be compared to a weather parameter, the probability of a particular number coming up with a climate parameter.

As a consequence of global warming, days with extraordinarily high temperatures have become more common in recent decades in Germany, just as the number six comes up more often if the die is loaded. But that does not mean that low temperatures have no longer occurred at all or that they will not occur again in the future. The probability of their occurrence has declined and will, in all likelihood, continue to decline in the coming decades. The example of throwing dice also illustrates that one cannot draw conclusions about humanity's influence on the climate from the occurrence of a single extreme weather event. A cold winter is not evidence against anthropogenic climate change, just as the number one coming up a single time is not evidence against manipulation of the die. On the other hand, an exceptionally hot spell is not proof of global warming, just as a single six does not provide any indication whether the die is loaded. Climate research is always about probabilities. Absolute statements are impossible as a matter of principle.

The atmosphere is not an isolated system, but interacts closely with other components of the Earth system: with the hydrosphere (oceans and the water cycle on the continents and in the atmosphere), the cryosphere (ice and snow, including permafrost), the biosphere (animals and plants), the pedosphere (soil), and the lithosphere (rock). These components define the climate system (see Fig. 1).

The various components of the climate system have drastically different physical characteristics, for example concerning density

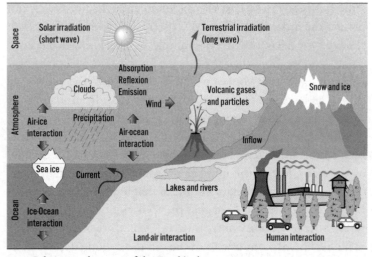

Fig. 1: Schematic diagram of the Earth's climate system.

or heat capacity. That is why their internal time scales vary widely. The atmosphere is a rapidly fluctuating component and responds quickly to disturbances, the oceans react much more slowly, and the continental ice sheets even more slowly to external stimuli such as anthropogenic greenhouse gas emissions. Because of the inertia of some system components, the climate will continue to change for centuries or even millennia, even if humans no longer cause greenhouse gas emissions. This is particularly true of the sea level. In addition, the atmospheric concentration of the most significant greenhouse gas emitted by humans, carbon dioxide (CO_2), will decrease only extremely slowly after CO_2 emissions have stopped. This is because the transport of the CO_2 from the upper layers of the ocean, which are in contact with the atmosphere, to the deep sea, the only long-term carbon dioxide sink, is very inefficient because of the ocean's strong stratification. Therefore, the climate effect of CO_2 remains a factor as well.

Climate variability

One of the climate's outstanding characteristics is its large range of natural fluctuation. One year is not like the next, one decade not like the previous one. The natural climate fluctuations make it more difficult to identify long-term man-made global warming and to prove anthropogenic influencing of the climate. Natural climate fluctuations can be observed on many different time scales, from months to millennia and beyond. In principle, one can differentiate two types of climate fluctuations, external and internal ones. Whereas external climate fluctuations are triggered by disturbances 'from the outside', internal ones originate within the climate system itself. The most well-known examples of external climate fluctuations are the ice ages. The reasons for these cold periods, which are accompanied by extraordinarily large expanses of ice, include fluctuations of the parameters of the Earth's orbit – for example, changes in the Earth's orbit around the sun or the tilt of the Earth's axis. External fluctuations also include changes in solar radiation due to fluctuations in the amount of energy emitted by the sun, as well as climate changes caused by volcanic eruptions. Anthropogenic climate influences, including emissions of greenhouse gases and aerosols as well as land use changes, are also considered external factors.

Let us take a closer look at the internal natural climate fluctuations, which do not need any external trigger. Although climate fluctuations in general are perceived as longer-term changes in the characteristics of the atmosphere around us, such as air temperature or frequency of precipitation, the causes of climate fluctuations are not necessarily to be found within the atmosphere, but often in its interaction with the slow-acting components of the climate system (Fig. 1) such as the oceans. According to the concept of the stochastic climate model proposed by Hasselmann in 1976,[5] the short-period

5   Hasselmann, K. (1976), Stochastic climate models Part I. Theory. Tellus, 28, 6, 473–

fluctuations in air temperature associated with weather activity induce long-period fluctuations in the ocean, analogous to 'Brownian motion'[6] in theoretical physics. The changes in the oceans, in turn, can impact the atmosphere. For example, fluctuations in the temperature of the ocean's surface can result in changes in the atmospheric weather processes. Reconstructions of the climate of the past millennia as well as instrumental measurements are evidence of the fact that climate fluctuations become stronger as the time scale increases, corresponding to Brownian motion. To illustrate, the temperature deviations in North and Central America between the pinnacle of the last ice age, approximately 20,000 years ago, and the beginning of the current interglacial, the Holocene, approximately 11,000 years ago, were much larger than the temperature deviations between the mediaeval interglacial and the following Little Ice Age which developed over some centuries.

Since industrialisation began, the significance of humans for the climate has grown immensely as we have emitted large amounts of persistent greenhouse gases such as carbon dioxide (CO_2), methane, (CH_4), halogenated hydrocarbons including chloro-fluorocarbons (CFCs), and nitrous oxide (N_2O), thus causing global warming which is already verifiable today. The energy sector is the most important anthropogenic source of greenhouse gases. In addition, large amounts of greenhouse gases are generated by agriculture and through land use changes such as slash-and-burn clearance of tropical rain forests or draining of moors. On the other hand, humanity is cooling the Earth by emitting aerosols, which are generated mostly through sulphur emissions from burning coal. Natural climate variability masks the anthropogenic trends. In other words, we must examine the interactions of natural and anthropogenic climate changes if we seek to understand the

---

564
6   https://www.britannica.com/science/Brownian-motion

development of the climate since the beginning of industrialisation and to predict it in the future.

The greenhouse effect

In order to understand how humans impact the climate by emitting greenhouse gases, we must consider the greenhouse effect. The optimum living conditions on Earth are due mostly to the composition of Earth's atmosphere, which is clearly different from those of other planets in the solar system. The main components of the Earth's atmosphere are nitrogen (N_2, approx. 78%) and oxygen (O_2, approx. 21%). Argon, an inert gas, makes up approximately 0.9%. Together, nitrogen, oxygen, and argon account for approximately 99.9%. Trace gases comprise the remainder of 0.1%. Among the trace gases are the greenhouse gases, and they are the ones with strong impacts on the Earth's climate as they influence the planet's radiation budget. The greenhouse gases produce the Earth's greenhouse effect whose name they bear, and it generates the mild temperatures and thus the favourable living conditions on Earth. In other words, the greenhouse effect is a natural characteristic of the Earth's atmosphere.

Without it, it would be bitterly cold on the surface of the Earth. The global average temperature increase due to the greenhouse effect is approximately 33°C. John Tyndall, an Irishman, described the greenhouse effect very vividly in 1862: 'As a dam built across a river causes a local deepening of the stream, so our atmosphere, thrown as a barrier across the terrestrial rays, produces a local heightening of the temperature of the Earth's surface.'[7] Tyndall

---

7   Tyndall, John (1873). Further Researches on the Absorption and Radiation of Heat by Gaseous Matter (1862). In: *Contributions to Molecular Physics in the Domain of Radiant Heat*, pp. 69–121. New York: Appleton.

also identified the gases responsible for the greenhouse effect. He found that most of the greenhouse effect is caused by the gaseous phase of water (H_2O), water vapour. Even back then, he also correctly observed that the contribution of the other gases, for example CO_2, was significantly smaller, but by no means negligible. We know today that water vapour is responsible for approximately two-thirds of the *natural* greenhouse effect and CO_2 for approximately one-fourth.

But how does the greenhouse effect actually work? Greenhouse gases are largely permeable to solar radiation, but not to thermal radiation. In a sense, energy is trapped at the Earth's surface and in the lower layers of the atmosphere, as in a greenhouse. In this simple analogy, the greenhouse gases take on the role of the glass. On an Earth without an atmosphere, the surface temperature would be determined exclusively by the balance between irradiated solar energy and the thermal radiation sent out by the planet's surface (albedo or backscatter ratio). At today's albedo, the global surface temperature would average around −18°C. Even an atmosphere consisting of pure oxygen and nitrogen – after all, these two components make up 99% of our atmosphere – would not make any significant change. Our planet would be an icy desert, and life as we know it probably never would have emerged. The average global temperature of the Earth's surface is currently approximately +15°C. Thanks to the greenhouse effect, the Earth has been able to enjoy fairly mild temperatures throughout almost all of its more than 4-billion-year history.

Let us go into more detail. Matter emits electromagnetic radiation[8] (emissions), and these emissions increase with the heat of the emitting matter. In addition, the maximum of this radiation is shifted toward shorter waves as the temperature of the

---

8 Electromagnetic radiation is radiation consisting of waves in which electric and magnetic fields are coupled with one another

body increases. At 6,000°C, the sun emits mostly short waves. The spectral range of solar radiation that is relevant in terms of energy spans roughly 0.3 to 3.5 μm[9], with a maximum of radiation energy at approximately 0.48 μm. This mostly provides for energy in the form of visible light on Earth. However, incidental electromagnetic radiation is also swallowed by matter (absorption) so that additional energy enters the environment, generally felt in the form of warming. At the temperatures of the terrestrial climate system, which are low compared with those on the sun, most of the electromagnetic radiation emitted by the Earth's surface and atmospheric components takes place in the non-visible long-wave infrared spectral range. The radiation emitted from the Earth is often called terrestrial radiation or terrestrial thermal radiation.

The two main gases of the atmosphere, oxygen and nitrogen, exhibit no substantial emissions or absorption relevant for the Earth's temperature.[10] In contrast, greenhouse gases such as water vapour and to a lesser extent carbon dioxide or methane absorb a small fraction of solar radiation and themselves emit infrared radiation. In the downward direction this additional thermal radiation from the atmosphere is greater than the solar radiation absorbed, making the energy input at the surface higher than it would be without such gases. This process warms the surface of the Earth and (as a consequence of various transport processes) the lower atmosphere as well. The warming of the Earth's surface increases the energy sent out, thus resulting in a balance of the radiation at the upper edge of the atmosphere; averaged over the longer term, the thermal radiation that the Earth emits into space must be equivalent to the short-wave radiation it absorbs from the sun.

---

9   1 μm corresponds to 10^{-6} m or one one-thousandth of a millimetre

10   Ozone (O_3), the triatomic form of oxygen, is an exception. Stratospheric ozone
     absorbs much of the ultraviolet radiation from the sun and warms the stratosphere.

Much of the thermal radiation emitted from the Earth's surface is absorbed by the greenhouse gases, and only a small fraction of it reaches outer space through the atmospheric radiation window, a spectral range of approximately 8–13 μm within which radiation from the surface can escape through a cloudless atmosphere. These gases emit energy themselves, depending on their temperature, yet since their temperatures fall with increasing elevation in the atmosphere, this energy is much lower than at the Earth's surface. For this reason, if the amount of greenhouse gases in the atmosphere rises and the Earth's surface temperature remains constant, less and less energy would leave the Earth for outer space in the form of thermal radiation. As the surface temperature rises, this deficit in the radiation budget is balanced by the Earth's surface emitting correspondingly more thermal radiation. So an increase of greenhouse gases in the atmosphere must necessarily result in warming of the Earth's surface and the lower layers of the atmosphere.

The increase in carbon dioxide since the beginning of industrialisation

Since the beginning of industrialisation, humankind has produced large amounts of greenhouse gases, reinforcing the terrestrial greenhouse effect. In other words, it would be correct to speak of the additional or anthropogenic greenhouse effect when we mean the intensification, by human action, of the (natural) greenhouse effect, which is so enormously important for the Earth's climate. The persistent greenhouse gases emitted by mankind remain in the atmosphere for decades and even centuries. The persistence of CO_2 averages approximately 100 years; it fluctuates strongly, depending on the process of removal. In 2015, the annual amount of CO_2 emitted globally by mankind was roughly 35 billion tons. During the decade from 2005 to 2014, the land regions took up 30% of

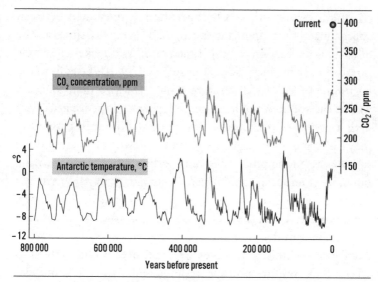

Fig. 2: The CO_2 concentration (ppm) in the air and the temperature (°C) in Antarctica, reconstructed from ice cores

the anthropogenic CO_2 emissions, the oceans 26%. The other 44% remained in the atmosphere. Since the sinks do not suffice to balance out the anthropogenic CO_2 emissions, the CO_2 concentration in the air had to increase. In pre-industrial times, it was approximately 0.028% or 280 ppm.[11] Today, at more than 400 ppm, it is around 40% higher than at the beginning of industrialisation. This value was last reached at least 800,000 years ago (Fig. 2).[12]

The historical composition of the air is known from ice cores drilled in Antarctica and analyses of the bubbles enclosed in them. Over the course of previous millennia until the early

11 ppm: parts per million
12 http://www.nature.com/nature/journal/v453/n7193/full/453291a.html

twentieth century, the CO_2 concentration fluctuated between approximately 170 ppm and 300 ppm. This range defines a scale of natural fluctuation for this time period and makes clear how extraordinary the increase of atmospheric CO_2 has been from the beginning of industrialisation to more than 400 ppm today, as well as the speed of the increase. In Figure 2, those ice age cycles with a period of roughly 100,000 years stand out in particular; they came about through changes in the Earth's orbit around the sun. At these long time scales, both carbon dioxide and methane function as important intensifiers of climate changes. When, for example, the Earth began to warm again following the last ice age, the temperature and the CO_2 concentration rose in parallel over the following millennia. For example, changes in the temperature, circulation, chemistry, and biology of the oceans caused them to release CO_2 into the atmosphere, and combined with additional intensifying processes, this caused even more global warming. Such intensifying processes are called positive feedback, and they explain why the global climate responds sensitively to relatively small disturbances.

For epochs further back in time than the last 800,000 years, scientists use methods that are less direct. The relevant proxies suggest that the atmosphere last reached a CO_2 concentration of 400 ppm about 3 to 5 million years ago, during a period when the temperature of the Earth's surface was about 2 to 3.5°C higher than in the pre-industrial period. About 50 million years ago, during the Eocene, the atmospheric concentration of CO_2 may have been about 1,000 ppm higher and the average global temperature about 10°C higher than today. Under the conditions prevailing at the time, there was hardly any ice on Earth, and the sea level was approximately sixty metres higher than today. In this context, it should be observed that the speed of the increase in atmospheric CO_2 concentration at the present time is greater than in the Eocene by orders of magnitude. For this reason, there is strictly speaking no real palaeoclimatic analogy to climate change as it exists today and is possibly to be expected as early as this century. Indeed, humans are conducting a large-scale and unique experiment with the Earth, as Roger Revelle stated more than 50 years ago.

Anthropogenic climate change

The fact that more greenhouse gases in the air intensify the natural greenhouse effect and result in global warming has been known for more than 100 years. As early as 1896, Swedish Nobel Laureate Svante Arrhenius published a paper titled 'On the Influence of Carbonic Acid in the Air upon the Temperature of the Ground'.[13] Arrhenius was actually referring to carbon dioxide, but at the time, the term used in the scientific literature was carbonic acid. Arrhenius calculated the change in the Earth's surface tempera-ture for the various latitudes and the different seasons for various atmospheric CO_2 concentrations. According to his calculations, doubling the atmospheric CO_2 concentration would induce global warming of approximately 5 to 6°C in equilibrium. Current-day climate models calculate average global warming of approximately 3°C[14] if pre-industrial CO_2 levels are doubled, whereby the results vary widely, from 1.5° to 4.5°C. Global warming defined in this way is called climate sensitivity in the scientific literature of today. Interestingly, even in his groundbreaking publication, Arrhenius speculated whether the climate effect of CO_2 that he had calcu-lated might be too high.

---

13 Arrhenius, S. (1896a), 'Ueber den Einfluss des Atmosphärischen Kohlensäuregehalts auf die Temperatur der Erdoberfläche', *Proceedings of the Royal Swedish Academy of Science*, Vol. 22, I No. 1, pp. 1–101

14 The equilibrium will be reached only centuries after the CO_2 concentration is doubled

But Arrhenius was interested in more than human influence on the climate. He was interested most of all in how ice ages come and go, as were many other scientists of his day. That is why he also discussed in depth how temperatures would change if the atmospheric CO_2 concentration were to drop by one-third. His results show a cooling of the Earth's surface by approximately 3°C. So he indeed identified an important process in the context of the development of ice ages (see Fig. 2). On the other hand, Arrhenius was able to identify positive aspects of increasing CO_2 concentrations in the atmosphere: '[The increase in carbonic acid] would allow our descendants, even if they only be those in a distant future, to live under a warmer sky.' Perhaps an understandable thought from the perspective of a Swede. We know today that global warming of several degrees Celsius would have dramatic impacts, for instance an increase in heat waves and heavy precipitation events, long-term sea level rise by several metres, or excessive acidification of the world's oceans resulting from their absorbing CO_2, with incalculable risks for marine ecosystems.

CO_2 alone does not have as strong an impact on the climate as the figures above suggest. It is the positive feedback loops that play an enormously important role in the context of anthropogenic climate change. For example, the concentration of water vapour in the atmosphere depends on the temperature of the air. And thus, atmospheric water vapour is also indirectly dependent on the concentration of greenhouse gases emitted by mankind in large amounts. For it is the greenhouse gases which are instrumental in determining the temperature of the planet. Water vapour has its own particular characteristics, completely different from those of carbon dioxide or methane, for instance. When moist air rises and reaches cooler layers of the atmosphere, it condenses, forming water drops that are visible as clouds and from which rain falls at times. For this reason, the atmospheric lifetime of water vapour is relatively short, only around 10 days. The warmer the

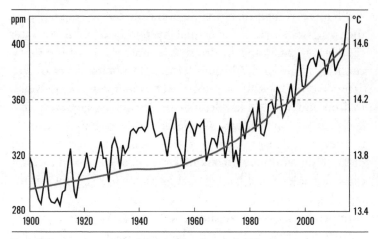

Fig. 3: CO_2 concentration of the air (ppm) and global average temperature (°C.) for the period 1900–2015. Wonsun Park, GEOMAR.

air becomes, the more water vapour the atmosphere can absorb before condensation begins. And as we know, water vapour is a very efficient greenhouse gas. Water vapour intensifies warming, and this in turn enables uptake of even more water vapour in the atmosphere. This has been the situation since the beginning of the twentieth century. Its characteristics include the increase of greenhouse gases in the atmosphere, especially CO_2, and an obvious increase in global temperature (Fig. 3).

Satellite measurements also provide evidence of the fact that the water vapour content of the air has increased continually over the past decades.

The water vapour feedback loop naturally also works in the opposite direction. American scientists conducted a kind of thought experiment with a climate model in which they set the concentration of carbon dioxide and methane, the non-condensing greenhouse gases, to zero. As expected, the Earth cooled, but much more strongly than would result from calculations based on the two gases' shares of the natural greenhouse effect. If the water vapour content in the air drops as a consequence of the initial cooling, a kind of death spiral of the greenhouse effect occurs. Temperatures continue to cool, water vapour content continues to drop, and, within a few decades, the Earth is covered with ice.[15]

Water vapour feedback is one of the most important positive feedbacks in the climate system and increases the impact of the CO_2 emitted by mankind by a factor of two to three. It can react quickly and has a global impact, which is why it is the most important feedback mechanism on the time scales on which anthropogenic global warming is developing. Another important positive feedback mechanism, which also reacts quickly, but has only a regional impact, is ice-albedo feedback. As a consequence of initial warming, perhaps induced by CO_2, the ice and snow covering areas of the Earth are receding. Light-coloured surfaces have a high albedo, which means that they reflect a large amount of solar radiation. If ice and snow recede because of a rise in temperature, albedo is reduced. For this reason, the Earth's surface can absorb more solar radiation in these areas, which further intensifies warming, which in turn makes the areas covered by ice and snow smaller. If we observe longer periods of many decades and beyond, then the positive feedback mechanism of the carbon cycle, which reacts quite slowly, becomes more important compared with the water vapour feedback and ice-albedo feedback mechanisms.

The question of whether mankind is changing the climate was answered long ago by the international climate research community. There are practically no more climate scientists today who would deny the existence of anthropogenic climate change.

---

15 Lacis (2010), Atmospheric CO_2: Principal control knob governing Earth's temperature. Science, 330, 356–359, doi:10.1126/science.1190653

Climate change is well underway, and its signs are unmistakable. The Intergovernmental Panel on Climate Change (IPCC)[16] plays a decisive role in collecting, evaluating, and communicating the scientific findings. It was established jointly by the World Meteorological Organisation (WMO) and the United Nations Environment Programme (UNEP) in 1988. Its remit is both to describe the scientific state of knowledge about global climate change and to provide international policy advice.

The IPCC has published five assessment reports since 1990. More than 830 of the world's leading climate scientists collaborated as authors on the four working group contributions to the most recent Assessment Report (Fifth Assessment Report, AR5), which were published in 2013 and 2014. In addition, thousands of scientists were tasked with reviewing the report. In its most recent Assessment Report, the IPCC writes in brief, succinct words: 'Human influence on the climate system is clear.'[17] Even the IPCC's Second Assessment Report (SAR), published in 1995, states: 'The balance of evidence suggests a discernible human influence on global climate.'[18] It is evident that there has been a great consensus in the international climate research community for years that our climate is changing and that mankind is the key actor.

Identifying mankind as the key actor

What brought this consensus about? Two things above all are to be mentioned in this context. First, the instrumental measurements and the proxy data show that the changes in climate since

---

16 http://www.ipcc.ch/

17 http://www.ipcc.ch/pdf/assessment-report/ar5/wg1/WG1AR5_SPM_FINAL.pdf

18 https://www.ipcc.ch/pdf/climate-changes-1995/ipcc-2nd-assessment/2nd-assessment-en.pdf

the beginning of industrialisation are extraordinary compared with the previous millennia. Secondly, the results of the climate models support exposing mankind as the main cause of these climate changes. It must be borne in mind that there are a number of natural and anthropogenic factors that impact the climate at the same time. Researchers introduced radiative forcing to compare the impacts of the various drivers on the climate system. It is a measure of the change in the Earth's energy balance due to external factors and is given in units of watts per square metre (W/m^2). An external factor may be an anthropogenic change in the atmospheric concentrations of greenhouse gases or aerosols, a change in the Earth's incident solar radiation, or changes in volcanic activity spanning decades, as well as other factors resulting in a change of the amount of energy absorbed by the Earth's surface. Other examples of external factors include a change in albedo resulting from land-use changes, for instance forest clearance. The anthropogenic increase in greenhouse gases in the atmosphere brings about positive radiative forcing, the anthropogenic increase in aerosols in the air negative radiative forcing. Positive radiative forcing results in warming the Earth, negative in cooling it.

In the following, let us look at the various radiative forcings that have occurred since industrialisation began (1750–2011) and which have been calculated using climate models and changes in concentration. There are of course great uncertainties in determining historical radiative forcings. We will review only the best estimates here; an extensive discussion of the uncertainties is to be found in the most recent IPCC Assessment Report.[19] Total anthropogenic radiative forcing since the beginning of industrialisation is positive and amounts to 2.3 W/m^2 (Fig. 4). That means that the human influence on the climate is warming, not cooling, if we consider all anthropogenic influences together.

---

19 IPCC (2013), Working Group I Contribution, Chapter 8

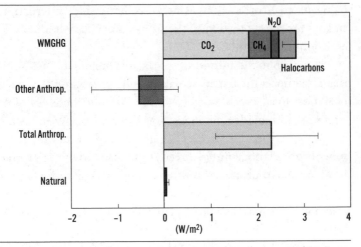

Fig. 4: Radiative forcings (1750–2011) for the anthropogenic and natural external factors,[20] in W/m₂ WMGHG, well-mixed greenhouse gases

The radiative forcing due to the persistent ('well-mixed'[21]) greenhouse gases totals 2.83 W/m². CO_2 is the most important component, contributing 1.82 W/m². Methane (CH_4) is the second-most important, contributing 0.48 W/m². It is formed by biological decomposition processes of organic material in the absence of air. There are numerous sources of methane. It escapes from rice paddies, landfills, coal mines, natural gas production, and from millions of head of livestock. Halogenated hydrocarbons, contributing 0.36 W/m², and nitrous oxide (N_2O), contributing 0.17 W/m², are the other persistent greenhouse gases produced by humans, and are in third and fourth place. CFCs' share of

20 IPCC (2014), Synthesis Report
21 Well-mixed greenhouse gases (WMGHG) are gases that remain in the atmosphere for at least one year, so they are mixed well throughout the atmosphere around the globe

halogenated hydrocarbons is now declining since international treaties for the protection of the ozone layer[22] have limited CFC emissions significantly.

Let us turn to the anthropogenic factors besides the WMGHG that also impact the Earth's radiation budget. Tropospheric ozone is a short-lived greenhouse gas and also contributes to global warming. Its radiative forcing is approximately 0.4 W/m², which roughly corresponds to that of halogenated hydrocarbons. Tropospheric ozone is not emitted directly by human activity; it is formed from precursor substances emitted by human activity, for example nitrogen oxides, carbon monoxide, and hydrocarbons. Human emissions of aerosols cool the planet significantly; their radiative forcing is approximately –0.9 W/m². It is composed of the aerosols' interaction with radiation and their impacts on clouds. The sum total of the radiative forcing by anthropogenic factors that are not persistent greenhouse gases is approximately –0.5 W/m².

The radiative forcing during the period 1750 to 2011 caused by natural external factors totals only approximately 0.1 W/m². But by no means does this indicate that changes in solar radiation and volcanic eruptions had no significant impacts on the development of the climate. An increase in the luminosity of the sun contributed to global warming during the first half of the twentieth century (Fig. 4). But then it decreased again, so the impact of the sun on the climate during the entire time period observed was small. The 1991 eruption of the Philippine volcano Pinatubo, one of the strongest of the twentieth century, caused cooling, but only briefly, in the following year. Finally, water vapour has no appreciable anthropogenic sources; it is, however, an important feedback gas in the climate system, i.e., it intensifies climate changes due to other factors, as described above.

---

22 CFCs destroy the stratospheric ozone layer, which protects us from ultraviolet radiation

Indicators of climate change

There are a number of indicators that make clear that the climate system reacts to positive anthropogenic radiative forcing. Compared with the time period 1850 to 1900, global surface temperature has increased by approximately 1°C[23] (see Fig. 3). Germany's temperature increase since 1881 is 1.4°C.[24] Globally speaking, 13 of the 14 warmest years since the beginning of comprehensive instrumental measurements have been in this century, and the warmest year to date was 2015. The link between global warming and the increase in atmospheric greenhouse gases, especially the increasing atmospheric concentration of CO_2, is obvious and is confirmed by all climate models. The warming cannot be simulated without taking greenhouse gases into account. Of course, there are natural fluctuations; but the long-term trend of the temperature is clearly upward. The number of hot days has increased globally, including in Germany. Additional trends can be discerned when examining all land regions together. For example, heavy precipitation events, flooding, and droughts are occurring more frequently.

Of all regions of the Earth, the strongest warming is to be seen in the Arctic. It is literally visible: the Arctic sea ice is melting at a breathtaking pace. The area covered with sea ice in the summer has already retreated by more than one-third since the beginning of satellite measurements in 1979. The minimum expanse of sea ice, which is reached in September, was only a good 4 million km^2 in 2015. In the 1970s and 1980s, the minimums still averaged a good 7 million km^2. The winter maximum, which is reached in March, is shrinking appreciably. For example, the smallest winter maximum since the beginning of satellite measurements was observed in March, 2016.

---

23 https://crudata.uea.ac.uk/cru/data/temperature/
24 http://www.dwd.de/DE/klimaumwelt/klimawandel/klimawandel_node.html

Another piece of evidence for climate change: the rising of sea levels. One reason is that the oceans are warming, which is why the ocean water is expanding. Another is that inland ice is melting. Since satellite measurements of the sea level began in 1993, the global average sea level has risen by approximately 8 cm[25]; since 1900, the historic measurements combined with the satellite measurements show a sea level rise of just under 20 cm. According to these figures, sea level rise has accelerated enormously during the past two decades. For a long time, thermal expansion of the water was the largest contributing factor. In the past 40 years alone, the oceans have taken up more than 90% of the warmth that has been held back because of the increase in greenhouse gases in the atmosphere.[26] However, the inland ice masses are shrinking faster and faster. The mountain glaciers are retreating in all latitudes; their losses of mass have accelerated even more since the beginning of this century.[27] The Greenland and West Antarctic continental ice sheets have started to melt,[28] accelerating the rising of sea levels. At present, ice melting contributes more to sea level rise than thermal expansion. It is important to mention in this context that there are major differences in sea level rise in different regions, which are mostly due to changes in ocean currents.

And finally, the oceans are becoming demonstrably more acidic because, at present, a good quarter of the carbon dioxide emitted by human activity is taken up and dissolved in sea water.[29] In total, the oceans have absorbed roughly one-third of the CO_2 emitted by human activity since the beginning of industrialisation, thus

25 http://www.aviso.altimetry.fr/en/data/products/ocean-indicators-products/mean-sea-level.html
26 http://www.ipcc.ch/pdf/assessment-report/ar5/wg1/WGIAR5_SPM_brochure_en.pdf
27 http://wgms.ch/latest-glacier-mass-balance-data/
28 https://nsidc.org/cryosphere/sotc/ice_sheets.html
29 http://www.globalcarbonproject.org/carbonbudget/15/hl-compact.htm

lessening the impacts of climate change. On average, ocean water is almost 30% more acidic[30] than in pre-industrial times because of the CO_2 uptake.[31] It should be borne in mind that cold water can take up a larger amount of gases than warm water. That is why ocean water is most acidic at high latitudes. In the event of unchecked CO_2 emissions, ocean acidity will more than double by the end of this century. The more acidic the oceans become, the less additional carbon dioxide they can take up from the atmosphere, and a larger fraction of anthropogenic emissions will remain in the air. This would further accelerate global warming. Warming and acidification of the oceans, as well as other factors such as pollution and overfishing, are already threatening life in the world's oceans and, thus, one of our key food sources today. It is simply no longer possible to turn a blind eye to climate change and its many and diverse consequences. It is time to act quickly.

Looking to the future

How far has climate change already actually advanced? To what extent can we still limit global warming at all? And what could future scenarios look like? One thing is virtually certain: limiting global warming to 1.5°C as stated in the Paris Climate Agreement is already practically impossible. If, for example, the CO_2 concentration of the air is to be 'frozen' at today's level, global CO_2 emissions would have to decline immediately by approximately 60 to 70% and continue to drop over time. Even in this case, the average global temperature would still increase by a few tenths of a degree Celsius. Only if global greenhouse gas emissions were to drop to practically zero immediately could it be possible to reach

---

30 This corresponds to a lowering of the pH value by approx. 0.1.
31 http://www.pmel.noaa.gov/co2/story/What+is+Ocean+Acidification%3F

the goal of limiting global warming to at most 1.5°C. These observations illustrate that even limiting global warming to 'well below 2°C', as the Paris Climate Agreement states, is still a truly Herculean task.

And rapid reduction of global greenhouse gas emissions appears anything but likely today. The outcomes of international climate mitigation policy to date are indeed sobering: global CO_2 emissions alone have increased by a good 60% since 1990 (Fig. 5). Aspirations and reality could not be further apart than they are in climate mitigation. Taking realistic scenarios for the future development of global greenhouse gas emissions as a basis, observers are sceptical whether the global community will reach the Paris goal. The world is not on a good course when it comes to climate mitigation. If one simply extrapolates the greenhouse gas emissions of the past decades into the future, it will lead us into a world that will be about 3 to 5°C warmer than the period 1850 to 1900. The impacts of such climate change, which would be unique in terms of its extent and speed, would be incalculable.

Optimistic scenarios assume that greenhouse gas emissions will stabilise in the coming years and decline significantly after that, but will drop to zero only during the second half of the century and will remain negative for the remainder of the century. Only then would there be a high probability of being able to limit global warming to less than 2°C. From today's perspective, that appears nothing less than utopian. Yet it remains a possibility. It would, however, require the will of all countries to solve the climate problem in a sustainable way, as well as strong solidarity among countries, especially between the industrialised nations and the developing countries and emerging economies.

Nonetheless, there is reason to hope that things will take a turn for the better in the coming years. In the meantime, the conditions for international negotiations on climate mitigation have changed.

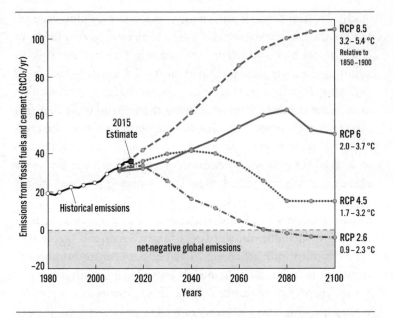

Fig. 5: Historical CO_2 emissions (GtC/year[32]) since 1980 and emissions scenarios through 2100 (left-hand scale). The numbers on the right indicate the expected changes in global near-surface average temperatures relative to the time period 1850–1900. The ranges of the equivalent CO_2 concentrations (CO_2-eq), i.e., if all greenhouse gases are converted to CO_2, are given at the top left. Negative emissions mean that more CO_2 is removed from the atmosphere than emitted to it. Source: Global Carbon Project (2015)

The discussion whether anthropogenic climate change exists is a thing of the past; all countries clearly committed themselves to climate mitigation in Paris. The damage caused by climate change is becoming ever more distinctly manifest in many regions of the

---

32 The unit indicated here is C (carbon). Multiplication of this figure by 3.67 yields the values in units of CO_2

world. However, renewable energy sources are gaining ground. In 2015 they accounted for about 25% of electricity worldwide, in Germany for even more than 30%, and their share is increasing. In addition, the energy and carbon intensity of the global economy is declining. As early as 2013 and 2014, more capacities were installed in the area of renewables worldwide than in the fossil fuel and nuclear energy sectors combined. Pope Francis took up the findings of climate research in his environmental encyclical in 2015 and called for political consequences. And finally, the G7 heads of state committed themselves to decarbonisation, i.e., to a global economy without fossil fuels, at the summit in Elmau in 2015.

Unfortunately, it proved impossible to reach a consensus in Paris about including the word decarbonisation in the Agreement. It merely mentions 'achieving a balance between anthropogenic emissions by sources and removals by sinks of greenhouse gases in the second half of this century....'. This amounts to a loophole: strictly speaking, countries do not need to phase out fossil fuels at all. Technical solutions are still possible, for example CCS (carbon dioxide capture and storage), whereby CO_2 from coal-fired power plants is captured and stored underground or in the sea floor, if this method is defined as a sink. Moreover, the wording of the Paris Agreement is very vague in many cases. '[G]lobal peaking of greenhouse gas emissions' is to be reached 'as soon as possible' – very non-committal wording.

We are faced with entirely new challenges today. Climate change is a systemic risk. We are living in a time of accelerated technological and societal development as well as increasing global networking in the realms of the economy, communications, politics, and culture. Simple cause-and-effect principles are no longer valid. An event considered harmless may have unforeseen consequences even across large distances or after a long period of time, and those consequences may endanger the ability of the international community of states to function. For the damages caused by unchecked climate change will not impact the environment alone, but may also concern the economy or global security architecture: a global recession would be likely and continually growing refugee flows might result as well.[33]

The Earth system is complex; surprises are inevitable. Science can show trends, but can calculate the detailed consequences of unchecked climate change only with great uncertainty. Systemic risks such as climate change are characterised by a high degree of complexity, uncertainty, and ambiguity. The precautionary approach is highly relevant when dealing with systemic risks: if we cannot calculate the impacts of our actions on the climate precisely, then we should minimise the disruptions caused by human activities as much as possible.

---

33 http://www.climate-service-center.de/science/projects/detail/062860/index.php.en

Our Threatened Oceans

Stefan Rahmstorf, Katherine Richardson

> Living with the sea forces us to think differently: to think in a
> new way and to act differently.
>
> *Elisabeth Mann Borgese, 1918–2002, pioneer of marine conservation*

Viewed on a geological timescale, the world's oceans are in a phase
of rapid and far-reaching change brought into focus evermore
clearly by new data and recent research. These changes concern
physical characteristics such as temperatures, sea levels, and ocean
currents; chemical characteristics such as acidity; and the plant
and animal life in the ocean. We humans are not only the cause
of this development, which is dramatic in many respects, but we
are also adversely affected by it: we are harming ourselves. It is
our responsibility to shape the future of the oceans. To this end,
we should first take a sober look at the scientific findings, and we
provide a brief overview of them in the following.

Ocean warming is continuing

Measurement data from around the world show that global
warming is continuing, as predicted by climatologists (see the
contribution by Mojib Latif in this book). This development is
also observed in the world's oceans. Figure 1 shows the measured
increase of average global ocean surface temperatures. It amounts
to roughly 1°C since the early twentieth century.

Viewing the temperature increase on a map of the world reveals

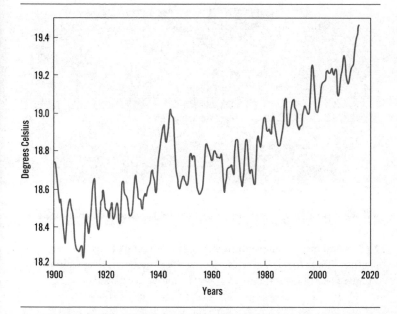

Fig. 1: Average global ocean surface temperatures from 1900 to 2015, as a moving average over 12 months. The relatively high values during World War II are probably artifacts of the data

distinct regional differences (see Fig. 2). A 'cold blob' in the North Atlantic south of Greenland is particularly conspicuous. This region has not only resisted global warming; it has even cooled slightly since the late nineteenth century. Its average temperature in 2015 even set a cold record: according to data from the US National Oceanic and Atmospheric Administration (NOAA), it had never been so cold there since the beginning of record-keeping in 1880. And that in the year which globally was the hottest by far!

An analysis of ocean temperatures published in 2010 by researchers from Bremen, Germany, attributes the 'cold blob' in the subpolar North Atlantic to a weakening of the Gulf Stream

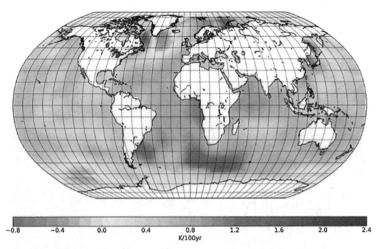

Fig. 2: World map of temperature change since the end of the nineteenth
century (linear trend of ocean surface temperatures in degrees Celsius per
hundred years). Graph: Levke Caesar (In colour: see plates)

system. 'The global conveyor has been weakening since the late
1930s,' they wrote in the Journal of Climate. A later analysis of
proxy data that permit the reconstruction of temperatures back
to the year AD 900 suggests that the weakness of the Gulf Stream
system in recent decades is probably unique in at least the past
1,100 years. Although such a weakening has been predicted by most
climate models, it appears to have occurred earlier than expected.
There is evidence that meltwater from the shrinking Greenland Ice
Sheet has contributed to it.

But back to global warming: not only are the temperatures at
the surface of the ocean increasing, but it is becoming warmer
at deeper levels as well. There is less warming at greater depths
since the warmth penetrates slowly from the surface to the deep
ocean. Named Argo Floats after the Greek myth of the argonauts,
about 4,000 autonomous measurement robots have been drifting

through the world's oceans since the year 2000, moving up and down the water column while taking temperatures, providing data with unprecedented global cover. The warming trend can now be documented down to several thousand metres depth. This warming impacts life in the ocean as well as its oxygen concentration, which will be discussed below.

An overall measure for the warming of the oceans is their increasing thermal energy content. More than 90% of the additional heat captured by the increasing amount of greenhouse gases in the atmosphere ends up in the oceans because of their great capacity to store heat. The average heat uptake of the world's oceans since 1971 is 200 terawatt – that is more than ten times the amount of total human energy consumption.

The sea level is continuing to rise

The global sea level has been measured by satellites since 1993. These data are available on the Internet, at *sealevel.colorado.edu*, for anyone to view anytime (as are many other data about the climate system). The curve shown in Figure 3 is constantly updated there.

According to these data, the global sea level rose by about eight centimetres – at a rate of three centimetres per decade – from 1993 until this book went to press. Besides this increasing trend, the curve reveals a few more interesting details. For example, there was a downward spike from 2010 to 2011, which initially baffled scientists (while climate deniers rejoiced). Yet the puzzle was solved with the help of other satellites: the main reason for the spike was that a huge amount of water was being stored on land after extreme precipitation and major flooding in eastern Australia. Elsewhere, such masses of water would drain off into the ocean, but in large parts of eastern Australia they flow inland to Lake Eyre, a salt lake. The sensitive instruments on the GRACE satellites can detect

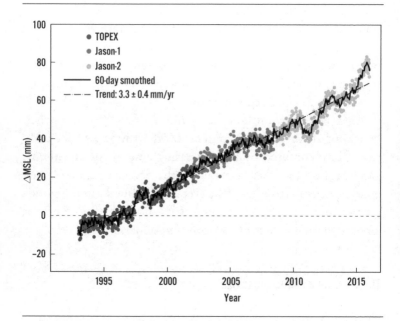

Fig. 3: Global sea level, measured by altimeters on the TOPEX, Jason-1, and Jason-2 satellites. Source: University of Colorado

such a water mass because it changes the Earth's gravitational field slightly. GRACE also weighs the shrinking of the continental ice sheets in this way.

More and more is becoming known about the history of sea levels before satellite measurements began – for one thing, of course, by using measurements of the sea level along the coastline, but going even further back by analysing proxy data. They permit reconstruction of the evolution of the sea level, e.g., from cores drilled in salt marshes along the coasts. Several groups of researchers have compiled a comprehensive database of such reconstructions from coasts on all continents over the course of recent decades, so a team headed by Robert Kopp of Rutgers University in the US was able to publish a global curve prepared on the basis of the database for the first time in early 2016. The data show that in none of the preceding 28 centuries did the global sea level rise even remotely as much as in the twentieth century. Instead, the typical pattern was that centuries with a few centimetres rise alternated with centuries with a few centimetres decline.

Based on the laws of physics, it is of course clear that global warming like that in the twentieth century must result in rising sea levels. For the warming of the ocean water described above causes thermal expansion – warmer water simply takes up more space. And a warming climate also melts continental ice, so that additional water enters the ocean. In fact, the contributions of ocean warming, disappearing glaciers, loss of ice in Greenland and Antarctica, and some smaller factors, all measured independently, add up to the actually measured rate of global sea level rise. The sea level has already risen by approximately 20 centimetres since the late nineteenth century.

Even this moderate rise is already causing considerable problems in many places, eroding coasts and exacerbating storm surges, as was the case with Hurricane Sandy, which flooded seven subway tunnels beneath the East River in New York, among other things, in October 2012. Or tropical storm Haiyan, whose storm surge in November 2013 devastated parts of the coast of the Philippines. In some places, it no longer even takes a storm: when the positions of the moon and the sun make the normal tides especially high, that is enough to put streets in Boston or Miami under water. Miami plans to spend half a billion dollars on protection against the rising water in the coming years – an undertaking that is futile in the long term because of the porous ground on which the city is built.

But what will the future of the sea level be? On the basis of new scientific insights, expectations have become significantly more pessimistic in recent years. The most recent 2013 report by

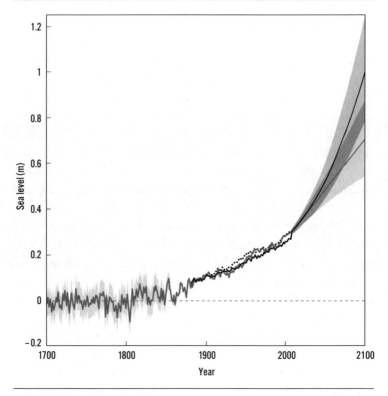

Fig. 4: The global sea level from 1700 to 2100. Source: modified following IPCC (2013)

the Intergovernmental Panel on Climate Change (IPCC), which is considered conservative, had to correct its projections to the year 2100 upward by about 60%, compared to the previous 2007 report (Fig. 4).

Even in the event of stringent climate mitigation, approximately 40 centimetres of sea level rise can be expected to occur in addition to the almost 20 centimetres since the beginning of the twentieth century, but according to the IPCC, it could also be an additional 70 centimetres or more. And that, too, might still be an underestimate. A survey of 90 renowned sea level experts from 18 countries, published in 2013, revealed that two-thirds of them expect a greater sea level rise than that estimated by the IPCC.

The more we learn about the behaviour of the large ice sheets, the more pessimistic the sea level predictions become. In March 2016, a group of US researchers headed by Robert DeConto presented the latest progress in the development of computer models of the Antarctic Ice Sheet in the leading science journal *Nature*. The researchers had taken account of insights from physics that describe better than before how shelf ice and large ice cliffs break up. They were the first to successfully reproduce the changes in the Antarctic ice mass in the Miocene (a geological era 23 to 14 million years ago), which are evidenced in geological data, with their model simulations. The same model gives reason to expect up to one metre of sea level rise in this century from Antarctica alone if greenhouse gas emissions continue unchecked; total sea level rise could even reach two metres by 2100.

And that, too, would only be the beginning, since sea level rise would continue at an accelerated pace for centuries after the year 2100. According to several studies published in recent years, the smaller West Antarctic Ice Sheet is probably already destabilised, and it will probably contribute to three metres of unstoppable sea-level rise over the course of the next few centuries. A similar fate is looming for parts of eastern Antarctica if warming continues.

Not least the small island states have been urging the global community for many years to limit global warming to, at most 1.5°C, so that they may still have a chance of survival. The Paris Climate Agreement reached in December 2015 includes this value at least as an aspiration.

Ocean life and climate change

Although the temperature increases recorded thus far in the ocean may seem small in our eyes, they are huge seen through the eyes of organisms living in the ocean. Therefore, climate change is already having enormous consequences for life in the ocean. Not only is temperature one of the most important factors controlling the distribution of organisms in the sea but it also influences physiological rates such as growth and respiration. It also provides important cues in the life history of many species, for example the onset of spawning and migration. Over the past ten years, numerous studies have demonstrated changes in the distributions of all types of marine organisms in response to changing ocean temperatures.

Fish are both the ocean organisms that most people are best acquainted with and for which we have the best long-term distribution data thanks to the monitoring done in connection with regulation of commercial fisheries. All over the world, we see changes in the distributions of fish species and fish communities emerging that were previously unknown to – or at least

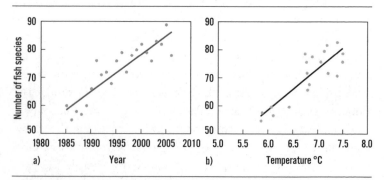

Fig. 5: Change in numbers of bottom fish species in the North Sea with time and temperature. Redrawn from Hiddink and ter Hofstede (2008). Climate induced increases in species richness of marine fishes. Global Change Biology 14, 453–460. doi: 10.1111/j.1365-2486.2007.01518.x

not recognised by – modern humans. The ~1.6°C temperature increase in bottom waters in the North Sea which has occurred over the last few decades has, for example, been accompanied by an increase in the number of fish species found there (Fig. 5).

The newcomer species are moving in from more southern waters as temperatures in the North Sea rise. At first, this may appear to be good news as it looks like climate change may, at least in the beginning, increase biodiversity in the North Sea. However, fish species differ greatly in terms of their size, their diets, their predators, their value in the commercial fishery and more. Of the fish species that have become more abundant in the North Sea, many are small sardine-like plankton eaters. The species that have become less abundant are generally larger fish, such as cod, which are associated with colder waters. This means that the structure of the ecosystem in the North Sea is changing such that there are more small fish that eat the tiny plants and animals floating in the water and fewer of the large fish that traditionally have been included in the northern European diet.

The massive redistribution of organisms in the ocean in response to climate change is creating communities and ecosystems comprised of organisms that, as far as we know, have not previously been found together. We do not yet know how well these new ecosystems will function – will they ultimately be dominated by single species? Will all life stages of the new (or old) members of the ecosystem be able to find food? Will these new ecosystems continue to supply valued services for human societies? Will they continue to perform within the Earth system in the same manner as earlier ecosystems? At present, we have no real methods to assess the functioning and 'health' of an ecosystem. Therefore, we have so far only been able to observe and describe the changes occurring.

Baltic cod in a changing climate

Given that cod has traditionally been a staple in the diet of northern Europeans, there has been much focus on this species over the past 10 years – not least of which in the Baltic. Given that cod is a cold water species, many have argued that it will disappear from the Baltic as it warms. Interestingly, however, fish bones recently recovered from prehistoric (7000 – 2900 BC) human waste dumps show that cod and the warm water swordfish have occurred simultaneously in the Baltic under warmer conditions in the past.

From what we know of cod physiology and life histories, it seems likely that they are less able to survive (are stressed) under warmer conditions but, apparently, they did remain in the Baltic under historical warm periods. That cod have survived in the Baltic under warmer conditions in the past is, however, absolutely not a guarantee that they will survive here through the current change in climate. The extremely fast (relative to those that have occurred in modern world history) rates of temperature increase currently being recorded challenge the adaptive capacities of species. Furthermore, cod in the Baltic today are facing other stressors that their ancestors did not. These include changed oxygen conditions, pollution, and – not least – heavy fishing pressure.

Just as our own bodies become weakened and less able to withstand disease or other challenges when we are dealing with multiple stressors so do all other organisms, including cod. We have historical evidence that the cod population can survive in the Baltic when dealing with warm temperatures when temperature increase presumably occurred as a single stressor. Whether or not cod can survive temperature increases in the face of all other current stressors, as said, remains to be seen. In any case, if we as a society want to maximise the chances of maintaining a cod population in the Baltic in the face of climate change, it would be prudent – in addition to mitigating human-caused climate change – to reduce all other stressors on the population, including the fishery.

Coral reefs are threatened by both climate change and increasing CO_2 in the atmosphere

Fish have been used here to exemplify how species are responding to climate change. Not all organisms are as motile as fish, however, and many are having difficulty keeping pace with ocean warming. Coral reefs comprise whole ecosystems that are permanently attached to the substrate. The little animals that form the reef itself, obtain their energy from tiny plants living within their tissues. When temperatures get too high, the coral animals expel their tiny plants – thereby losing both their energy source and their colour. We call this 'coral bleaching'. We have seen huge coral bleaching events (see Fig. 6) all over the world in recent years, and these are intensifying as ocean temperatures increase. In early 2016 the worst bleaching event ever was recorded on Australia's Great Barrier Reef. Over 90% of the reef showed signs of bleaching. Bleaching does not necessarily mean that all the corals die, but many do. Bleaching is probably also something that has always occurred, at least occasionally, but events are so intense and are happening so rapidly now that coral reefs do not have time to recover from a bleaching event before a new one sets in. This makes the future of the ocean's coral reefs very uncertain. It is worth noting, however, that it is estimated that a half a billion people the world over are, to a greater or lesser extent, dependent on coral reefs for their livelihoods. About 30 million of these (mostly living on coral atolls) are considered to be entirely dependent on coral reefs.

As if bleaching wasn't a big enough problem in itself, corals are also threatened by changes in ocean chemistry.

Fig. 6: A diver documents dead corals near Lizard Island, Great Barrier Reef, Australia, May 2016. Courtesy of XL Catlin Seaview Survey

Ocean acidification

An often-ignored side effect of our emissions ('the other CO_2 problem') is the acidification of surface waters of the ocean. The gases in the waters of the surface ocean and the atmosphere are constantly exchanging and coming into equilibrium between the two media. Therefore, when the CO_2 concentration in the atmosphere increases, so does the concentration of CO_2 in the surface ocean. When CO_2 dissolves in water, carbonic acid is formed. This means that the surface ocean 'acidifies'. The Intergovernmental Panel on Climate Change reported in 2013 that the current rate at which the ocean is acidifying is faster than at any time in the past 65 million years and possibly the last 300 million years. While we cannot predict exactly how organisms will respond to ocean acidification, we know that during the Earth's history, some acidification events with lower rates than observed today were linked to mass extinctions of marine biodiversity.

Many marine organisms are sensitive to changes in ocean acidity but those producing structures of calcium carbonate are especially susceptible as calcium carbonate dissolves under acidified conditions. The more the ocean acidifies, the more readily calcium carbonate dissolves. In addition to corals, molluscs and echinoderms (i.e., starfish and sea urchins) are believed to be most sensitive to ocean acidification; aquaculture facilities along the northeast Pacific coast are already suffering fatalities of oyster larvae due to acidification. Coral reefs are comprised of the chemical form of calcium carbonate that is most sensitive to acidification and, also here, changes are already being seen in natural coral communities that can be attributed to the increase in dissolved CO_2 in the surrounding water. These changes can only become more intense in the coming decades as atmospheric CO_2 concentrations continue to climb.

The ocean as a carbon sink

It has long been known that the ocean is an incredibly important player in the global carbon cycle. As the root cause of climate change is human perturbation of the carbon cycle, much focus during the past 10 years has been on getting a better understanding of the biological, physical, and chemical processes that contribute to ocean carbon cycling. We have known for some time that the ocean has, since the Industrial Revolution, taken up between one third and half of CO_2 emissions deriving from human activities. For a long time, it was thought that this uptake was primarily due to physical and chemical processes. Biological processes are now also recognised to be important and much progress in understanding how plants and animals contribute to the ocean carbon cycle has been made in the last 10 years.

It has, for some time, been assumed that biology primarily contributes to the ocean carbon cycle – and the ocean's ability to take up and store CO_2 from the atmosphere – through the sinking of biological materials formed through photosynthesis carried out by the tiny plants called phytoplankton. CO_2 is taken up from the surrounding waters via photosynthesis and converted to more complex molecules containing carbon. The cells containing these carbon molecules (or the organisms that ate those cells) then sink deep into the ocean. CO_2 is again produced when this material is degraded by bacteria but, if this bacterial activity occurs in the deep waters of the ocean, i.e., in a water mass that is not in direct contact with the atmosphere, then the CO_2 concentration becomes higher than that in the atmosphere. In other words, 'extra' CO_2 can be stored in deep ocean waters.

This process, which is known as the biological pump, is a passive process, i.e., it happens all by itself as dead and dying material obeys the laws of physics and sinks to the bottom of the sea. To our great surprise, it has been shown recently that biology can also contribute *actively* to the transport of carbon from surface waters to the deep ocean. *Calanus finmarchicus*, a large zooplankton species found over the entire North Atlantic, has a life cycle whereby it hibernates during the winter at depth (up to about 1 km) in the open ocean. Before swimming downwards for its winter nap, however, it produces large quantities of lipids (fat). All winter as they hibernate, the animals burn off these lipids and release CO_2 to the surrounding waters. It turns out that the carbon transported from surface to deep waters in the North Atlantic by this one species alone may be of the same order of magnitude as the biological pump in this region!

Despite these new discoveries the biological pump remains an important process and new information has been obtained in the past 10 years as to how it works and what it is sensitive to. One particularly interesting bit of news here is that 'biodiversity matters'!

We have, as a rule, when considering the biological pump, simply considered phytoplankton as a black box and used bulk parameters that describe the average condition of the phytoplankton community present. We now know that that approach just doesn't work! Some species contribute much more readily to the biological pump than others. Often, it can be the case that the species most important for driving the vertical transport of phytoplankton in the water column are not necessarily those that are most abundant in the surface waters. The bottom line is that if we want to understand why the biological pump is efficient in some areas and not others, we need to actually better understand what phytoplankton species are present, their life histories, and their sinking characteristics.

While this is daunting, it is not an impossible task owing to another great innovation that has become readily available for marine biological work over the past 10 years, one that allows the identification of organisms present using molecular genetics. This means that it is now possible to identify plankton communities without relying solely on time-consuming, laborious and expensive microscopic quantifications (which, in any case, did not allow proper identification of the smallest species present). The introduction of molecular genetics to the study of plankton has changed our entire way of thinking about life in the ocean. Where we before thought that plankton species must be well mixed in the world's oceans (i.e., given enough time everything will, presumably, get everywhere), the new molecular genetics approaches have shown much greater genetic diversity in the plankton world than we ever would have suspected. How is this diversity maintained? Obviously, not everything is mixing everywhere! When so much of nature in the ocean is so small, it has been very difficult for us to observe it and to record the changes that might be occurring in response to global change. Molecular genetics has given new tools to address such questions and the next 10 years will be very exciting indeed!

The ocean's ability to act as a carbon sink is probably decreasing

It has long been predicted that warming of the ocean's surface layer will lead to a reduction in the amount of biological material produced via photosynthesis owing to a reduction in the amount of nutrients being introduced from bottom to surface water via mixing and upwelling. Nutrients are scarce in the surface layer, as they are used-up there and sink down in the form of dead biological materials. The warming of surface waters due to climate change inhibits mixing, as warmer water tends to float on top. This reduction in material produced is likely to lead to a reduction in the strength of the biological pump.

During the last 10 years, however, several other processes by which a warmer ocean will potentially lead to a reduction in the strength of the biological pump have been recognised or quantified. New research suggests that the phytoplankton community will change and become smaller in response to both the reduced nutrient availability in surface waters and increased temperature. Small organisms are generally lighter and, therefore, less likely to sink into deeper waters than larger cells.

Finally, the sensitivity to temperature of the bacterial breakdown of biological material sinking through the water column has been quantified. We have long known that increasing temperature would increase bacterial activity, but we have not been able to include this term in modelling of the carbon cycle in a warmer world because it was not known to what extent temperature would affect the bacteria. These new numbers show us that even if we manage to constrain human-caused global warming to within the politically agreed $2°$ C guardrail, the increased bacterial activity in the surface ocean resulting from increased ocean temperatures will substantially reduce the ocean's capacity to take up and store CO_2 from the atmosphere, and, thereby, make it even harder for humans to constrain climate change.

Oxygen depletion

Just as for life on land, oxygen is vital for all animal life in the oceans. Unfortunately, human activities are increasingly leading to the depletion of oxygen in parts of the oceans. The main reason is nutrient input in coastal waters (e.g., from the runoff of fertilisers used in agriculture). However, recent research shows that global warming can also lead to the spread of oxygen-depleted zones in the open oceans.

At the ocean surface, oxygen is in plentiful supply as it enters from the atmosphere through air/sea gas exchange and is also produced by photosynthesis that occurs near the surface, where sufficient sunlight is available. Enrichment of stratified coastal waters, such as those found in the Kattegat, with nutrients (mostly nitrogen, N, and phosphorus, P) entering through rivers stimulates photosynthesis in the surface layer of the ocean. The resulting increased phytoplankton biomass in the surface layer decreases the amount of light penetrating farther down in the water column and, thereby, decreases photosynthesis in the deeper layers. And all of the organic material produced in the surface layer that sinks to deeper layers is decomposed there by bacteria, a process which uses up oxygen. This leads directly to a reduction of oxygen in the deeper layers and causes the spread of 'death zones' where no fish or other animal life can survive. These zones are concentrated along coastlines of high population density and intensive agricultural production.

This is not the whole story, however. Evidence is now emerging that changes in the vertical distribution of photosynthesis due to nutrient input are accompanied by changes in the biodiversity of the phytoplankton present in the water column. In particular, it appears that phytoplankton in the surface waters are smaller than those in the bottom layer. Food webs are different depending on whether phytoplankton populations are dominated by large or small species. When phytoplankton are large, they can be eaten directly by large zooplankton or even fish larvae. Thus, there are only 2–3 steps in the food web from phytoplankton to fish. Small phytoplankton are, on the other hand, not retained in the feeding structures of large zooplankton. They are eaten instead by protozoans, which are then eaten by small zooplankton that then can be eaten by large zooplankton. Thus, when phytoplankton are small, there are many more steps in the food web before the energy they contain arrives at the level of fish. For every step in the food web, about 90% of the energy contained in the prey is lost. Therefore, foods webs with many steps are much less efficient at transferring energy up though the food web than food webs with only a few steps. Thus, when fertilising the ocean results in changes in the size structure of the phytoplankton this will lead to fundamental changes in the ecosystem.

The second type of oxygen depletion is caused by global warming. When ocean waters get warmer this decreases their ability to take up oxygen. And as the surface waters warm most and thereby become lighter than in deeper layers, the mixing of oxygen-rich surface waters with deeper waters is reduced. Thus, less oxygen is brought down to subsurface layers where it is already in short supply. While this mechanism is predicted by climate models, such a forced decline in open-ocean oxygen levels is not yet apparent in the sparse observational data, given that large natural variations in oxygen content of ocean waters also occur. A detailed modelling study published in 2016 suggests, however, that already in a few decades, by 2030–2040, the oxygen loss forced by global warming will be so strong and widespread that it will clearly emerge from the natural variations.

Using the ocean as a rubbish dump

Humans continue to either deliberately or by accident use the ocean as a waste receptacle. All forms of toxic waste remain a problem in the ocean, but the last 10 years has seen a rise in the appreciation of ocean threats posed by plastic pollution as well as several dramatic pollution events.

Plastics

When plastics became readily available in the 1950s, they were heralded as time and money savers given they could simply be thrown away when they had performed the service for which they were designed. It was already known at that time, however, that bacteria do not degrade plastics and that they, therefore, have a very long life (though plastic can be broken into smaller and smaller pieces with the interaction of light, heat, and mechanical action such as waves). It seems odd that no one apparently worried at that time (or until very recently) about where all of this discarded plastic would end up.

It turns out that much of it finishes its life in the ocean. Around 8 million metric tons of plastic waste is believed to enter the ocean from land every year and it is feared that this number could increase significantly by 2025. This is in addition to other plastic materials, such as fishing gear, originating from activities taking place at sea that are knowingly or inadvertently disposed of in the ocean. Pieces of plastic in the ocean are problematic for a number of reasons, entangling creatures and also being mistaken for food by birds and ocean animals. Many are aware of the common and often repeated myth of the supposed 'plastic island the size of Texas' in the Pacific. In fact, there are several regions located in and near subtropical ocean gyres where floating litter (plastic as well as other forms) can accumulate. The size and location of these litter patches varies, though nowhere do they actually create real islands.

While large plastic litter in the ocean is an eyesore and the sight of ocean animals entangled in plastic waste is heart-breaking, we should, perhaps, be even more concerned about the plastic pollution in the ocean that we cannot see. Tiny micro-plastic particles originating from larger plastic pieces that, over time, are broken down by wind and weather, or that originate from the plastic 'beads' common in cosmetics and toothpastes, are found in oceans and on beaches around the world. These micro-particles are no less threatening; tiny animals at the base of the food web, and filter feeders such as clams and mussels, ingest them as food. Furthermore, some of these plastic particles appear to accumulate some particularly toxic pollutants on their surfaces.

Major pollution events

Two major ocean pollution events occurring during the last 10 years deserve special mention here: the Deepwater Horizon oil catastrophe in the Gulf of Mexico (Fig. 7), and the release of radioactivity from the Fukushima nuclear reactor in Japan.

The Deepwater Horizon oil spill is believed to, by far, have been the largest accidental oil spill ever occurring. After the explosion of a BP operated oil rig, oil gushed directly into the deep ocean (1,525 m) for 87 days. Official US Government estimates place the total amount of oil spilled at 4.9 million barrels with devastating consequences for flora, fauna, and the local fishing and tourist industries. In a report to the US President on the incident, it was concluded that the accident could have been avoided. Likewise, the report concluded that 'Scientific understanding of environmental conditions in sensitive environments in deep Gulf waters, along the region's coastal habitats, and in areas proposed for more drilling, such as the Arctic, is inadequate. The same is true of the human and natural impacts of oil spills'. While it will probably take decades for the local environment around the Deep Horizon accident site to recover, we can hope that the sheer magnitude

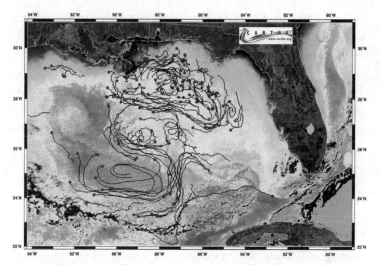

Fig. 7: CARTHE research consortium scientists analyse the paths of the oil pollution from the Deepwater Horizon disaster using drifters released in the Gulf of Mexico. The lines show the movements of the drifters four months after being released at the scene of the accident. The shades of grey show surface-level ocean temperatures. Courtesy of the Consortium for Advanced Research of Transport of Hydrocarbons in the Environment, CARTHE

and horror associated with such an accident will improve safety procedures surrounding oil extraction in the future and increase scientific effort aimed at understanding fragile marine areas.

A year later in March 2011, following an earthquake-generated tsunami, the nuclear reactors located in Fukushima malfunctioned. Ocean water was used to cool the overheated cores, resulting in approximately 80% of the radioactivity released entering the ocean. Ocean water carrying (weak) radioactive signals from Fukushima has been found off the west coast of North America, and the concentration of radioactivity in fish and other marine animals located near the accident site increased up to 1,000 fold (but, with notably few exceptions, never reached levels considered dangerous for human health). Today, small amounts of radioactivity are still leaking into the ocean from the site and fishing is still prohibited within 10 km of the accident site. Such a catastrophe emphasises how the ocean (and the atmosphere) interconnects us all. Although it was a Japanese decision to create and maintain the reactors in Fukushima, the effects of their failure were felt far from Japanese territory.

Harvest of marine resources

The picture regarding fisheries remains much the same as it did 10 years ago. Globally, the capture of wild marine fish has remained stagnant (or has possibly declined) since about 1990, but this is not due to lack of effort. According to FAO, only 3% of global fish stocks are underexploited. Over 50% are fully exploited and almost 25% are overexploited or depleted. The increases in harvest of marine organisms recorded in recent years have been due to an increase in marine aquaculture activities. These, however, do not come without an environmental price. Over 30% of the globally sold shrimp are produced through aquaculture. In all, it is estimated that 1–1.5 million hectares of coastline have been appropriated for this purpose. Much of this production occurs in Southeast Asia where mangrove forests are often removed to accommodate it. Of the 1–1.5 million hectares devoted to shrimp farming, it is estimated that 20–40% have resulted in the destruction of mangroves. Loss of mangrove forest not only results in loss of habitat for unique species, but mangroves also serve as vital barriers to large (weather or tsunami created) waves as they approach the coast. The loss of mangrove forests may therefore leave local coastal populations more vulnerable to the weather extremes predicted to accompany climate change.

Several policy initiatives have, however, been instigated during the past 10 years relating to the establishment of marine protected areas. The Aichi biodiversity targets agreed during the 2010 Conference of the Parties subscribing to the UN Biodiversity Convention include the establishment of 'a conservation target of ... 10% of marine and coastal areas'. The Sustainable Development Goal 14 ('Conserve and sustainably use the oceans, seas and marine resources for sustainable development'), adopted by the UN General Assembly in September 2015, reiterates this target: 'By 2020, conserve at least 10% of coastal and marine areas, consistent with national and international law and based on the best available scientific information.' While these targets are not legally binding and do not specifically suggest that fisheries should be prohibited in these areas, more and more protected areas are being created around the world and many of these have either forbidden fisheries or only allow forms that are believed to be gentle on the environment. Thus, there appears to be some hope that pressure on some fish stocks will be relieved in the coming years.

It is not only living resources that are harvested from the ocean; sand and stone have been harvested for centuries as building materials and, not surprisingly, shallow areas have been the most popular for this type of harvest. Significantly, shallow areas are where light from the sun can penetrate to the bottom, making it possible for anchored seaweeds to grow. Such areas are therefore extremely productive and are habitats for myriad different species. Recent years have seen some attempts at restoring stone reefs, which have been decimated by the human removal of stones for building purposes. The first EU-supported marine nature restoration project was to recreate a stone boulder reef in the Kattegat. The project ('Blue Reef') cost 4.8 million euros and was completed in 2013. Already, the project is having a distinctly positive effect on the distribution of young fish in the region.

Another 'harvest' from the ocean of which few are aware of the marine environmental consequences is 'land reclamation', where shallow coastal waters are filled in to create new land area. In northern Europe this technique was used in the nineteenth and early twentieth century to increase agricultural area. Today, it is used to develop coastal areas around the world, most notably for tourism. Again, because they allow light to penetrate to the bottom, shallow waters are highly productive. For a land-reclaimed area north of Funen in the Kattegat, it has been estimated that the shallow coastal waters locally produce up to 20 kg m^{-2} organic matter annually. As this material is potential food for fish and other marine organisms as well as birds, the conversion of shallow marine waters to land resulted in the loss of an enormous amount of food for marine organisms and bottom feeding birds. As in the case of the re-establishment of the stone boulder reefs, it may be possible to restore reclaimed land to its original marine state.

This is, of course, unlikely to happen when hotels have been built on the reclaimed land, but owing to the changing economics surrounding agriculture combined with the rising sea levels associated with climate change, some agricultural land created through land reclamation over the last two centuries is not economically viable for farming today. This means the restoration of some of the shallow marine areas sacrificed to land reclamation may, actually, be a possibility. A private Danish fund is currently attempting to restore a coastal lagoon by re-flooding ~350 hectares of reclaimed land on the north coast of Funen. If successful, this project could pave the way for the creation of similar nature restoration projects as coastal lands recede in the face of sea level rise.

What can we do?

The insights described above demonstrate clearly that the world's oceans are changing rapidly and with far-reaching effects. The health of the oceans and their biological wealth are massively threatened by simultaneously exacerbated environmental burdens: global warming, acidification, oxygen depletion, pollution by garbage and toxic substances, overfishing, and other unsustainable forms of use. It is difficult to get an overview of how well or poorly the various ocean regions are faring.

A 2008 study in the journal *Science* attempted to quantify and map the global human impact on the oceans. The data were updated again in 2015 (see Fig. 8). Nineteen environmental impacts were studied, including overfishing, climate change, and pollution. According to the study, not a single ocean region is unaffected by human uses. The polar waters and the tropical Pacific display the lowest impact. High to very high impact (red colours) is found especially in the North Atlantic (including the North Sea) and the North Pacific. Between the two studies, the impacts worsened in two-thirds of the world's ocean regions, especially because of progressing climate change. Regions showing improvement are reason for hope: destructive forms of fishing have declined in many European waters, for instance.

A group of more than 30 ocean researchers proposed a different approach in the journal *Nature* in 2012: an Ocean Health Index.[1] This index encompasses ten categories, including water quality, biodiversity, coastal protection, tourism and recreation, and food provision. The ideal considered here is not the ocean's natural state, but instead its optimal utility for us human beings. Uses such as tourism and food provision are considered positive, provided they are sustainable – which is why a coast visited by only a few tourists

---

1   See www.oceanhealthindex.org

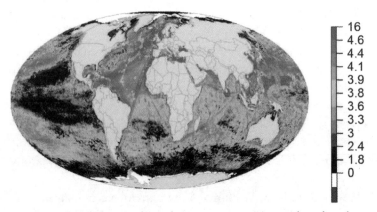

Fig. 8: Impact on the oceans due to human activities. The numbers describe the overall impact based on 19 categories. Source: Halpern et al. (2015) Nature Communications 6, 7615. (In colour: see plates)

gets a poor score in this category. In contrast, good scores were usually given for biodiversity – not because marine life along our coasts is even remotely as rich as it was just a few centuries ago, but because the situation is mostly stable and only a few marine animals are threatened by extinction. The data were evaluated on a scale of 0 to 100% for each coastal nation – these data can be viewed individually or as an overall score. The world's oceans overall were assessed as 60% healthy in this sense. A score greater than 70% was achieved in only 5% of all countries (including Germany at 73%). One can, of course, argue about the individual evaluations – above all, the authors intended to spark a debate about sustainable use of the oceans and to present a list of criteria that could then be further developed as research and societal discussion progress.

Ultimately, it is about the essential question of how our oceans and coasts can be managed well in light of global warming and the strong pressures to use them – in UN jargon: ocean governance in the broadest sense. The German Advisory Council on Global

Change (WBGU) presented an expert report on this in 2013 and developed a number of proposals.

The guiding principle is to view the world's oceans as the common heritage of mankind (as is already the case for Antarctica). This notion is not new. It was proposed as early as the 1960s by Arvid Pardo and Elisabeth Mann Borgese in the course of the negotiations concerning the UN Convention on the Law of the Sea. In concrete terms, this guiding principle means that no single actor, or company, or nation can claim an unlimited right to use the oceans. Instead, rules must be put in place that permit sustainable and just use of the oceans as a common good, and prevent short-term exploitation and overuse, guaranteeing their health and preservation for future generations. It may sound utopian today to enshrine the principle of the common heritage of mankind in international law – but a basis for this is already laid out in the Law of the Sea, and we consider it likely that a visionary reform of the Law of the Sea would find the support of the wider public in many countries.

An important guiding principle on the path toward this goal is the systemic approach. The ocean ecosystems are such complex networked systems that separate management of individual sectors (such as shipping, ocean energy, fishing, tourism) cannot do them justice. The third guiding principle is the precautionary approach. Safety margins taking account of the complexity and uncertainties as well as the danger of the irreversible collapse of ecosystems should be built into the system of marine management (for example when determining fishing quotas).

The global threats to the marine ecosystems from climate change and acidification, which must be averted as rapidly as possible, are of central importance. Both are caused by our carbon dioxide emissions. That is why one historical turning point giving rise to hope is the Paris Climate Agreement of December 2015: it is binding under international law and had already been signed by 177 states in New York on 22 April 2016 – the earliest possible day, unprecedented for a UN Convention. The agreed goal was to limit global warming to 'well below 2°C' (we have already caused warming of about 1°C). This means that we must reach net zero emissions of greenhouse gases in the second half of this century – which the Agreement explicitly calls for. What matters now for preserving the oceans is that the national governments not only implement their reduction pledges, but also make them significantly more ambitious in the future.

The future of the oceans is in our hands. There are depressing developments, just as there are signs of hope. Every one of us – including those of us far away from the coasts – can make a contribution, for example by preventing emissions and plastic waste, by making informed purchasing decisions about ocean products, through political work, by membership of ocean preservation organisations, or simply as a voter.

Overcrowded world? The global population and international migration

Rainer Münz and Albert F. Reiterer

This contribution discusses the history and current state of humankind from the perspective of population development and international migration. It also takes a brief look at future developments in the twenty-first century.

We are all part of the population of a town, a country, a continent – and thus part of the global population. The starting point is a person's place of residence, which defines this aspect of belonging. The population is constantly changing because of reproduction, mortality, and migration. Children are born, residents die, people move to a town, others move elsewhere. At the same time, the individuals within a society are ageing. All this works to change the size and the structure of societies.

It is also clear that we as humankind are part of a superordinate ecosystem. Swedish naturalist Carl von Linné was the first person to place human beings into his 'system of nature' as *Homo sapiens* in 1735, and he did so practically without comment. In place of the extensive descriptions he used to characterise the other species, he wrote simply 'know thyself'. Since then, biology considers us human beings to be a 'species' and thus part of evolution, even though this is still debated in traditional-religious circles to this day.

The relationship between humans and the environment has changed over time. Human beings have spread across vast areas of our planet's land mass. They have developed cultural technologies – from agriculture to the use of fossil fuels – that have enabled them to settle and survive practically anywhere. In this context, human history can also be interpreted as an emancipation of humans from nature. This in turn has quite significant consequences for the ecosystem.

What do we know about the population?

In principle, it is easy to determine a country's population figure: all we need to do is count heads. Until recently, more highly developed countries periodically conducted censuses and then updated their population data. By now, the administrative data about individuals, births, deaths, and migration is so well networked in some countries that their statistics offices conduct register-based censuses. This permits them to ascertain the status and development of the population practically at the touch of a button. However, the unregulated migration of a large number of refugees across Europe in the years 2015–16 showed that existing registration systems are unable to handle all situations.

Births and deaths are relatively well documented in developed countries and are also registered statistically. What is less clear is the number of people moving in and out. Not all those moving away from a country inform the authorities. But some immigrants also attempt to avoid registration: especially those lacking legal residence status. Finally, there are ambiguous cases. Does the Polish nurse or cleaner who commutes between her work in Frankfurt am Main and her family in the High Tatras belong to the German or the Polish population? And what about a young man who works as a skiing instructor in the Austrian Alps in the winter and as a sailing instructor on the Baltic in the summer?

The problems are much greater in less developed countries lacking a well-functioning administrative system. Quite a few countries do not record all births and deaths, let alone migration in and out of the country. There, we must rely on sample surveys and estimates. In other words, what we know about the global population is based only in part on official data, and otherwise on additions of such estimates.

A brief history of the global population: from Lucy and the Turkana Boy to 7.5 billion

How long has the population been growing? In order to answer this question, we must first clarify: since when have human beings actually existed? The beginnings of humanity date back two million years if we have history beginning with *Homo erectus*. It cannot be proved that we descend from a single couple – Adam and Eve, as it were – but genetic analyses show that we all originate from a relatively small group of developed hominids, who lived in Eastern Africa 2 million years ago. However, they shared only basic anatomy with current-day human beings. It has not been fully determined when language developed – 200 years ago, Wilhelm Humboldt called this making 'infinite use of finite means'. The same is true of the first occurrence of symbolic forms and objects. In any case, there is evidence of this that is approximately 300,000 years old: near Tan-Tan in Morocco and Berekhat Ram on the Golan.

We can only speculate about the number of people in prehistoric times. Regardless of all the uncertainty, one thing is clear: the numbers were initially very small. But there was long-term growth even back then. It took place in surges, which were followed by phases of stagnation (cf. Zahid et al., 2015). During shorter periods, there were numerous declines in population as well as events leading to the disappearance of entire groups, and at times almost the extinction of humanity.

The last three major surges can readily be placed in their historical context. The fact that some of our ancestors left Africa approximately 100,000 years ago marks the point when anatomically modern humans began to settle on other continents as well:

first in Western and Southern Asia, then in Eastern Asia, perhaps as early as 60,000 years ago in Australia, and about 45,000 years ago in Europe. Humans arrived in North and South America only later, at a point in time not known exactly. This global expansion was the first precondition for the growth of humanity to 3–4 million at the end of the Palaeolithic Age.

The next decisive change began 14,000 years ago; it concerned our lifestyle, which had been exclusively nomadic until then, and was so radical that it is called the 'Neolithic Revolution' (Childe, 1958). Up until then, all human beings had been hunters and gatherers. The first groups of people became sedentary during a period of global warming at the end of the last Ice Age. That was when agriculture and animal husbandry developed in the Middle East, first with sheep and goats, later with cattle (Cauvin, 2013). Societies with a division of labour developed on this basis. Humans who had become sedentary had more children and systematic food production also enabled more people to survive. Subsequently, population growth increased.

Seven thousand years ago, an estimated 7–10 million people already lived on our planet. The first cities emerged at the time, and around them the first states – first in Mesopotamia, somewhat later in India and China, significantly later also in Central and South America. These urban societies expanding into their hinterland were based on complex social, political, and military organisation, which enabled a greater division of labour. Population growth accelerated in these societies, so population figures rose steeply in some parts of the world.

It is likely that approximately 240 million people lived on Earth at the beginning of the Common Era. The Roman Empire, China, and India were each home to one-quarter of them. There was probably a significant decline in population in all three of these global regions in the following centuries. The rest of the world was, and remained, sparsely populated. In Europe and the Mediterranean region, this decline was a consequence of the step backward in civilisation in late antiquity – euphemistically called the 'barbarian invasion'. With the end of the Western Roman Empire, the political framework and the uniform legal system disappeared. The economic area and the infrastructure also disintegrated over time (Pirenne, 1985).

Only after the year 700 did population growth begin anew. In China, the population increased from 60 to 120 million within three centuries. Following a cooler phase in Europe, temperatures rose again. And around the year 1000, the so-called Medieval Climatic Optimum left its mark on life in Europe. Increased settlement and political reorganisation of Europe beginning in the Carolingian era enabled an expansion of production. The population began to grow again. But when the climate once again cooled from the fourteenth century on – this period, lasting into the nineteenth century, is called the Little Ice Age – it became difficult to feed the European population with the cultivation methods of the day.

Following military action in the Crimea, the Genoese introduced the plague to Italy in 1347/1348. The disease spread with lightning speed across almost the entire continent, whose population was already weakened by a lack of food.

More outbreaks of the plague and other epidemics such as cholera and typhus followed. The often underestimated mobility of people in the late Middle Ages, with wandering journeymen, pilgrims, artisans, harvest workers, and mercenaries, contributed to the rapid spreading of the 'Black Death'. The enormously densely populated mediaeval and early modern cities with their lack of sanitation were ideal breeding grounds for all these diseases. For example, 7 hectares of urban area in sixteenth-century Innsbruck probably housed 5,000 people – this amounting to more than 700 people per hectare.

One-quarter, perhaps even one-third, of all Europeans died of epidemics during the transition from the Middle Ages to the modern period (Bulst, 1979), in some regions even about half. The fourteenth-century author, Giovanni Boccaccio, in his collection of novellas *The Decameron,* begins with a powerful description of the Black Death, but other events of the modern period would decimate the population; for example, the Thirty Years' War killed almost 40% of the German population between 1618 and 1648.

The next surge of global population growth followed from 1750 onwards – a surge that has continued into the twenty-first century. During the Ch'ing (Qing) Dynasty, the population of China grew to 300 million. The Industrial Revolution began in Western Europe, and the first demographic transition spread from Northern Europe: a true epochal watershed that laid the foundation for the lifestyle and form of economic activity dominant today.

As early as 1800, the global population reached the threshold of one billion. At the time, a good 60% of humanity lived in Asia. Yet the Industrial Revolution began in Europe, and that is where the strongest population growth in the world occurred. Part of this growth was exported 'overseas' during the major emigration movements of the nineteenth and early twentieth century.

The European societies of the day would have been confronted with substantially larger social problems if they had not been able to rid themselves of part of their 'excess' workers and population. However, this was not a one-way street, as some people certainly did migrate back. One example is the poet Nikolaus Lenau, who grew up in what is today Romania. He went to the US in the summer of 1832 and bought a handsome piece of land: 400 acres, or more than 100 hectares. But just half a year later, he turned his back on the land of his dreams, deeply disappointed.

A broad working class emerged at the time in Europe and North America, mostly consisting of workers with poor training or none at all. Most of their relatives had originally migrated from rural areas – for example Poles to the Ruhr area or Czechs to Vienna. It took them about a generation to begin to take their destiny into their own hands, not least under the political influence of the rising labour movement.

In the mid-1920s, the global population crossed the threshold of two billion. In 1960, it was already three billion. In 2017, the figure was in the region of 7.5 billion. In contrast to the nineteenth and early twentieth century, this growth has been concentrated in the less developed countries of the world since 1945 – in recent times especially in Asia, where roughly 60% of all people live today.

Projections by the United Nations and other institutions show that the global population will continue to grow for a while. The 2015 revision of the UN projections expects more than 9.7 billion people in 2050; the medium-variant projection estimates an increase to just over 11.2 billion in 2100.

In the future, growth will no longer be strongest in Asia, where the population is expected to peak in around 2060 and then decline. In 2100, Asians should make up only 44% of humanity. Shrinking populations are to be expected, especially in China, Japan, and Korea. The same is true of many European countries, even though the development will be slowed because of immigration.

In contrast to developments in Europe and Asia, Africa's population will roughly double by 2040 and increase fourfold by the end of the twenty-first century. As a result, the demographic weight of the continents and country groups will shift. The countries highly developed today will therefore become relatively less important, whereas more and more people will live in countries that are currently less highly developed. In 1950, the European population still accounted for almost 22% of the global population; in 2015, only for 10%; and in 2050, presumably just 7%. The opposite is true of Africa, whose share of the global population is increasing the most rapidly. In 1950, only 9% of humanity lived in Africa, in 2015 16%, in 2050 presumably 26%, and in 2100 probably even 39%.

For less highly developed countries, strong population growth can amount to a development trap. They would urgently need

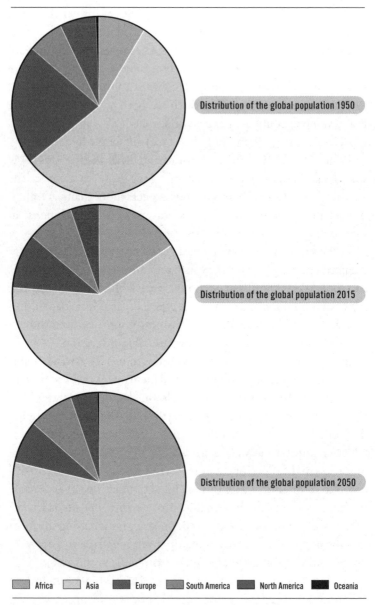

Fig. 1: The distribution of the global population is shifting

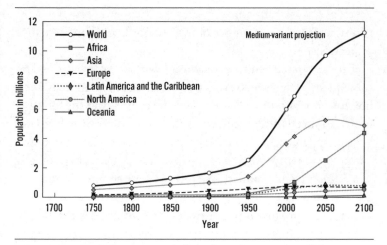

Fig. 2: Global population 1750–2100 (Source: UN Population Division, World Population Prospects, Rev. 2015)

their resources for investments in production and infrastructure to generate more prosperity. Yet a considerable portion of these resources has to be used for securing the basic needs of a rapidly growing population.

What is decisive for future development, however, is whether sufficient funds are available for school education and vocational training for children and youths. For investments in human capital are the only way to create the opportunity for sustainable economic development beyond the subsistence economy. At the same time, better education for girls and young women generally brings about lower numbers of children per family.

Prognoses and projections: looking ahead to the future

The United Nations has been preparing longer-term population projections since 1951, which demographers as well as many politicians and planners in poorer countries turn to for reference. Most developed states, in contrast, prepare their own prognoses. In addition, there are a number of institutions that offer alternative projections.

The UN published its projections every five years at first and subsequently has done so every two years since 1978. Initially, their horizon was 'just' three decades into the future. And the forecasts underestimated the dynamics of global population growth. It later became apparent that the UN statisticians assumed a global population figure for 1950 that was too low. Shortly thereafter, roughly 100 million people more than expected were counted in the 1953 census in China.

Later, the prognoses were extended to 2050, today through to 2100. The medium-term prognosis was repeatedly corrected up or down.

In 2010, the UN prognosis for the twenty-first century was 9.3 billion people in 2050 and 10.1 billion in 2100. The 2015 prognosis corrected the expected global population upward: to 9.7 billion in 2050 and 11.2 billion in 2100. This amounts to a difference of no less than roughly 300 million (more than 3%) and 1.1 billion people (more than 10.1% of the previous figures), respectively. Only for the period after 2100 do very long-term projections expect the number of people on our planet to stabilise or even decline.

It is important not to overlook the difficulties of such long-term projections and thus to regard them with a certain amount of scepticism.[1] In general, it is true that projections are as good as the available data and the assumptions on which they are based. Apparently, future numbers of births were estimated more accurately than the development of life expectancy. In the early days, too little consideration was given to the fact that a decline in mortality is not only dependent on the standard of living, but that in less-developed societies, such a decline could be 'imported'

---

1   Cf. on this Keilman (1998); also, e.g., Khan and Lutz (2007)

through targeted measures by the community of states and their organisations – for instance through mass immunisations, prevention of epidemics, and famine relief. Population science has the most difficulty with prognosticating future migration flows.

The projections have improved because over time, more complete initial data have become available. What is decisive, however, is the insight that more people will have to share our planet, its resources, and its ecosystem in the future. This raises the question regarding more equitable distribution of the available resources. But we must also ask: which forms of economic activity and life can be sustainable for a significantly larger global population?

The demographic transition: modern populations are emerging

The societies of the past were 'wasteful' from a demographic point of view: many children were born, but half of them died before adulthood. Mortality was high among adults as well. Today, the situation is exactly the opposite in Europe, North America, and East Asia. Life expectancy is high. Almost all children survive and reach adulthood. Compared with the situation 200 years ago, however, the numbers of children per family are low. At least in the most prosperous part of the world, our current-day societies are demographically 'sparing'.

Attitudinal changes also known as the 'demographic transition' occurred between these two situations. A decline in mortality was decisive, especially infant and child mortality. As a result, parents had more surviving children than expected. They reacted by limiting the number of births – with a time lag of a generation in most societies.

A large number of births and high mortality brought about only low population growth in premodern societies. In years with famine, epidemics, or devastation from war, the population figures even dropped. As mortality declined, population growth increased since fertility remained at the old, high level for a time. We saw this first in Europe and North America, then in Asia and Latin America, and today especially in Africa.

Even if the number of children per woman declines, the population continues to grow for a while: after all, many more young people reach the age for starting a family, in other words, have children themselves, even if significantly fewer than their parents and grandparents had. This is called demographic momentum.

It takes time for low numbers of children to slow down growth. Today there are significantly fewer than two children per family in almost all highly developed countries, above all in Europe, but also in Japan, Korea, and Singapore. The children's generation is thus smaller than that of their parents. Population growth occurs only if immigrants enter the country in larger numbers. They often come from less-developed societies, and it is also not uncommon for them to have more children, thus contributing to the population of their new homes in two ways.

In a growing number of countries with low numbers of children, the population figures are already on the decline. This is true not only for parts of Southern and Eastern Europe, but also for Russia and Japan. The population of China will also begin to drop soon.

Even after a good two centuries, the demographic transition has by no means come to an end. Since the middle of the twentieth century, a reduction in the numbers of children has been observable in the countries of the global South, but with a time lag. Yet some societies are still experiencing rapid demographic growth, especially in Africa and Western Asia.

The process is also following a somewhat different course in poor countries and emerging economies than it did in Europe at the time. After all, there are global efforts to disseminate family planning and birth control, to combat epidemics, and to reduce maternal and child mortality today. Famine and disaster relief, which function almost everywhere in the world, contribute significantly to keeping the number of fatalities low in the case of droughts, failed harvests, and humanitarian crises.

Life expectancy and mortality

The decline of mortality began in the North and West of Europe and was closely connected to better standards of living. Expansion of food production and improved transportation and sanitation (especially the construction of water supply, sewer, and waste disposal systems) enabled life expectancy to rise.

Some interventions were banal from today's perspective. For example, when physician John Snow (1813–1858) removed the pump handle from a tainted well in Broad Street in London's Soho district in 1854, the neighborhood was less than pleased. People had to fetch water from far away. But the cholera epidemic in the area was brought to a standstill.

People's changing attitude toward life itself and toward children as (future) people also played a role: children received more care, attention and affection, especially in the bourgeoisie of the more highly developed European societies from the late eighteenth century on. This too resulted in declining mortality of infants and children of all ages, and their better chances of survival caused the population to begin to grow.

Other factors also played a role in the twentieth century. Effective control of epidemics was decisive. Mass immunisations made diseases practically disappear – polio, for example, and, at least in today's developed countries, tuberculosis as well (though some of these diseases are spreading again today because of increased travel). The likelihood of surviving a heart attack has increased significantly and the decline of hard physical labour, fatal work, and traffic accidents, as well as greater health awareness, means that increasing numbers of people are healthy when they reach older age.

The highest life expectancy is currently not in Europe however (2010–15: 77.0 years, both sexes together), because of the

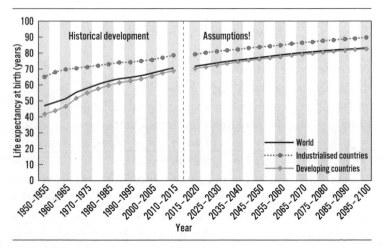

Fig. 3: People are living longer on average

disparities in different European countries' levels of development.
North America ranks first (79.2 years), whereby this is mostly
due to Canada. Life expectancy continues to be lowest in Africa
(59.6 years). It is expected that life span is continuing to increase;
the global average has risen from 47 years in the 1950s to 70 in
2015. The increase was above average, especially in Asia and Latin
America. On average, it was greater in less-developed countries
(from 41 to 69 years) than in highly developed societies (65 to
77 years), which had already previously accomplished some of the
improvements leading to longer lives.

What can be concluded when we compare continents becomes
even more distinct when we compare countries. Life expectancy
rises as prosperity increases. This link was first modelled in the
form of a curve by US economist Samuel Preston in 1974. But
today, the Preston curve shows that the link becomes progressively
weaker as per capita income rises above 30,000 US dollars per
year. Then, other factors play a larger role. One of them is social

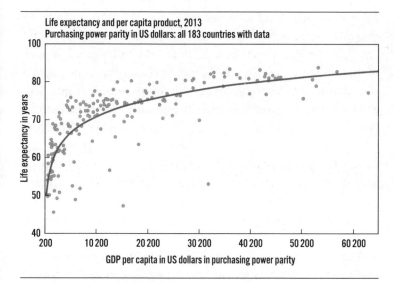

Fig. 4: Today's Preston curve

inequality: for example, the US is one of the countries with statistically the highest level of prosperity, but the degree of inequality is approximately that of a developing country. And until recently, the US was the only highly developed country without health insurance for all. That too reduced life expectancy in comparison with similarly prosperous societies.

It can be said in general terms that at a particular level of development, societal institutions and political decisions affect average life expectancy. In other words, material wealth is just one of several parameters. And besides its level, the distribution of wealth within a society is decisive, even if some experts – for example 2015 Nobel Laureate for Economic Sciences Angus Deaton (1994, 2013°) – doubt the impact of inequality in developed societies on life expectancy.

Family size and number of children

Historically, the decline in the number of children began in Northern and Western Europe. Yet it did not start simultaneously in each of the individual social strata. The middle classes were almost always the forerunners. Various forms of birth control were used quite discreetly. An open debate about family planning was met with strong resistance by the clergy and the political community. Physician Charles Knowlton (1800–1850) from Massachusetts wrote *The Private Companion of Young Married People* in 1832 and had to spend a few months in jail for it, but was acquitted on appeal. Decades later, there was a sensational court case in England against the English publisher of his writings. Only in 1877 was it decided in favour of the publisher. The dissemination of this sex education pamphlet, whose audience was mostly lower middle class, benefited immensely from this scandalisation. Only about 1,000 copies had been sold prior to the lawsuit. Afterwards, sales jumped to 250,000 in a single year.

Urban blue-collar workers generally began to limit the numbers of their children with a certain time lag after the middle classes. However, the question was discussed openly in the emerging labour movement in Great Britain quite early, as early as 1800. Richard Carlyle (1790–1843), a self-taught tinsmith and the son of a shoemaker, promoted both expanded suffrage and responsible parenthood and had to spend a number of years in jail for this reason. He and other authors were motivated by Malthus's famous *Essay on the Principle of Population* (1798).[2]

The trend of reducing the number of children reached Europe's peasant population particularly late. Just two generations ago, it was not uncommon for families in rural areas of Central Europe to have four or five, or more, children.

---

2   An Essay on the Principle of Population by Thomas Robert Malthus was a prophetic
     piece of writing that predicted a bleak future of famine and starvation with
     population growth far outstripping increases in food production.

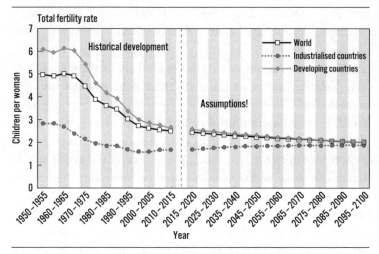

Fig. 5: Children per woman in the highly and less developed world

In Southern and Eastern Europe, the development began much later than in the North and West. But the difference was not only in the number of children, but also in the type of family. In Southern and Eastern Europe, marriage tended to occur more frequently and at a younger age, in the Northwest, less frequently and at an older age, even in premodern times. A larger part of the population of the old European agrarian societies in the Northwest of our continent remained unmarried throughout their lives. This was not the case in the Southern and Eastern parts of our continent. The boundary between the two regions is called the Hajnal line, for the US social historian John Hajnal. Historically, it ran roughly from Trieste to St Petersburg.

Around 1950, the average number of children per woman was approximately 5 worldwide; by 2015, it had dropped to just 2.5. In the developed countries, the number shrank from 2.9 to 1.8 children during this period, and, in the less developed countries, from just over 6 to 2.7. The numbers of children are highest in Africa, where the decline began only in the 1970s and is progressing more slowly overall.

One reason for this decline is a radical change in the relationship between the generations. In premodern societies, children were needed for their labour in the family. At the same time, adult children were responsible for caring for their parents if they were ill or elderly. In contrast, the incentives to have as many children as possible diminished in capitalist society and the modern welfare state. The social welfare systems provide protection against the most important risks today. But even in societies without social welfare systems, there are more reasons to have fewer children. Urban lifestyles and formal labour markets becoming more widespread are contributing factors here. Especially in parts of Asia and Latin America, the notion is beginning to prevail that fewer, better educated children can provide superior care for their parents in old age. Besides, the majority of people in Europe rely on public pension programmes and health insurance.

In parts of Asia – especially in China and India – there is an additional topic that deserves attention: a highly distorted imbalance between the sexes in the younger generation because, for at least 25 years, selective abortions of pregnancies with a female fetus have resulted in significantly more boys than girls being born. In the countries affected, one long-term consequence is that young men, especially those from the lower strata of society, cannot find female partners.

Demographic ageing: the facts and the debate

All premodern societies had young populations. The numbers of children per woman were high, as was mortality – especially infant and child mortality. As a consequence, there were relatively few older people. Modernisation then brought about better living conditions and declining mortality. A larger number of children survived, which is why population growth accelerated. But families subsequently adapted their family planning to the declining child mortality rates and had fewer children. In particular, women had, and still have, a strategic role here.

The topic of ageing is different today. Increasing life expectancy and reproduction rates that have dropped far below the reproduction level of 2 children per family resulted in advanced demographic ageing especially in Europe and Japan. Because older people are living longer and longer and fewer children are born at the same time, the average age is increasingly climbing upwards. In the US, ageing is curbed to a certain extent because the numbers of children are somewhat higher and because of substantial immigration, particularly from South America and Asia. But there, too, the same trends are to be seen among the population of European descent.

The process of ageing is becoming noticeable globally as well. In 1950, the number of people of prime working age (15–65 years) was not even twice as large as the number of children under 15. In contrast, there will be three times as many 15- to 65-year-olds in 2050 as children under 15. In the future, the number of older people will grow most rapidly, almost tripling between 2015 and 2050.

Demographic ageing is the downside of increasing life expectancy. In principle, it is based on a positive development in almost all 'post-transitional' societies. Never before was there a time when people lived so long on average. However, this is considered a problem for various reasons because the labour markets, social welfare systems, as well as health care and care of the elderly need to be adapted to this change. Having to tackle such reforms creates stress in political and economic systems.

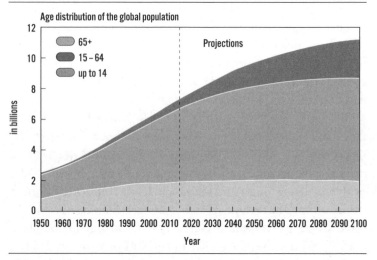

Fig. 6: The numerical relationships between the generations are shifting

Demographic ageing: two examples

Compared with other highly developed states, Germany has particularly low numbers of children and its population is therefore ageing especially quickly. The unification of the former German Democratic Republic and the old Federal Republic of Germany accelerated this process because the numbers of children in East Germany were particularly low for a longer period of time. This was caused by a rapid increase in the age at which East German women had their children to the West German level. At the same time, life expectancy in East Germany increased especially rapidly following unification.

In the past 25 years, the percentage of children, youths, and young adults under 30 declined from 38% in total (1992) to 32% (2015). In the coming years, this group's share will no longer decrease as much for the reason that the majority of immigrants are under 30. In contrast, the group of older people is growing

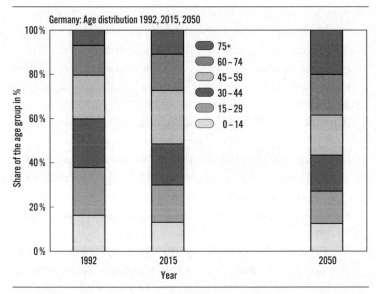

Fig. 7: Germany: Age distribution in a highly developed country

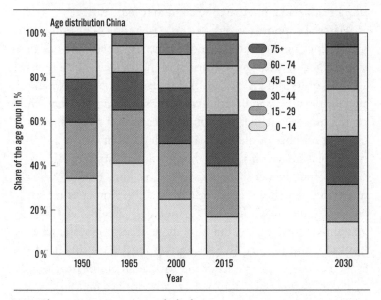

Fig. 8: China: Ageing in a particularly dynamic emerging economy

rapidly. In 1992, just 20% of Germany's population was over 60 years old; in 2015, the figure was already 28%. And the prognosis for 2050 is that just under 40% will then be over 60.

Ageing is not limited to the highly developed countries. This, too, is evident in the country on Earth with the largest population by far: China.

After the Second World War, China was not very different from other developing countries of the time. In 1965, 41% of the population were under 15. By 2015, this group's share had dropped to 18%. In contrast, only about 5% were over 60 in 1965. In 2015, older people already accounted for 16% of the population. And this percentage will continue to rise. At the same time, it is to be expected that China's population will shrink after 2030.

In China, the change in the age distribution is not only a result of societal modernisation, but also of the policy of limiting births, which has been in place since the 1970s. This 'one-child policy' was officially abolished only in 2015, even though quite a few couples had already had more than one child in recent years.

Material support for older people is an unsolved problem in China since neither the state nor former employers provide pensions or health care for the majority of the population. As in other societies of Asia and Africa, caring for their older parents was traditionally the task of adult children. A consequence of the one-child policy, however, is that the younger generation has to support a growing number of older relatives today and in the future. This means that better-off Chinese households are attempting to save a significantly higher share of their income 'for a rainy day'. So the question is whether it is possible to establish a functioning social welfare system in China. This is not only about social welfare guaranteed by the state, but also about access to public schools, hospitals, and municipal housing. Up until now, this has been available only to people from the particular city or province. In light of high internal mobility, there are 200–250 million Chinese from the poorer provinces of Western China who are living in the economically more attractive southern and eastern regions of the country without the rights of local citizens.

The paradox is, with its high economic growth, China is making a particularly strong arithmetical contribution to reducing the global inequality between the less developed and the highly developed countries at the country level. At the same time, its highly underdeveloped and discriminating welfare model is contributing to increasing internal inequality rather than alleviating it.

Migration

Migration is more than spatial mobility. It means temporarily or permanently changing residence. Such a change within a country is called internal migration. In contrast, international migration involves crossing a boundary into another country. Nomads who have no permanent residence are therefore mobile, but not migrants. Many 'mass migrations' in antiquity and the early Middle Ages were not migrations as we understand them today, but occupation and settlement of land by militarily superior groups.

Migration gained an additional dimension with the development of the modern state, its fixed borders, and its unified concept of citizenship combined with demands that citizens and subjects be loyal. A person going abroad is a foreigner there. Privileged emigration from a person's home country to a colony no longer exists. However, some countries grant certain groups of people a right to privileged immigration: this is true in Israel for Jews; in Germany during the Cold War and up until a few years ago for ethnic Germans; in Russia today for ethnic Russians from other successor states of the former Soviet Union.

People from Western Africa or Albania and Kosovo who leave their home country for Germany or Scandinavia are giving up not only their lifeworlds by moving away, or trying to do so, but also a number of clearly defined political rights. Migration may improve their material situation rapidly, but they will enjoy the same political rights only after acquiring citizenship in their destination country.

Mass migration in the modern period

When the *Mayflower* left Plymouth on 6 September 1620 and landed at Cape Cod two months later, on 11 November 1620, this group migration began a tradition lasting for about three centuries. The 'Pilgrims' were not exactly fleeing, but they were leaving a country where they could not live their religion freely. Moreover, they were seeking more plentiful livelihoods in this new Jerusalem beyond the Atlantic than they had had in Europe, but that was not their overriding motivation. In contrast, France's Protestant Huguenots really did have to flee after the revocation of the Edict of Nantes, as did the Puritans after the restoration of the monarchy in England in 1659/60. But economic motivations were much more important for many other emigrants.

Because of Europe's colonial expansion, modern immigration societies developed in which the immigrants dominated the political, business, and cultural communities. From the late eighteenth century on, a small but increasing flow of individuals and families from Europe began to migrate to North and South America, Algeria, Palestine/Israel, Southern Africa, Australia, and New Zealand, but also to Siberia and Central Asia – 70 million people in total. They sought freedom and better material living conditions in the colonies of the 'New World' and then in the states that had gained their independence. Many of these people were not from the lowest stratum of society – which is, incidentally, also true of many migrants and refugees today. The poorest could not and cannot afford the journey and also often lacked the self-confidence necessary.

Other regions of the world were subjected to European colonisation, but were not settled by Europeans. This is true of India, large parts of Africa, and Southeast Asia.

This mass emigration of individuals and families was not limited to Europe. But other mass movements were less voluntary than the emigration of European subjects and citizens.

Enslavement and shipment of Africans, especially to North and South America and the Caribbean, were closely linked to European colonial history. The Spanish conquest of what is today Latin America not only brought about the collapse of the great (Aztec, Inca) empires there. It also effected a brutal exploitation of the native population, as well as its infection with newly introduced diseases, resulting in enormous population declines. But the colonial rulers and their plantation economy needed workers. The same process was repeated with a time lag in North America, especially in what is the US today (Daniels 1992; Stannard 1992). The native population there not only died of newly introduced diseases; it was also persecuted, displaced, and robbed of its livelihood in a targeted fashion through the last third of the nineteenth century.

Its place was taken by Africans who were hunted down, enslaved, and sold to European and American businesspeople by local potentates. The demographic and social impacts on the societies of the so-called Gold and Slave Coasts of Western Africa, but also on those of Eastern Africa, were tremendous. This was not only about the 12 million slaves who were abducted and taken across the Atlantic between the sixteenth and the nineteenth century. There was 'collateral damage'. For, in addition, a large number of people who were intended to become enslaved fell victim to these hunts and transfers. Western businesspeople and their customers on the other side of the Atlantic were not the only profiteers; agents and rulers from the Arab world played important roles in the slave trade.

The global transfer of cheap Indian workers within the British Empire was also closely connected with the colonial plantation economy. They were fleeing from hunger and adversity on the

Indian subcontinent. Some came alone and intended to return, while others came with their families and settled. In the early years, these labourers were not free to select their work, but were bound to a certain employer. One could call this temporary servitude. The kafala (sponsorship) system, which is widespread to this day from Saudi Arabia to Qatar to Dubai, places similar limitations on foreign workers in the Gulf Region.

This labour migration is the cause for today's large Indian diaspora from the Caribbean and Guyana to South Africa, Mauritius, and Malaysia, to the Fiji Islands. Larger parts of the population of Indian descent in Eastern Africa, who had been there for several generations, were motivated to emigrate after the end of the colonial period or were simply driven out. This policy was carried out most radically in the 1970s under the rule of Idi Amin in Uganda.

The context of the recruitment of cheap Chinese workers is similar to that of the Indian labour migration. They were used both in agriculture in Southeast Asia and for cutting timber and building railroads in the western parts of the US and Canada. And they were the first group of migrants who were openly discriminated against after the end of slavery in the US and finally suffered a ban on further immigration.

Flight and displacement in the twentieth and early twenty-first century

The situation changed in the twentieth century. Labour migration became less important from the First World War on. Classic countries of immigration – most notably the US – introduced restrictions on immigration. Instead, the first half of the twentieth century was marked by mass flight and displacement. The causes were the drawing of new boundaries after World War I and World War II as well as the establishment of states on an ethno-national basis, which entailed forced resettlement of minorities.

The first major displacement took place between Turkey and

Greece. Although Greece had been granted a generous amount of Ottoman land on the coast of Asia Minor (Ionia) in the first peace treaty of Sèvres (August 1920), Greece attacked Turkey the following year and tried to conquer a large part of Anatolia militarily. But the invaders suffered a major defeat. The fact that a new Greek government had the responsible ministers and generals put on trial and shot did not help the situation, either. The 'catastrophe of Asia Minor' ran its course. In the Treaty of Lausanne (24 June, 1923), Turkey and Greece agreed on an exchange of populations. Roughly 1.5 million Orthodox Greeks had either already left Asia Minor or were forcibly resettled. A larger part of the Muslims living in Greece also had to resettle in the new Turkey. This affected another half million people. Some 200,000 Greek residents of Istanbul and the islands of Imbros and Tenedos as well as Muslims in Western Thrace were exempted from the forced resettlement. Kemalist Turkey did not abide by this agreement later on, however. In the 1960s and 1970s, the last Greeks were urged to leave, and only a few thousand live in Turkey today.

There were further displacements and forced resettlements during World War II. Most of them were coercive measures by Nazi Germany and the Stalinist Soviet Union. Much more important in terms of numbers were those forced resettlements, however, that the Allied powers decided upon directly after the end of the war in 1945 at their Potsdam Conference. They affected 10 million ethnic and East Germans as well as 1.5 million Poles.

Further mass displacements occurred in the process of decolonialisation. European powers withdrew from Africa, the Middle East, the Indian subcontinent, and Southeast Asia between 1948 and 1975. This brought about the return of the military, civilian personnel, and white settlers to the European metropolises as well as massive movements within the regions themselves. In the short term, both the partition of Palestine and the founding of the state of Israel on the one hand, and the partition of British India in majority-Hindu India and by now almost exclusively Muslim Pakistan on the other, brought about large waves of flight and displacement. Algeria's independence forced almost all residents of European descent as well as a large part of the Jewish population to leave for France and Israel, respectively, in 1961–62.

There was also a case of dual displacement in Europe after the United Kingdom had granted its colony Cyprus independence. Turkey intervened militarily following a Greek coup against Makarios, the first elected president. The Turkish occupation of the northern part of the island in the summer of 1974 brought about displacements of the Greeks there and then flight and displacements of the remaining Turkish population from the south. One need only compare the map of settlements before and after the occupation: a linguistically, ethnically, and religiously mixed island was transformed into two parts, with a militarily drawn border that now separates the two population groups. Even potential formal reunification would not change this.

In the last quarter of the twentieth century and the early twenty-first century, regional conflicts and international military interventions were the most important cause of massive refugee movements. The defeat of the US in South Vietnam made approximately 1.5 million boat people flee across the South China Sea to neighbouring countries from 1975 on. More than 5 million people fled to neighbouring countries after the Soviet military intervention in Afghanistan in 1980, the following war between the Islamic fighters supported by the West, Taliban rule ensuing after the Red Army pullout.

Civil wars or the collapse of state order also brought about mass refugee movements from Rwanda, Burundi, Eastern Congo, Sudan, and Somalia in the 1990s. Here, too, the refugees were mostly taken in by neighbouring countries. The same was true in the case of Syria from 2011 on. In 2016, there were more than 6.5 million internally displaced people in the country, while more than

4.5 million Syrians had fled abroad – mostly to Jordan, Lebanon, and Turkey.

Europe's most recent ethnic 'cleansings' took place in the 1990s. The collapse of Yugoslavia and the following wars resulted in the displacement of hundreds of thousands of Bosnians, Serbs, Croats, and Kosovo-Albanians, as well as Sinti and Roma. More recently, Europe has been confronted with the effects of violent conflicts and civil wars of our Asian neighbours. Since 2014, larger numbers of refugees have been coming to Europe from Afghanistan, Iraq and Syria, as well as Eritrea and Somalia on the Horn of Africa. In 2015, the large number of people crossing borders irregularly became a dominant political issue, and not least because many did not apply for asylum in the first EU country, but travelled on to Germany, Austria, or Sweden. When such large numbers of people are involved, it is often difficult to differentiate whether they are migrants or refugees fleeing persecution.

Migration and labour mobility

Labour migration became more important again after 1950 when the postwar economic boom generated greater demand for it. The scarcity on the labour market was exacerbated by two demographic factors. For one thing, the Second World War had decimated the number of men of working age in quite a few countries. For another, women had more children during the baby boom, and many interrupted or stopped gainful employment altogether. It was not yet a matter of course in all strata of society for women to work outside the home. In this situation, several Western European countries decided to recruit foreign workers from Southern Europe, the Maghreb, and Turkey. The only Communist country to permit such recruitment was Yugoslavia. Other countries in the part of Europe under Communist rule at the time lacked workers themselves. For this reason, Vietnamese workers were sent to the German Democratic Republic and Czechoslovakia.

Recruitment was based on international agreements. Workers were to remain for a limited period of time and were to rotate back home and be replaced by others. Over time, however, some of the so-called guest workers stayed. Only years after entering the country did they become de facto immigrants, bring their families, and settle in Western Europe. However, accompanying measures to support their integration were usually lacking.

Those countries in Europe that still had significant overseas territories after 1945 experienced further immigration to their labour markets as well. In the course of decolonisation, it was not only officials, soldiers, and settlers of European descent that came to their respective motherlands. They were also followed by people from the Asian, African, and Caribbean states that had gained independence between 1948 and 1975. Knowledge of European languages and a culture oriented toward the former metropolises made this migration easier.

The recruitment of workers from other parts of Europe and from neighbouring countries, as well as the postcolonial migration, changed the composition of the population of Western Europe long term.

For about 400 years, emigration had been dominant in Europe in the course of the colonial expansion. At the same time, there was a longer period of politically desired ethno-cultural homogenisation from the nineteenth century on. Old resident minorities were to assimilate, switch to the language and religion of the majority, or emigrate. At the same time, most of the states founded in the nineteenth and twentieth centuries – from Greece to the Balkans and Eastern Central Europe to Germany – considered themselves national homes for members of their own ethnic groups living abroad. Only since the 1960s has there been appreciable immigration to Europe. And only since 1985 has the total number of immigrants to EU countries been significantly larger than the number of Europeans leaving, which they of course continue to do. As a result whilst the societies of Western and Southern Europe have become more diverse in terms of religion, language, and culture, but inequality has also increased.

Following a longer phase of intentional homogenisation, new minorities and diasporas emerged in the Northwest and later also in southern Europe. The insufficient integration of some immigrants reinforced this development and resulted in the emergence of parallel societies in some metropolises.

During the same period, the classic countries of immigration in North America and Oceania also became more diverse. Between 1965 and 1975, they brought an end to their restrictive immigration regimes that had been oriented toward people of European descent and opened their borders to immigrants from other parts of the world, especially Asia and Latin America. This will have considerable consequences in the long term. In the US and Canada, people of European descent will no longer form the majority after 2050. This is already the case in California.

International migration of workers is by no means only toward Europe, North America, and Russia. Large numbers of workers are migrating within Africa, Asia, and South America. The Arabic Gulf States, South Africa, Malaysia, and Singapore, for example, have become important destination regions of this South-South migration. In several Gulf States, the immigrant workers now form the majority of the population. A large part of this migration is occurring on the basis of recruitment and workers' strictly enforced return to their home countries. The overwhelming majority of the recruited workers have no prospect of remaining or bringing their families, much less of obtaining citizenship.

Since the beginning of the twenty-first century, the number of international migrants has been growing more rapidly than the global population. In 2000, there were 175 million people in the world who did not live in their country of birth, or 2.8% of the global population at the time. In 2015, it was already 244 million, or 3.2%.

The most important destination regions of international migration are North America (US, Canada), the European Union (especially Germany, the United Kingdom, and France), Russia, and the Gulf States (especially Saudi Arabia and the United Arab Emirates), as well as Australia.

The most significant countries and regions of origin are South Asia (India, Bangladesh, Pakistan), Mexico, and China. There has also been considerable emigration from Russia since the 1990s.

Increases in the numbers of migrants from Asia have been particularly large, namely from 68 million in 2000 to 104 million in 2015. The increases in numbers of migrating Europeans (from 52 to 62 million), Latin Americans (from 26 to 37 million), and Africans (from 23 to 34 million) were smaller during this period.

A larger part of international migrations occur within individual continents. In 2015, 52% of the 34 million African migrants continued to live in Africa. Important destination countries included Egypt, Nigeria, and South Africa, but just over one-quarter of them (27%) came to Europe.

Of the 104 million Asian migrants, 60% stayed in another Asian country. Their most important destinations were the Gulf States, Singapore, Malaysia, and India. Europe was in second place, taking in 20%, and North America in third, with 16%.

Of the 62 million Europeans who emigrated, 66% lived in a different part of Europe (including Russia) in 2015. Their most important destinations were European Union countries – above all Germany, the United Kingdom, and to a somewhat lesser extent France – as well as Russia.

The same is true of the 2 million emigrants from the Pacific islands of Oceania. Almost 60% of them lived in Australia and New Zealand in 2015, but no less than 19% in Europe.

In contrast, of the 37 million mobile Latin Americans and Caribbeans, emigration to another continent has been the rule so far. The large majority went to North America (70%) and Europe

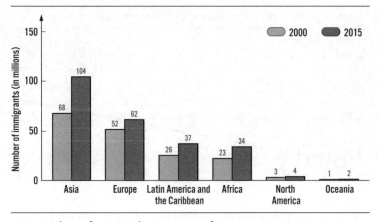

Fig. 9: Numbers of migrants by continent of origin, 2000–2015

(12%). Just 16% lived in another Latin American country in 2015. North America is not included in this comparison because mobility between states of the US and Canadian provinces is considered internal migration.

Push and pull: Migration from poorer countries to richer ones
It seems reasonable to assume that the same dynamics – resulting from differences in prosperity – that determine numbers of children and life expectancy (see the Preston curve in Fig. 10) also influence migration movements. As prosperity increases, mortality declines, and the need to emigrate seems to decline as well. At the same time, the incentive to immigrate increases. This is evidenced by a global comparison of those countries for which data are available.

In fact, net migration (derived from immigration and emigration figures) is dependent on the level of prosperity. If a country's annual per capita GDP is less than 9,000 US dollars, then on average there is more emigration from than immigration to that country. If it is between 9,000 and 15,000 US dollars, immigration

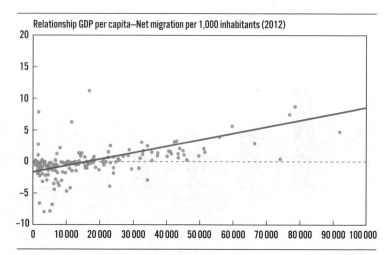

Fig. 10: A new 'Preston curve': Net migration (per 1,000 inhabitants) as a function of the level of prosperity (GDP per capita), 2012

and emigration are balanced on average. If it is more than 15,000 US dollars, immigration tends to outweigh emigration.

This is a general statistical correlation across all countries, but does not apply to every single one. After all, the majority of migrations are regional, not transcontinental. In Africa, people from very poorly developed countries such as Burkina Faso, Niger, or Mali do not migrate primarily to Europe, but to Nigeria, for example, where per capita GDP is somewhat higher, even though Nigeria, too, is among the poorer countries compared with the rest of the world.

In Europe, migration often occurs from middle-income to high-income countries. Yet migration is driven not only by differences in prosperity, but also by individual opportunities. Obstacles to migration have been largely removed within the EU, and mobility exists between prosperous countries, too. The situation in the labour market plays an important role here. That is why the predominant direction of migration can switch, sometimes rapidly.

Up until 2008 – that is, before the beginning of the financial and sovereign debt crises – countries such as Ireland, Spain, Portugal, and Greece recorded substantial immigration. From 2009 on, net migration reversed rather quickly. First, there were no new immigrants from abroad because of a lack of opportunities, and then quite a few immigrants who had lost their jobs left these countries. They were followed by younger natives of these countries seeking work in Germany, the United Kingdom, or overseas.

How does international migration work?

Paul Collier and other economists see the decision to migrate as a kind of investment that is supposed to pay off over the course of a person's life. This investment is all the greater the higher the obstacles on the way to the potential destination countries are, and the higher the number of migrants who have to give up their livelihoods in their countries of origin. But who bears these costs? Partly the migrants themselves, but partly it is also their families, clans, and even those who help raise the funds for travel costs, visas, documents and translations, employment agencies, often also for human traffickers. The social costs of the separation of spouses or of parents and children must be borne by entire families as well.

This also means that migration can bring about substantial obligations. A person whose migration is paid for by others is no longer free, but must attempt to pay back these expenditures in some way as soon as possible. Then, emigrants must try to earn appreciably more than they would have been able to at home. At least in the initial years, they send as much of their income as possible 'back home'.

In summary, remittances from successful migrants are many times higher than all international and multilateral development aid. This amounts to a significant contribution to many countries' macroeconomic performance. The distributional effects are important as well. After all, private remittances flow directly to private households and strengthen their purchasing power. A large part is used for ongoing consumption. But these remittances are also invested in school fees, medical expenses, construction of houses, or the purchase of means of production.

In the destination country, so-called pioneer migrants often function as footholds, serving as base camps or contact points for others following from the same area. As long as the difference in prosperity remains, following migration is all the stronger the larger the diaspora in the destination country is (cf., for example, Carrington et al., 1996). But it does not grow limitlessly. For one thing, people move away. For another, every diaspora loses some of its potential members through cultural assimilation when individuals with immigrant backgrounds feel restricted by the rules and social control within their diaspora and try to emancipate themselves from it.

Part of the global diaspora plays an important role in the relations between their countries of origin and their destination countries: as lobbyists for certain issues in their old homes, as brokers of commercial relations, as investors. In the past, many a diaspora also involved alternative elites who supported national independence or regime change in their countries of origin and at times returned there in order to continue their efforts.

Emigration always entails a certain brain drain. But it can also have a stabilising effect for the countries of origin, particularly when many – especially young – people cannot find work at home. Emigration then provides a 'safety valve' reducing the number of malcontents. But some of the low-skilled and socially disadvantaged population in the destination countries see new immigrants as threatening competitors for jobs and social benefits, creating tension among the low-skilled native population of the destination country and migrants who have been living there for a longer time. But there are also members of the better secured middle classes

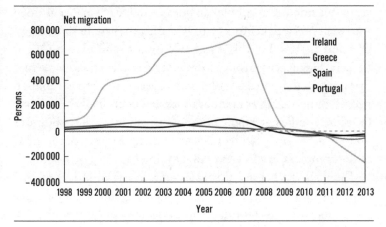

Fig. 11: Short-term changes in net migration in the developed world; the examples of Ireland, Greece, Portugal, and Spain (Source: EUROSTAT)

who mobilise against immigration. They may not see threats to their professional status, but to their identity and outlook on life. The reaction is unpleasant xenophobia.

The global population and the Earth's 'carrying capacity'

The global population has grown in a series of surges since the Neolithic Period. The twentieth century saw the strongest growth. Around 1990, the number of people on Earth rose by more than 90 million per year. In total, the number of people on our planet increased fourfold between 1900 and 2000. This was unique in world history. Such growth in just 100 years had never occurred before, and it will not take place again in the future. Global growth is slowing down even now.

Long-term projections come to the conclusion that population growth on our planet will come to a standstill in roughly 80 to 100 years. The number of people can be expected to be smaller again in the twenty-second century. This is already the case in some countries and regions. But this is not an answer to the question about the carrying capacity of our ecosystem. After all, in the late twenty-first century, the global population is expected to be 10 to 11 billion people, or half again as many as today. It will probably be possible to secure a sufficient supply of food. But can we create conditions under which Earth can handle the burdens arising from 10 or 11 billion people over a longer period of time?

The question behind this is about a universal model for the economy and society. Poorer societies are guided by a development model that is to bring them to the level of Europe, the US, and Japan in terms of material wealth and resource consumption. From an ecological perspective, however, this model is anything but sustainable. Even for today's highly developed societies, it is questionable how long this path can be sustained. If 10 billion or more people desired to produce and consume at this level, such limits would be confronted quite rapidly. Yet we are criticising this from the perspective of privileged people who have already benefited from resource dependent material wealth.

Bibliography

For a more comprehensive bibliography, please refer to Münz and Reiterer (2009) listed below.

Bulst, N. (1979), Der Schwarze Tod. Demographische, wirtschafts- und kulturgeschichtliche Aspekte der Pestkatastrophe von 1347–1352. Bilanz der neueren Forschung. In: Saeculum. Jahrbuch für Universalgeschichte 30, 45–67.
Cameron, R. (1989), A Concise Economic History of the World. From Paleolithic Times to the Present. New York: Oxford University Press.
Carrington, W./Detrachiage, E./Vishvanath, T. (1996), Migration with endogenous moving costs. In: American Economic Review 86, 4, 909–930.

Cauvin, J. (2013 [1997]), Naissance des Divinités, Naissance de L'Agriculture. Paris: Biblis.

Childe, V. G. (1958), The Dawn of European Civilization. New York: Knopf.

Collier, P. (2013), Exodus: How Migration is Changing our World. Oxford/New York: Oxford University Press.

Daniels, J. D. (1992), The Indian Population of North America in 1492. William and Mary Quarterly, 3rd Series, Vol. 49, 298–320.

Deaton, A. S. (2013), The Great Escape: Health, Wealth, and the Origins of Inequality. Princeton: Princeton University Press.

Hondrich, K. O. (2007), Weniger sind mehr. Warum der Geburtenrückgang ein Glücksfall für unsere Gesellschaft ist. Frankfurt a.M.: Campus.

Keilman, N. (1998), How Accurate are the United Nations World Population Projections? In: Population and Development Review 24, Supplement: Frontiers of Population Forecasting, 15–41.

Khan, Hafiz T. A., Lutz, W. (2007), How well did past UN Population Projections anticipate demographic trends in six Southeast Asian countries? Oxford Institute of Ageing Working Papers 507.

Klein, H. (1960), Das große Sterben von 1348/49 und seine Auswirkungen auf die Besiedlung der Ostalpenländer. In: Mitteilungen der Gesellschaft für Salzburger Landeskunde 100. Vereinsjahr. Salzburg: Gesellschaft für Salzburger Landeskunde, 91–170.

Lesthaeghe, R. and Surkyn, J. (2007), When History Moves On: The Foundations and Diffusion of the Second Demographic Transition. In: Jayakody, R., Thornton, A., Axinn, W., eds., International Family Change. Ideational Perspectives.

Münz, R., Reiterer, A. F. (2009), Overcrowded World? The Global Population and International Migration. London: Haus Publishing

Pirenne, H. (1939), Mohammed and Charlemagne. London: G. Allen & Unwin.

Preston, S. H. (1975), The changing relation between mortality and level of economic development. Population Studies 29 (2), 231–248.

Reher, D. S. (2004), The demographic transition revisited as a global process. Population, Space and Place, 10 (1), 19–41.

Shennan, S., Downey, S.S., Timpson, A., Edinborough, K., Colledge, S., Kerig, T. (2013), Regional population collapse followed agriculture booms in mid-Holocene Europe. Nature Communications doi: 10.1038/ncomms3486.

Stannard, D. (1992), American Holocaust. The Conquest of the New World. Canada: Oxford University Press.

Stoto, M. A. (1983), The Accuracy of Population Projections. Journal of the American Statistical Association 78, 13–20.

United Nations Population Division (2015), World Population Prospects: The 2015
    Revision, Volume I: Comprehensive Tables. ST/ESA/SER.A/379. New York.
Zahid, H. J., Robinson, E., Kelly, R.L. (2015), Agriculture, population growth,
    and statistical analysis of the radiocarbon record. Proceedings of the National
    Academy of Sciences of the United States of America Vol 113, No. 4, 931–935.
    doi 10.1073/pnas.1517650112.

Feeding the planet: environmental protection through sustainable agriculture

Klaus Hahlbrock and Wolfgang Schuchert

Background

Following publication of the book *Feeding the Planet: Environmental Protection through Sustainable Agriculture* (Hahlbrock, 2009), we were often asked how many people the planet could feed. However, this question was neither posed by us nor implicitly answered. The only possible answer is an indirect one: it depends on how we deal with each other and with the resources available to us. For this reason, the book began with the key question of how to secure food for humankind long term in spite of continuing population growth and advancing environmental destruction, and arrived at the conclusion that the imbalance of hunger and overabundance, poverty and wealth, overuse of resources and ecological stability is becoming increasingly severe.

Today, a decade on, hardly anything about this general description of the situation has changed in principle except for the certainty that resolving the imbalance is exceedingly urgent. A large gap apparently exists between certain knowledge and consequential action. Not even the dramatically increasing streams of migrants and refugees from the regions of Africa wracked by war, drought, hunger, and poverty have been able to shake up the prosperous countries' self-centred stance, which is out of touch with reality. In addition, almost a billion people are hungry, and millions are starving to death even though there is enough food for all. For they are not hungry because of a lack of food, but because of poverty and a lack of access to everything that most of us take for granted: a wholesome diet; safe drinking water; schooling and vocational education; social, economic, and technical infrastructure; medical care; and financial provision for old age.

It is true that the UN Millennium Development Goal of halving the number of people suffering from hunger between 1990 and 2015 was reached at least in 11 African countries (BMEL, 2015a). However, since population growth has continued unchecked during the same period, this is only a relative success in some countries on the basis of their situation in 1990, while the total number of people going hungry has hardly changed.

The extent to which the production and universal availability of qualitatively and quantitatively sufficient food is linked to our past and future social and ecological behaviour is described in depth in *Feeding the Planet*[1], as well as in two survey articles.[2] The following sections will draw on these publications to show how the prospects for feeding the world have developed over the past decade and which conclusions are to be drawn.

Important aspects – especially the development of the climate, the availability of water and energy, ecological stability, and population growth – are discussed in separate chapters of this volume, so that we can limit our analysis to their relevance for human nourishment and its fundamental prerequisites.

The biosphere, the climate, and water

Like all other living creatures, all domesticated crop plants and livestock are subject to the basic laws of biology. Each has its own

---

1   In the complementary book *Natur und Mensch: Der lange Weg zum ökosozialen Bewusstsein* (Hahlbrock, 2013)

2   Hahlbrock (2011)

species-specific needs concerning ecological complexity, nutrients, and water, as well as climate and soil characteristics. Together with all other organisms of their habitat, they form an ecosystem in which every part is both a beneficiary and a competitor.

On the one hand, all plants – cultivars used in horticulture, forestry, and agriculture as well as the naturally occurring wild types – are beneficiaries of a multitude of diverse small animals and microorganisms that improve the soil for root growth and nutrient uptake, pollinate their flowers, or eliminate pests, as well as animals large and small that eat their fruit and spread the seeds. On the other hand, they have enemies who desire to live at their expense or in their place, just as they themselves are enemies, or competitors, of all the many other species whose potential habitats they occupy.

Numerous organisms have adapted to beneficiary partners in this ecological complexity, often to the extent that they are dependent on each other. Familiar examples include some of our fruit species and the honey bees that pollinate them and live on their nectar; certain species of fungi that occur only in symbiosis with the root network of certain tree species (birch bolete, false saffron milk-cap, and others); and the panda, threatened by extinction, whose sole source of food is the leaves of a particular species of bamboo which is also endangered.

For such specialisations to develop, all the species in an ecosystem must occur with sufficient population densities that account for the needs of the individual species to the greatest extent possible, even though the composition of species is constantly fluctuating in detail. A continuously changing balance emerges in which the rising or falling numbers of individual species generally result in the same behaviour of their partner organisms.

This is true especially of agriculture, forestry, and horticulture, particularly if the initial situation is changed massively by the cultivation of just one, or a few, crop plant species for several years on a single piece of land, combined with intensive fertilisation and herbicide and pesticide application. After all, while the natural dynamic is a stable ecological process of species-rich biocenoses, the stability of ecologically impoverished cultures must be maintained artificially through interventions by mechanical and chemical means (herbicides, pesticides, and fertilisation), and often also through irrigation. This applies analogously to uniform stocks of livestock and the conditions under which they are kept.

Older people still remember the many colourful fields of flowers and similarly colourful varieties of bird and butterfly species. Most of them have vanished because of modern agriculture and forestry, as have countless less conspicuous animal and plant species. A few grass species and dandelions are practically the only plants to grow on meadows and fields over-fertilised with slurry, and 'weeds' and 'insect pests' are eradicated from fields with herbicides and insecticides. Many species of butterflies and other insects that are specialised for certain wild plants that are now downgraded to weeds are thus lacking a source of food, and the majority of birds can find neither enough insects nor suitable plant seeds.

The cleared areas of the tropical rainforests are examples of particularly profound and long-term ecological degradation. Once sites of a unique abundance of species surpassing all other ecosystems in terms of opulence and duration over time, and constantly regenerating themselves from their own resources through cyclical genesis and demise despite meagre soils, they have become large-scale monocultures of soy, sugarcane, or corn that are cultivated and harvested by machine. On the same area where millions of species of microorganisms, animals, and plants had established a stable ecological network with a natural nutrient and water cycle across long periods of time, only a single species of crop plant is grown which is dependent on fertilisers, herbicides, pesticides, and often also on artificial irrigation. Such single crop farming is disastrous for the diversity of natural species and the stability of the biosphere and the climate. From the perspective of mass production of food and feed oriented exclusively toward profits and economic growth, this system is imperative, though prone to collapse before long.

In the absence of intensive agriculture relying on breeding for high yields and high quality, which extends back to the Neolithic Period, it would not have been possible to feed several billion people. Yet the ecological and spatial limits of this development have long been reached in most places and irreversibly overstepped in particularly sensitive regions such as the tropical rainforests, many desert fringes, and previously wooded mountain slopes. Besides their key role for the entire biosphere, the wooded ecosystems in particular fulfil another function indispensable for human life: together with the major areas covered with water, snow, and ice, they are the most important stabilisers of the global climate and thus also of high-yield agriculture; this is especially true of the tropical rainforests.

All high-yield varieties used in agriculture are adapted so specifically to the climatic, geological, and other factors in the places where they are cultivated that their yields would suffer under changed conditions or it would be impossible to grow them at all. In every stage of development (from germination of the seed through the growth of shoots and leaves, formation of flowers and fruits, to maturity), every variety has certain demands of its habitat that are specific to the species and the variety. Especially in sensitive stages of development, every large deviation of the environmental conditions from the norm (extreme heat, cold, flooding, drought, severe weather, etc.) has negative impacts on growth and maturation and thus also on the yield – and in the worst case, total crop failure.

Enhanced plant growth is sometimes mentioned as having a positive impact of the increasing carbon dioxide concentration in the atmosphere. However, enhanced growth also requires larger amounts of nutrients and water as well as favourable conditions for growth in every other regard. Most importantly, though, growth in size is not a yardstick for the amounts of nutrients, vitamins, or aromatic or other substances in the plant. Many of the varieties of fruits and vegetables common today, which have been bred for size, transportability, and shelf life, have significantly lost flavour, the immediately perceptible characteristic, compared with the older and smaller varieties. And even if all this did not matter, one small, and in any case questionable, advantage would nonetheless be countered by the many serious disadvantages of global warming in other realms.

Especially in numerous emerging markets and threshold countries, deforestation and the overuse of previously fertile soils as contributing factors to global climate change have partly dramatic, if regionally highly different, impacts on agricultural productivity and other living conditions. Not least, they exacerbate the pressure to migrate because of hunger, poverty, and war. Even if the rapidly increasing carbon dioxide concentration of the air rightly plays an important role in the current climate debate, we should not lose sight of two hardly less alarming developments: soil erosion and desertification, which are increasing in many places, as well as depletion or pollution of the natural water resources.

One of the main causes for this development, including climate change, is the constantly progressing transformation of natural ecosystems and water cycles that emerged over long periods of time into monocultures requiring large amounts of water, energy, plant protection, and other management measures and which are productive only in the short term. Besides food crops, this also increasingly concerns feed and energy crops, rubber, coffee, palm oil plantations, and many others. The impacts are alarming: dwindling water resources; nutrient depletion or desertification of soils through overgrazing, nutrient removal, and salinisation, followed by wind erosion; pollution or contamination of rivers, lakes, and oceans; drying up of wetlands; and diverse forms of soil sealing.

Fig. 1: Illegal slash-and-burn clearance of land for soy cultivation in the Gran Chaco in Argentina (top), and siltation of vegetable fields in the oasis Kebili in Tunisia (bottom)

Particularly drastic examples include the once fish-rich Aral Sea and Lake Chad, which have almost completely dried up, shrinking to less than 10% of their original size and turning into barren salt flats within a few decades; the ongoing large-scale annihilation of valuable tropical rainforests (currently approximately 12 million hectares per year); and the expansion of deserts and semi-deserts because of overuse and climate change in parts of Africa and Asia (see Fig. 1).

Agriculture is not only a direct or indirect cause of this development, but is also negatively impacted by it: as an important contributing factor to global warming by producing large amounts of carbon dioxide, sulphur oxides, and nitrogen oxides from slash-and-burn clearance; burning wood, grass, or straw; and emitting nitrogen oxides from fertilisers, and methane from rice paddies and the stomachs of ruminants. The substantial amount of energy used, and the corresponding amount of carbon dioxide emissions, for cultivating the fields, transporting, processing, and storing the harvest, including cooling or freezing numerous intermediary or final products during transportation and storage, must be added to this. Agriculture is also responsible for approximately 70% of global water consumption, more than all other users.

This description of the current situation could have been similar ten years ago: the awareness of and the knowledge about the constantly growing dangers of this development have existed for a long time, yet there is still a lack of willingness to take decisive action. Many cautionary reports and analyses have been prepared by the UN, the World Bank, scientists, governments, and others (e.g., BMEL *Nahrung für Milliarden*, 2015a; *Meat Atlas*, 2014; *Soil Atlas (Bodenatlas)*, 2015; IFOAM EU *Feeding the People*, 2015; *UN Convention on Desertification*, 2014). Yet the unanimously invoked radical turnaround can be detected at best in small signs of hope that are still much too small for a real trend reversal.

An important reason for this may well be the widespread failure to see the bigger global picture. Hardly any other region of

Fig. 2: Traditional methods of threshing (top) and drying (bottom) grain in Southern India. The asphalt surfaces are avoided by automobile traffic when grain is dried on sunny days

the world enjoys conditions as favourable as those in Europe for high agricultural productivity: a balanced climate with changing seasons and day lengths, regular rainfall, nutrient-rich soils, and a robust biosphere. In few of the major non-European cultivation areas are the wheat yields, for example, even remotely as high as in the regions of Western Europe near the Gulf Stream.

Against this background, Europeans often fail to understand the major differences in productivity between Europe and all the other continents – especially the vast areas in Africa and Asia with little water. Yet it is by no means only the advantages of the geographical location that are responsible for this difference. The tremendous socioeconomic gap, exacerbated, if not caused, by political, infrastructural, and technological failings, contributes considerably to the fact that agricultural productivity does not fulfil its potential in many developing countries (see Fig. 2).

Breeding plants and animals

When domestication of plants and animals began, so did breeding. Although it was probably not an intentionally pursued goal at first, domestication/breeding is always based on selecting those individuals for use and reproduction that are the healthiest and promise the highest-quality yields. Thus, over the course of several thousand years, the high-performance crop plants and livestock that make up the indispensable basis of our diet today were developed from the wild varieties that had originally been gathered or hunted and that were suitable for domestication.

Approximately one hundred years ago, the efficiency of this traditional form of selective breeding was increased enormously by intentional crossing of varieties with desired characteristics following Mendel's laws. Despite the high yields of many modern high-performance varieties, which often reach the limits of physiological

Fig. 3: Yields of modern high-performance varieties in comparison with related wild types: barley and a wild relative from the Anatolian highlands (left), corn and its Mexican precursor teosinte (top right), bred and wild potatoes from the Andes (bottom right)

tolerance, cross-breeding combined with selection continues to be the indispensable foundation of plant breeding (Fig. 3).

Besides its permanent task of maintaining valuable varieties and adapting them to different habitats, breeding constantly produces new varieties with new characteristics. To increase the mutation rate and thus the probability of success, seed can be treated with radiation or a substance triggering mutations (mutagen). Besides further improvements in quality and yield, the primary goals include characteristics such as resistance to the most important plant diseases and pest insects as well as various kinds of stress tolerance. These highly desirable traits are often either weakly expressed or absent from the beginning, or have been lost over the long history of breeding.

New methods of molecular biology were developed and adapted to breeding in the 1990s. For example, genes for certain characteristics can be detected early by using marker-assisted selection with known molecular markers, which speeds up plant breeding. At the same time, both the efficiency and the fundamental possibilities of plant breeding in particular were increased further through plant genetic engineering. It was used to introduce genes for desired characteristics into varieties even across the boundaries of species. As early as 1995, a virus-resistant papaya variety and an insect-resistant cotton variety, which were developed using genetic engineering, were cultivated commercially for the first time. Since then, the cultivation of genetically engineered plants has increased annually by up to 10%.

According to a report by the International Service for the Acquisition of Biotech/GM Applications (ISAAA), genetically engineered plants were grown on a total of 181.5 million hectares, or 12% of the world's arable land, in 28 countries in 2014. The largest areas were in the US (73 million hectares), followed by Brazil (42), Argentina (24), India (12), and Canada (12). The figures for Europe were very small in comparison: Spain (0.1), Portugal, the Czech Republic, Slovakia, and Romania (<0.05 each). Corn, soy, and cotton were the main crops (in the US, 90% of total cultivation of each of these plants), all with genetically engineered insect resistance and/or herbicide tolerance. According to this study, the economic and ecological gain amounted to an average saving of 37% in pesticides and herbicides, a 22% increase in yields, and a 68% increase in earnings, especially of small farmers. Since 2011, the amount grown in developing countries has been greater than that in industrialised countries.

None of these breeding results would have been possible with conventional methods alone. Over time, many more plant varieties with additional genetically engineered characteristics have been developed, above all in the US (pumpkin, sugar beet, alfalfa) and China (papaya, poplar, pepper, tomato), and recently for the first time also in Bangladesh (eggplant). Building on now over 20 years of experience, the number of countries employing genetic engineering and the number of breeding goals pursued using genetic engineering have grown significantly faster than in the initial phase, not least because no disadvantages of any kind have come to light that genetic engineering per se could have caused. In view of numerous claims to the contrary and the widespread critical stance particularly in Europe toward genetic engineering, this assertion must be stated more precisely.

It is important to differentiate between the method with which a variety was bred and the way in which it was applied. Every instance of cultivating uniform cultures, regardless of whether the plant was bred with or without the help of genetic engineering, is a massive intervention in the natural dynamic balance of the ecosystem affected that can have serious consequences. The more intensive the artificial management measures are, the more serious the ecological consequences. Reducing precisely these consequences as far as possible is the goal of genetically engineered changes – for example, the resistance of 'transgenic' cotton against bollworms, which would otherwise have to be combatted with even more insecticides.

However, independent of the breeding method, large genetically uniform cultures are ideal playgrounds for the mutational acquisition of resistance by insects or pathogens, or of herbicide tolerance by weeds, and should be avoided as much as possible.

The decision about whether and how to cultivate the variety bred in an ecologically and socially acceptable way, including management measures, irrigation, and further processing, is also independent of the type of breeding. As a matter of principle, genetic engineering should be employed only if it provides more advantages than disadvantages for the environment, human nourishment, or human health, and the breeding goal cannot be reached in any other way.[3] However, such reservations should apply in general for any intervention in nature. Every case of sexual reproduction, and thus also every form of breeding, results in a coincidental new combination of genetically determined traits. Every individual designated for further development must therefore be tested in terms of its advantages and disadvantages as well as its suitability for cultivation in a process of cross-breeding, backcrossing, and selection until a variety developed from it is genetically stable and suitable for the mandatory testing procedure conducted for licensing. Although genetic engineering can shorten the initial phase of this process, it then continues for transgenic plants exactly as for any other case of breeding – except that particularly strict conditions apply.

And one more thing is usually not taken into account when valuating genetic engineering: that undesired side effects may occur when genes are transferred. Yet this possibility exists all the more in the case of mutations caused by radiation or mutagens, and also in conventional breeding, where thousands of genes of two crossing partners are combined with each other – and with a result that cannot be prognosticated in any detail. Only selection and further breeding of suitable individuals can result in a uniform variety that can be licensed and cultivated, regardless of whether the result was achieved in a conventional manner or with additional help from genetic engineering, radiation, or a chemical mutagen.

Although there is evidence of ecological advantages for all plants produced with genetic engineering and used in agriculture so far (see above), these advantages are merely relative and must not hide the fact that agricultural land is still being lost in many ways, that more and more new land is accessed at the expense of

---

3   Hahlbrock (2007), pp. 209 ff

valuable natural ecosystems, usually only for short-term commercial gain, and that large-scale monocultures always require artificial plant protection. All the more are hopes directed to genetic engineering supporting further breeding of stress-tolerant, insect- and disease-resistant varieties in order to reduce yield losses. Several such varieties are in the advanced stages of development.

A completely new breeding method might result from CRISPR/Cas9 technology, which was first prescribed in 2013 and has already been applied successfully many times in basic research. Like previous genetic engineering procedures, it too is based on modified application of natural biological processes. In this case, it is a bacterial immune response to infectious viruses, which was discovered only recently and in which the genetic material of the virus is removed in a pinpointed way in a multi-step process leaving no residues. The CRISPR/Cas9 technology ('genome editing') developed on this basis permits not only removing genetic material in a targeted fashion, but also exchanging, modifying, or introducing it, or influencing its activity.[4]

Although it appears that this process occurs naturally only in bacteria, it is transferable to all other classes of organisms in the genetically altered form. The technology opens up entirely new prospects for breeding in comparison with the previous form of genetic engineering. CRISPR/Cas9 technology has already been applied successfully to several species in initial model experiments, including the model plants *Arabidopsis* and tobacco as well as rice, wheat, corn, and millet, which are especially of interest in relation to breeding. Since CRISPR/Cas9 technology leaves no residues and thus cannot be ascertained after the fact as the cause of the change, it is necessary to determine the rules and regulations for its practical application.[5] On the basis of experience to date, it is

---

4   Doudna and Charpentier (2014)

5   Huang et al. (2016)

vital to inform the public without delay, and in a generally comprehensible way, about the implications of the decisions arrived at and the pros and cons of applying the technology.

In animal breeding, genetic engineering has been used outside the realm of research only in the case of a transgenic salmon. The 'AquAdvantage' salmon, which grows especially quickly, was approved for consumption, with restrictions, in the US in 2015. In contrast, artificial insemination and animal cloning have already been standard methods for decades. As CRISPR/Cas9 technology is opening up new possibilities, including treatment of hereditary diseases in humans, the range of methods available in animal breeding may also be broadened in the near future. So a legal framework – desirably also a societal consensus – would be all the more important as a precondition for its use. Yet for the time being, practical application of genetic engineering is limited to breeding plants, the above-mentioned salmon, and some microorganisms used in producing pharmaceuticals and foods.

Directly or indirectly (via the use of isolated enzymes), genetically engineered microorganisms, especially bacteria and yeasts, play important roles in the production of bread, cheese, beer, wine, fruit juices, vitamins, and other additives. For instance, during cheese production, milk is treated with the enzyme chymosin, which previously had to be sourced from the stomachs of calves and is today produced by transgenic microorganisms; the enzyme pectinase, which is now produced in a similar way, is used in manufacturing fruit juices; and many foods contain added vitamins, amino acids, citric acid, colourants, or the flavour enhancer glutamate, often as the products of transgenic microorganisms.

Another breeding goal for food crops is adaptation of valuable varieties to other environs, namely ones that have been limited to certain regions, whose cultivation in their traditional form has been difficult, or that are not competitive on the global market.

Quinoa and amaranth, two nutritionally valuable plants from the South American highlands, are often mentioned as examples.

In the case of agricultural livestock, the most important breeding goals are in principle the same as for plants: quality and quantity for human nutrition. As a result, some extremely high-performance varieties of a few breeds of the most important livestock – none of which would be able to live in the absence of intensive human husbandry are now prevalent around the globe. In the US, for example, the particularly high-performance Holstein-Friesian cow accounts for more than 80% of all dairy cows. Since animals, in contrast to plants, can experience suffering physically and psychologically (at least as humans perceive the matter), the extreme breeding goals and levels of performance aimed for are becoming increasingly questionable – as is the handling of animals in factory-farming producing eggs, meat, and milk. However, consumers also play a substantial role in these developments owing to their preference for and habituation to consumption of cheap foods and their meat-based eating habits.

Food production, consumer behaviour, and eating habits

The globalisation of markets is bringing about a constantly advancing transformation at all steps along the way between producer and consumer. On the production side, this began above all in the industrialised countries and a few emerging economies with a concentration on large farms, including factory or large-scale farming. It is now continuing with land grabbing at the expense of dispossessed or displaced small- or micro-scale farmers in some developing countries, unabated clearing of primary forests, and speculation with agricultural land and raw agricultural products. Multinational corporations and supermarket chains dominate wholesaling and retailing. In Europe, for example, 10 companies account for about 40% of the market share for food.

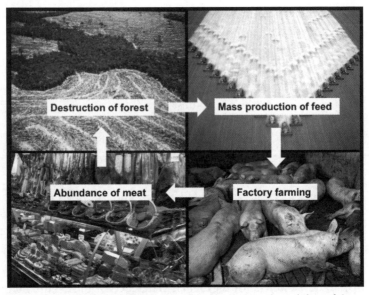

Fig. 4: Negative feedback of high meat consumption on the stability of the biosphere and the climate, the productivity of soils and, thus, agricultural productivity in many important cultivation areas. Several individual impacts intensify each other. For example, soil productivity declines under intensive agricultural use of nutrient-poor soils which previously sustained a self-regenerating primary rain forest, and cheap meat offered to consumers stimulates demand, which in turn intensifies the pressure for further clearances for cultivating feed crops, and thus the overall decline of soil fertility and the climate changes – increasingly to the detriment of effective agriculture

In recent times, a large part of cleared forest land has been used for cultivating energy and feed crops, the latter mostly for factory farming. The total amount of agricultural land (about 4.9 billion hectares, approximately 1.5 billion hectares of which are under cultivation), however, has hardly changed despite ongoing large-scale slash-and-burn clearance (approximately 12 million hectares per year). The gains are more than offset by the losses due to desertification and soil erosion, as well as land-use changes for urban development, and for transportation, industrial, and recreational projects. Desertification alone is responsible for the loss of approximately 12 million hectares of productive agricultural land. This development – especially in relation to the excessive and still increasing production of meat, which requires immense amounts of feed – is neither ecologically nor economically sustainable and shows every indication of looming self-destruction (Fig. 4).

Factory farming further worsens the negative energy and climate scorecard at all stages of the production and processing chain as large amounts of feed are transported from the main growing areas in South and North America to the major purchasers in Europe, China, and Japan. The environmental burdens and the energy required are particularly serious because of high water consumption, the production of enormous amounts of slaughterhouse waste, and the massive use of antibiotics, vaccines, and growth hormones. In Germany alone, a centre of factory farming, approximately 750 million animals were slaughtered in 2012: roughly 628 million chickens, 58 million pigs, 38 million turkeys, 25 million ducks, 3 million head of cattle, 1 million sheep and goats, and half a million geese – three-quarters of a billion animals raised for their meat for a human population of approximately 80 million and their export profits.[6]

This is not the place to go into more detail about the ethical considerations and protests against the conditions under which the animals are kept and transported alive, the slaughter methods, and the dangers of transmitting diseases (bird flu, swine flu, BSE). Two further issues, on the other hand, are associated particularly closely with the outlook for human nutrition to be discussed here: a wholesome diet and the long-term availability of arable land under acceptable climatic and ecological conditions.

6   Meat Atlas (2014)

From a nutritional perspective, excessive consumption of meat and animal fat causes strain on the metabolism, owing to the high content of nucleic acids, protein, and saturated fatty acids. Painful and often chronic diseases such as rheumatism or arthrosis can also be triggered by immoderate consumption. The globally increasing consequences of an unhealthy diet and lifestyle ('lifestyle diseases' such as obesity, heart attacks, strokes, diabetes, and many others) would be worth a chapter of their own. The advancing development of resistance against the antibiotics used on a massive scale in animal farming (approximately 15,000 tons per year in the US alone), whose use in human medicine is thus seriously devalued, and the negative impact of hormone residues consumed with the meat would merit an extensive discussion.

Particularly remarkable in this context are the large-scale production and excessive consumption of foods of animal origin at the expense of a considerable share of the grain and soy harvests, which could be used directly for human nutrition. About one-third of the global grain harvest, and in industrialised countries even more than two-thirds, are currently used as animal feed. Depending on the type of animal, the land area required for meat production is three to ten times as large as that required for the same amount (by weight) of wheat. Besides the other inputs (plant protection products, fertiliser, energy), meat production also requires large amounts of additional water, many times more than for growing plants: approximately 15,000 litres/kg of beef, compared with 1,000 litres/kg of wheat and 250 litres/kg of potatoes.[7]

'Energy crops' are now another competitor for agricultural land besides factory farming. Sugarcane and corn are cultivated on a large scale for ethanol production, and rapeseed and palm oil for biodiesel. Especially in the tropical and subtropical countries of South America (corn and sugarcane fields) and Asia (palm

---

7   Meat Atlas (2014); BMEL *Understanding global food security and nutrition* (2015c)

oil plantations), further tropical forests have been destroyed to produce ethanol and palm oil either for the domestic market (mostly the US and Brazil) or for export.

In the short term, this development is at the expense of the biosphere and the climate, in the long term also at the expense of food production, which is vulnerable in any case. In the first decade of the twenty-first century alone, global production of bioethanol from sugarcane increased by a factor of five, and production of biodiesel by more than a factor of ten. In Germany, for example, a total of 2.2 million tons of biofuels were produced in 2013 from domestic wheat, rapeseed, and sugar beets.

According to UN FAO estimates, biofuels will account for approximately 6% of global grain consumption in 2015/2016. Roughly identical amounts will be used for human nutrition (44%) and animal feed (35%), of which almost half will be consumed by poultry and about one-quarter by pigs and ruminants respectively, according to Alltec-Information (2015).

Since roughly two-thirds of global agricultural land is grazing land, even doing away completely with factory farming would not amount to a diet without meat, egg, and milk products. What drives the mass production of additional foods of animal origin is not a nutritionally justifiable *need* – it is the constantly increasing amounts offered at bargain prices that change consumer behaviour and eating habits. Although this trend has mostly stabilised in recent years in the industrialised countries, it is still continuing, especially in the most populous emerging markets and threshold countries of Africa, Asia, and South America. Meat consumption is often considered a status symbol.

With the exception of a more efficient feed conversion ratio, the same is true of fish and crustaceans, more of which are also being consumed. Since the oceans have mostly been fished to the limits of maintaining stocks, or beyond those limits, and many inland waters are overly polluted with waste and toxins, numerous edible fish and crustaceans have been mostly or almost exclusively raised in aquacultures in recent years and generally marketed frozen.

The insight that this development with all its facets cannot be sustainable and, the longer it endures, will have all the more serious and long-term consequences for the biosphere, the climate, and future human living conditions, seems to be becoming more prevalent over time, especially with some of the younger generation. Many corresponding changes in behaviour are to be observed. Rejection of factory farming, a growing interest in a healthy diet, and a preference for products manufactured in an ecologically and ethically acceptable way are becoming more widespread and nourish the hope that these tendencies will gain even more general popularity.

Alternative resources and renaturation

In various regions of Central America, Africa, and Asia, insects and insect larvae that have been dried, roasted, smoked, or prepared in other ways are consumed as protein- and fat-rich foods. The spectrum ranges from bee larvae and ants to butterfly caterpillars as thick as a finger and giant locusts (Fig. 5). Eating them is above all a question of culture and dietary habits, besides their availability and the rest of the food supply.

As early as the fifth century BC, Greek historian Herodotus reported about desert dwellers who ground dried locusts into flour which they then mixed with milk to form a paste, and John the Baptist is said to have lived on locusts and honey in the desert. Today, roasted locusts, grasshoppers, or ants are not unusual in China, and fried bee larvae are considered a special delicacy.

Some regions are home to a few dozen, others up to several hundred edible insect species, depending on the climate and geographical location. The number of insects that are edible and

Fig. 5: Ready-to-eat insects at a market in Bangkok

nourishing is far greater than that of animals usually kept for meat. In addition, cultivating them is significantly easier and requires fewer inputs. Europeans, however, who have never become familiar with such foods, generally refuse in disgust to eat insects, just as some Asians shudder at the idea that some Europeans eat snails.

The situation is similar for algae. They are a ubiquitous part of the diet in East Asia, whereas they are uncommon in Europe. Sushi wrapped in algae is just as commonplace for Japanese diners (and recently also for Europeans) as dolmadakia or dolmas wrapped in grape leaves are for Greeks and Turks. In China, and even more in many places in South Korea, algae are a firmly established part of the daily diet.

Both groups of organisms, insects and algae, are ubiquitous and account for a large part of the animal and plant mass on Earth, and yet, little research has been conducted on their vast species diversity. This is true even for the many microscopically small single-cell organisms belonging to the groups of phyto- and zoo-plankton that are fed on by many fish and small animals as well as some whale species in the oceans and other water bodies. Both algae and insects, which are nutritionally valuable, can make an important contribution to the human diet, even in places where people are not accustomed to them and reject them simply for that reason.

On the basis of a comprehensive study, the EU's European Food Safety Authority (EFSA) has classified potential risks from consuming insects as being no different from risks from consuming other kinds of animals (Finke et al., for EFSA, *Journal of Insects as Food and Feed*, 2015).

Improving cultivation methods, distribution, and storage in developing countries offers further significant potential for opti-mising the global food situation without requiring additional land. The diet of approximately 2 billion people in Africa and Asia currently depends on half a billion small- or micro-scale farmers each with 2 hectares or less of land under cultivation. Their har-vests, which are already small, are threatened by additional losses, especially on the meagre soils of sub-Saharan Africa, because of climate change, increasing scarcity of water, and a lack of infra-structure. Even today, they must spend up to 80% of their income on food (compared with less than 20% in the EU). Many do not have access to clean water and are also threatened by conflicts over the few and shrinking water resources.

Increases in agricultural productivity in these regions require improvements in all the relevant areas: technical training, social and technological infrastructure, property rights, status of women, political stability, and natural resource conservation. However, these are such fundamental and urgent demands of national and international policy that they go far beyond the problem of the current and future global food situation, which is the topic here. In the context of this overview, a few concrete examples and considerations must suffice.

More than 80% of the food consumed in developing countries is produced locally on about 500 million small- or micro-scale farms. Most of them rely on sufficient rainfall to irrigate their fields or small plots of land, yet it is becoming increasingly common for rains to fail to arrive. Targeted support projects for sustainable water use in the context of sustainable land management in some particularly rain-poor regions of Niger and Ethiopia vulnerable to drought have proven to be significantly more effective, cheap, and sustainable than far more costly humanitarian aid measures that are not sustainable.[8]

This and many similar examples exemplify countless projects with different motivations and funding structures supporting successful capacity building with long-lasting impacts. The at times dramatic effects of advancing desertification and the depletion of water resources, both exacerbated by persistent global warming, call for a rapid and sustainable increase in agricultural yields and social safety nets. And they do so not least in order to lessen the increasing migration pressure triggered by hunger, poverty, lack of resources, and civil wars in many parts of Africa and the Near East.

Besides the above-mentioned external conditions, the most urgent measures include conservation of the remaining water resources and returning to variegated cultivation of numerous field and garden crops adapted to the local conditions, combined with integrated animal husbandry. This type of mixed cultivation, i.e., several species of crops on the same land (vegetables, root crops, grain, fruit trees, etc.) along with animal husbandry adapted to the amount of land on which feed is grown, has a long tradition across all continents, especially on small farms. Up to the present

---

8   *UN Convention to Combat Desertification* (2014)

day, smallholder farming in developing countries is mostly purely subsistence agriculture with every farm producing primarily for its own consumption and any surpluses being traded or bartered locally; historically, this system was commonplace everywhere.

This form of food production, which has a rich tradition and uses a large number of species and varieties, is far superior in ecological terms to large-scale cultivation of monocultures, and even more to factory farming. In areas with little water and poor infrastructure, it also provides the opportunity for integrated and thus economical water use and low waste production as well as a stable societal structure tied to the locality, whereby short distances and cycles provide social and economic advantages complementing the ecological ones.

The above-mentioned political measures, however, are indispensable preconditions. Training for technical and methodological improvements can be provided by national and international research institutions, agencies, and aid organisations. Conversely, the area's experienced farmers can contribute their own knowledge and experience.

This kind of 'agro-ecological' agriculture has the potential to counter the increasing destabilisation of the biosphere and climate change and to contribute to an extensive and sustainable lifestyle and economic activity, even in many regions currently still under intensive cultivation. It is also an essential component of the new trend to consume regional and seasonal foods produced organically, including urban gardening.

Another important alternative measure to counter desertification, global warming, further losses of species and, as a consequence, also loss of food security, consists in protecting the still remaining natural habitats and renaturating ecologically impoverished ones. Ongoing projects in Niger and Northern China are remarkable examples of comprehensive renaturation measures. Following an extreme drought in 1975, the practically treeless Galma region in

Niger was renaturated to such an extent that three decades later, more trees grew there than had previously been the case. A similar large project in China, the country with the highest reforestation rate in the world, is combating desertification Northwest of the greater Beijing region, which is threatened by sandstorms and water scarcity, with comprehensive programmes for renaturation of the arid areas and securing the groundwater sources.

According to UN estimates, roughly 2 billion hectares of land in total could be gained or reclaimed for human use through renaturation. In the drought-stricken regions of Niger, Mali, and Burkina Faso alone, the renaturation of 5 million hectares of land has enabled the recovery of a large amount of parched agricultural land and ended migrations caused by hunger.[9]

Renaturation projects whose purpose is not directly agricultural can also make important indirect contributions. Above and beyond their actual goal, they can raise awareness for just how much time and effort may be needed to reverse ecological damage that has been caused – to the extent they can be reversed at all – regardless of whether they were caused by agriculture or other factors.

A fitting example is the end-to-end renaturation of the Emscher River in Germany, which had deteriorated into an open wastewater sewer connecting the major cities of Dortmund, Bochum, Gelsenkirchen, Duisburg, and Oberhausen with the Rhine – a project started in the early 1990s with 2020 earmarked as the date for completion of the main work. A 400 km long sewer tunnel up to 40 m deep is being built through the densely populated Ruhr area in order to liberate the river from its concrete bed and return it to a condition as close to its natural one as possible; the project costs will amount to 4.5 billion euros. The green landscape emerging as a result of this project will doubtless achieve the desired impact on the people affected – and the same is true of the numerous

---

9   *UN Convention to Combat Desertification* (2014)

rivers, lakes, and former opencast mining sites that can be used for recreational purposes following renaturation.

Similar renaturation measures, as well as privately or publicly funded information events on topics relevant to food production and the environment, have increased significantly in number and breadth in recent years. Two examples with the same goals, but realised at different times and about different subject areas are a large permanent exhibition hall inaugurated during the International Horticultural Show in Kunming, China, in 1999 featuring chilling wall-sized images of the consequences of environmental destruction, and a major travelling exhibition in 2016 in various places in Germany titled 'Variety counts' about the value and the looming loss of biodiversity.

All direct and indirect projects to secure human nutrition and other living conditions can be sustainable only if they are flanked by two further measures which are urgently required in any case: the still remaining natural ecosystems must be protected effectively from degradation, and any waste of resources must be prevented. Not only when it comes to consumption of natural resources, water, and energy or to electrical and plastic waste but also and especially in relation to food, the amount of waste is barely lesser in scale than the amount of what is actually needed. Harvest and post-harvest losses to pests and germs are high, especially in humid areas, and require comprehensive countermeasures, in particular technical and agro-ecological improvements as well as increased efforts in resistance breeding.

Waste and shelf life

In the industrialised countries, up to half of harvests are lost before reaching their destination. End consumers alone discard one-third of all food on average, depending on its type and price, because they purchase too much. Food is then discarded during the preparation phase, as well as leftovers, and also because the best-before date is commonly misinterpreted as a definite date after which the food should no longer be consumed. Additional losses occur during manufacturing as well as in wholesaling and retailing. In manufacturing, they mostly arise due to quality problems during or after manufacture, and in wholesaling and retailing because of incorrect storage or passing the best-before date.

Many foods can be used days, weeks, or even months after the date indicated without significant losses in quality, provided they are stored properly. Handling food mindfully in every respect – from shopping to the plate to waste – would be a decisive contribution to resource conservation and securing the future, and it would not even require restrictions, much less giving anything up. However, expenditures of less than 20% of average income on food at historically low food prices across the EU are anything but an effective incentive to prevent waste.

As in all other areas of our lives, the observation made at the outset applies here as well, namely that it depends on our current behaviour as to whether our Earth will still be able to feed humanity in the future. This appears more than questionable in the absence of a change of direction toward sustainability.

Prospects

The prospects for changing direction arise from this stocktaking. A broad spectrum of developments in the past decade has become apparent, with the negative significantly outweighing the positive. At least it is possible to formulate a number of minimum requirements and starting points for successfully changing course on this basis. In their totality, the threats to future food production, some of which have been foreseeable for decades and are still constantly intensifying, are an urgent warning:

- the continued annihilation of biodiversity and ecological stability because of forest clearance and other forms of trans-formation of natural ecosystems into land for agricultural and other uses, including draining wetlands and sealing soils
- the overuse and degradation of soils and water bodies, causing desertification, wind erosion, and climate changes, especially in arid regions and regions vulnerable to drought
- large-scale cultivation of crops with little or no rotation of crop species and varieties, without islands of biodi-versity, habitat network systems, food supplies, resting places, and corridors for birds and other small and large animals, aggravated by excessive use of plant protection and fertilisers
- mass production of meat, eggs, and milk in factory farming, with correspondingly high consumption of land, feed, and water, and production of slurry and other wastes as well as the danger of the emergence and spreading of diseases and resistances to antibiotics
- additional competition for land and environmental pollu-tion through the growing of feed and energy crops
- genetic impoverishment in crops and livestock through concentration on a few high-performance varieties
- mindless wasting or discarding of food and many other limited resources

This list of acute threats to food production is balanced at least to some extent by a list of promising developments:[10]

- a significant increase in demand for foods produced regionally and in an environmentally friendly way, and

---

10 In more depth in Hahlbrock (2013), pp. 188 ff

at the same time (i) a rejection of products of factory farming and (ii) corresponding changes in dietary habits

- provision of information in the media about diet, health, production methods, and waste in the food system as well as about the value and vulnerability of ecosystems
- efforts by private foundations, and increasingly also by municipal and state institutions, to protect valuable habitats and vulnerable species and to realise sustainable lifestyles and a sustainable economic system
- efforts by numerous research institutes, universities, and non-governmental organisations toward capacity building for improving agricultural productivity in developing countries
- general international treaties on nature conservation and climate mitigation as well as specifically on the protection of vulnerable fish species and the establishment of fishing quotas
- giving more weight to environmental protection and nature conservation measures in EU agricultural policy by designating ecological focus areas

This juxtaposition delineates the most important deficits and assets in the field of food that must serve as starting points for the change of direction. Two categories of high-priority measures to secure human nutrition result from it. The first and highest category concerns politics, both at the national level (the authority to make laws and set policy guidelines) and at the international level (treaties). Similarly to the most recent climate treaty, further international treaties (and compliance with them!) are urgently needed for the protection of the still remaining centres of biodiversity and for expanded environmental protection and nature conservation, as well as for the renaturation of degraded and suitable land areas and water bodies.

Such measures to secure human nutrition require concrete laws, guidelines, and support measures to orient all areas toward a form of economic activity that is sustainable in agro-ecological terms as described above. This cannot imply abandoning intensive agriculture entirely, especially in light of continuing population growth – mostly due to poverty – and the need to supply major cities and megacities with food. The most recent research findings must be applied as well as longstanding experiential knowledge about the ecology of the individual cultivation areas. Indispensable preconditions for sustainable development include the greatest consideration possible for agro-ecological factors and fair trading conditions both within states and between industrialised and developing countries.

Some particularly serious developments are already irreversible, above all the loss of tropical rainforests, formerly arable soils, and water resources, as well as climate change, which is due in part to these factors. Plant cultivation and livestock production are already affected by climate change in many ways. Crops and livestock must be adapted to regions with heightened risks of drought, heat, severe weather, or flooding – provided they can still be used for agriculture at all – and to population shifts of pests and germs due to climate change, which require additional focus on resistance breeding. In most cases, extreme climate conditions diminish not only yields, but also the quality and shelf life of the harvest.

This is partly balanced on the positive side by several pioneering developments that mirror two basic tendencies complementing one another: increasing awareness of the acute threats to future quality of life, and the gradually increasing willingness to orient one's own lifestyle towards taking remedial measures and taking the initiative on even the smallest of scales at the grassroots level to counter the major problems existing at the global level.[11]

---

11 Hahlbrock (2013), pp. 201 ff

Preconditions for sustainable food security

The political and business communities
- Sustainable protection of the biosphere and the climate as well as sustainable use of all resources (sustainable intensification)
- Capacity-building for development and fair global trade with particular consideration for the socially and economically disadvantaged populations in developing countries
- General schooling and vocational education (including women) in developing countries, among other things to combat poverty and population growth and to increase agricultural productivity
- General support for agro-ecological agriculture as well as support for agricultural research, especially for and in developing countries
- Securing the priority of biodiversity, climate, and food production over the cultivation of feed and energy crops
- Prevention of land grabbing, further concentration on large farms, and speculation with land or agricultural products
- General teaching of basic knowledge within and outside school settings about ecological, economic, and social interdependencies in the areas of agriculture, nutrition, and health

Agriculture
- Environmentally friendly procedures in plant cultivation and animal husbandry
- Integration of ecological focus areas
- Expansion or preservation of the biodiversity of crops and livestock, including the use or reintroduction of plant varieties and animal species adapted to the local conditions
- Production of wholesome, high-quality foods
- Expansion of regional marketing

Personal behaviour
- Acquiring, evaluating, and passing on the above-mentioned basic knowledge
- Varied diet of foods produced in an environmentally friendly way
- Preference for seasonal products from the region or from fair trade
- Mindful handling of food and prevention of unnecessary waste
- Getting involved and serving as an example (according to the motto: If you want to change the world, you have to change yourself first).

For food production, wholesaling and retailing, and consumption, this juxtaposition gives rise to a package of measures for sustainable action in the political and business communities as well as in terms of personal behaviour (see box above). It is true that in the absence of a corresponding change in direction in other realms of life, these measures alone will not suffice to secure the future of human nutrition. But without them, any attempt to do so would appear futile.

To emphasise the main point once again: the number of people that the Earth can feed depends decisively on our behaviour now and in the future. Each and every one of us is responsible. We, and our diet, are part of the diversity and the internal dynamics of the Earth's biosphere – beneficiaries of its abundance and dependent on its well-being and its limits.

Bibliography

Alltech (2015), Global Feed Survey, info@alltech.com.

BMEL (2015a), Nahrung für Milliarden, Federal Ministry of Food and Agriculture, Berlin.

BMEL (2015b), Ökologischer Landbau in Deutschland, Federal Ministry of Food and Agriculture, Berlin.

BMEL (2015c), Understanding Global Food Security and Nutrition – Facts and Backgrounds, Federal Ministry of Food and Agriculture, Berlin.

Doudna, J. A. and Charpentier, E. (2014), The new frontier of genome engineering with CRISPR-Cas9, Science 346, 6213.1258096.

FAO (2012/2013), The Contribution of Insects to Food Security, Livelihoods and the Environment, 2012, and Edible Insects – Future Prospects for Food and Feed Security, www.fao.org/forestry/edibleinsects.

Finke, M. (2015), The European Food Safety Authority – Scientific opinion on a risk profile related to production and consumption of insects as food and feed, Journal of Insects as Food and Feed 1, 245–247.

Meat Atlas (2014), Facts and Figures about the Animals we Eat. Heinrich Böll Foundation, Berlin.

Hahlbrock, K. (2009), Feeding the Planet: Environmental Protection through Sustainable Agriculture. Haus Publishing.

Hahlbrock, K. (2011a), Scenario Ernährung. In: K. Wiegandt (ed.): Perspektiven einer nachhaltigen Entwicklung. Frankfurt: Fischer Taschenbuch Verlag.

Hahlbrock, K. (2011b), Nach 10 000 Jahren auf neuen Wegen – Pflanzenzüchtung für Ernährung und Umwelt. Naturwissenschaftliche Rundschau 64, pp. 61–72.

Hahlbrock, K. (2013), Natur und Mensch – Der lange Weg zum ökosozialen Bewußtsein. Munich: Allitera Verlag.

Soil Atlas (2015), Facts and Figures about Earth, Land and Fields. Berlin: Heinrich Böll Foundation.

Huang, S., Weigel, D., Beachy, R. N., Li, J. (2016), A proposed regulatory framework for genome-edited crops. Nature Genetics 48, 109–111.

IFOAM EU Group (2015), Feeding the People – Agroecology for Nourishing the World and Transforming the Agri-food System, www.ifoam-eu.org.

James, C. (2014), Global Status of Commercialized Biotech/GM Crops. ISAAA Brief No. 49. Ithaca, N.Y.: ISAAA.

Kocar, G., Civas, N. (2013), An overview of biofuels from energy crops: Current status and future prospects. Renewable and Sustainable Energy Reviews 28, 900–916.

Smith, R., Barnes, E. (2015), PROteInSECT – Insects as Sustainable Sources of Protein. Minerva Health & Care Communications.

Spektrum der Wissenschaft Spezial 4/2013 – Wertvolle Ökosysteme (2013), www.spektrum.de.

Teillant, A., Laxminarayan, R. (2015), Economics of antibiotic use in U.S. swine and poultry production. Choices, 1–11.

UNESCO (2015), Water for a Sustainable World. The UN World Water Development Report, Paris.

UN Convention to Combat Desertification (Dec. 2014), Desertification – The Invisible Frontline. www.unccd.int.

Credits

Fig. 1 top: Florian Kopp, bottom: Yann Arthur-Bertrand

Fig. 2: Klaus Hahlbrock

Fig. 3: Max-Planck-Institute for Plant Breeding Research

Fig. 4 top left: Yann Arthur-Bertrand, top right: Reuter, bottom right: Roland Geisheimer, bottom left: Jürgen Held

Fig. 5: Jürgen Held

The future of resource water – revisited

Wolfram Mauser

Almost a decade has passed since my book *Water Resources: Efficient, Sustainable and Equitable Use* was published. Time to take it up again and consider where we stand today, with respect to how long global water resources will last and which of the statements made in the book are still true and where something must be added or modified.

The world has changed substantially in the past ten years. At this point, I would like to mention just a few aspects I think important as background to assessing the global scarcity of water today. Neoclassical economic theory, the dominant system of thought for justifying economic activity prevailing in 2007, outlived its usefulness with the global economic crisis of 2008. Nonetheless, it is not dead, and we are struggling globally to find a successor that can combine sustainable economic activity, material prosperity, and equity. In 2007, the dynamics of the digitalisation of all areas of life were largely underestimated. One person in two is now a cell in the newly emerging superorganism of global social networks. The prosperous part of humanity is now aware that the outcome of the ferment of globalisation, digitalisation, and rationalisation is not, as was often assumed in 2007, generating only winners and a world that is happier overall (but certainly not automatically sustainable). Middle-class citizens in these countries are just realising the extent to which they are becoming socioeconomically devalued by a global oversupply of labour and all-encompassing digitalisation of all processes that make up life.

Unlike times past, global population growth is becoming

manifest in more than just abstract numbers. It has become concrete through conflicts around work, meaning, and global positioning. As a consequence, Europe too – after the US, India, Australia, and Southeast Asia – is now in a painful struggle to find a stance towards refugee and migrant flows that corresponds to the continent's cultural roots. Economic development in the emerging economies has proved temporary, in contrast to the optimistic view of it prevailing in 2007. Although it is true that Brazil, Russia, South Africa, China, and India are making progress with their economic development, albeit in very different ways, the ghosts of corruption, mismanagement, and poor governance are far from retreating, there as well as elsewhere. On the other hand, the fall in the price of renewable energies (solar and wind) that was to occur in the following ten years was simply inconceivable in 2007. It was a major factor contributing to the success of the COP21 Climate Conference in Paris in December 2015: for the first time in history, a credible economic rationale complemented the moral ones for phasing out the carbon economy.

We know now what we could not even imagine in 2007: carbon soon becoming history as an energy carrier and the simultaneous birth of information as a commodity will impact regional lifestyles and development prospects of people, cultures, and nations at their core. What does the unavoidable phase beginning now in which we will refrain from consuming almost all carbon resources in the world signify for the local fate of those who do or do not have them? Saudi Arabia's quest for a new role in the world, combined with the current development of the price of oil, and the country's decision to end production of intensively irrigated wheat are initial and contradictory evidence. The transformation, which still seemed relatively abstract in 2007, is now generating multifaceted images of the future that are not only positive. Geopolitical and geostrategic analyses based mostly on protecting the interests of nation-states and long thought to have been overcome have become socially acceptable again and are the subject of intensive discussions and widely circulated publications (e.g., Marshall, 2015). They would have us believe that it is possible to ignore the increasing globalisation of trade and information and to return to the seemingly idyllic nineteenth-century world of nation-states dominated by Europe.

I conclude from this brief analysis that the question of how long water resources will last has lost none of its relevance. But we must brace ourselves for having to seek answers to the question in a very different environment. It seems as if long-term global challenges such as water scarcity, climate change, the global food supply, and sustainable development are increasingly being pushed aside in a world in constant crisis mode. And yet they constitute the cosmic background radiation, so to speak, from which crises emerge. Nonetheless, one thing is certain in this world of uncertainties: the global challenges will still exist when the currently high degree of nervousness triggered by a more realistic perception of the societal consequences of globalisation and digitalisation has calmed down.

What does all this mean for a current-day view of water consumption as a scarce resource? Has water scarcity itself changed, or only perceptions of it? Do we have any new insights? In order to discuss these questions systematically, it makes sense to review the core statements from 2007.

The core statements from 2007

I would like to summarise my insights about water scarcity on Earth as of 2007 as follows:

1. We differentiate between blue water, which flows in rivers, and green water, which flows through vegetation and enables it to grow. We source water for drinking,

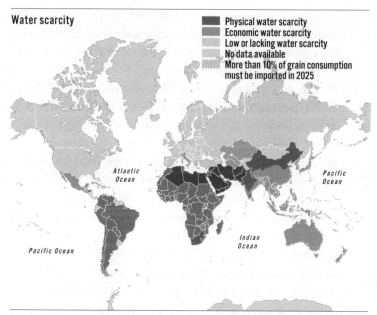

Fig. 1: The map shows the countries projected to suffer from physical and economic water scarcity in 2025 (changed following IWMI, 2000)

sanitation, and industry from the blue water flows, and food mostly from the green water flows. 96% of the water used by human beings is for food production, so management of the green water resources is decisive for whether or not water is scarce. The international community of states established the Dublin Principles for handling the supply of clean water for drinking and industrial uses, with the goal of every person being able to access clean drinking water.

2. Water use is characterised by regional conflicts between upstream and downstream users. Sometimes, use of river water as green water and massive engineering interventions for food and energy production bring about

enormous damage to the environment and society (e.g., Aral Sea). It is often imputed that wars are fought over water, but this cannot be proven with certainty.

3. All eminent institutions predicted that the Earth was heading toward a water crisis that would affect most of the world's population and that broad areas of the Earth would suffer from economic or physical water scarcity in 2025.

4. Figure 1 shows the notion prevailing at the turn of the millennium about how the global water crisis would develop. The map, which I used in my 2007 book, was published by the International Water Management Institute (IWMI) in Sri Lanka. Economic scarcity means that water resources are not available in abundance and must therefore be factored into economic considerations. Physical water scarcity exists if more than 40% of the available blue water is diverted to green water flows for food production. The core areas of the predicted water scarcity are mostly in the Middle East, in the Maghreb states, and in northern China. In addition, the entire global South will be affected by economic water scarcity. In other words: gloomy prospects.

5. In the best case of water-efficient grain production, 1 kg of food requires 500 times that amount of green water. It is tied to grain production in the form of 'virtual water'. This amount increases practically without limit as food is processed. For example, 1 kg of beef contains 16,000 litres of virtual water. No other sector of the economy consumes even remotely as much water as agriculture. Therefore, food production and our eating habits are decisive for water scarcity on Earth.

6. If we assume that the amount of green water required to generate the global population's daily calorie requirements (3,000 kcal per person per day) remains constant,

that all people have sufficient food, and that the Western world maintains its level of water consumption, then the amount of green water needed would double. Yet global water resources cannot double because hardly any additional opportunities exist for expanding agriculture and irrigation. The only practical solution to the problem is to increase agricultural water productivity ('more crop per drop'). There are various options for doing so; the most effective is yield increases in rain-fed agriculture, especially in Africa and Asia. Increasing yields in these regions to the European level would make it possible to produce sufficient food without using more green water, or so it was thought in 2007.

7. Food is traded worldwide. Virtual flows of the water that was needed to produce it in its original location thus accompany the traded foods around the globe. Guiding these virtual water flows enables us to cut back on real water use. This is based on the fact that the production of a certain amount of food in arid areas requires comparatively much more water than in regions with abundant water. Concentrating food production in the moist regions of the Earth and simultaneously increasing agricultural trade makes it possible to save water and protect ecosystems in the arid areas.

In 2007, I gave a cautiously optimistic answer to the question as to how long water resources will last: 'If we learn to manage water resources globally, they will last a long time. Water is not like crude oil: it renews itself constantly. Water, the natural resource that is most likely to become scarce first, will be the resource to show us if we are capable of sustainably managing the Earth system's important cycles of matter. Only in this way can we do justice to the responsibility that we have already acquired through appropriation and possession. More and more scientists and technicians from around the world are addressing these topics, more and more politicians are asking for solutions, and more and more people need a solution.'

In the following, I employ three core areas to illuminate the changes of the past ten years: (1) the global water crisis, (2) the role of green water in securing the global food supply, and (3) the situation regarding global water governance.

What do we know now about global water scarcity?

The scenarios on global water scarcity that were designed and examined around the turn of the millennium tell us a lot about the knowledge available and the ideas about the future at the time. Crises that have been proclaimed generate attention; if they are proclaimed for the future, the advantage is that they do not have to be substantiated by observable reality – simplification increases acceptance. For example, the analysis was based on simply extrapolating population growth. By now, we know that that assumption was too simple; it would mean that the stabilisation of the global population by the end of the century, which is becoming apparent, would not come about. The population development of the past ten years has impressively confirmed the initial trend of a constant decrease in the population growth rate. On this basis, it is now considered certain that the global population will stabilise at approximately 9.5 to 10 billion people in this century. Without exaggeration, this can be considered a turning point in the assessment of the future. After all, a sustainable development of the relationship between human beings and their environment in the future is not compatible with constant population growth. Rapid stabilisation of the population makes all further efforts to stabilise water use all the more meaningful.

Has the global water crisis been called off?

So how do matters stand now with respect to the water crisis? Can it be called off or postponed to a later point in time in light of this altogether encouraging development of the global population? A great deal has happened in this regard, and it is worthwhile taking a closer look at this quite ambivalent development.

Humanity has developed effective early warning systems over the past ten years. This is evidence both of increasing global awareness of the crisis and of the determination not to submit to crises. For example, the largest natural disaster of the new century, the 2004 tsunami in the Indian Ocean, which caused more than 230,000 deaths, triggered the development of an early warning system that evaluates measurements from around the world in minutes, thereby ensuring that information about the directly imminent threat reaches the affected population before it is ravaged by a tsunami. Hardly noticed by the general public, the European Union and the US have installed a fleet of satellites in the past ten years that observe changes in the environment regularly and with great precision. Like global 'sensory organs', their sensors are continually monitoring the planet, its oceans, fields, forests, lakes, and cities. Independent of national borders and the will of many a country to conceal looming catastrophes, they point out dangerous developments early on. Like the tsunami early warning system, they are an integral component of the beginning of the Information Age. Even today, every human being has free, open, and complete access to all the data from the environmental satellites. Large data streams about the global condition of the environment are already flowing, and they will accompany us into the future as well. The knowledge we gain from them will be an important factor in deciding about how we develop solutions for the major global challenges.

We are just learning how to interpret these new global environmental satellite observations and how to place them in wider

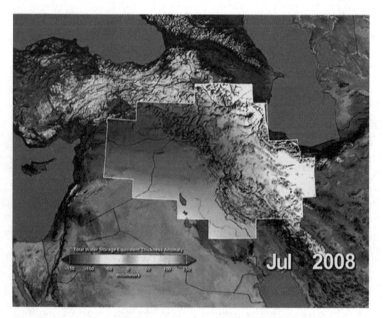

Fig. 2: The image shows the extent and magnitude of the decline of groundwater reserves between 2002 and 2008 in the Middle East in equivalent anomaly of altitude, measured with the GRACE satellite (from NASA, 2013) (In colour: see plates)

contexts. For example, Figures 2 and 3 show the large-scale deple-tion of groundwater and reservoirs in the Middle East between 2002 and 2008, and between 2003 and 2010 respectively. This large-scale image of massive environmental changes was the product of two satellites' continuous and extremely precise measurement of the Earth's gravitational force. Whenever mass increases anywhere on Earth (e.g., because of the presence of more water in the groundwater bodies), the force of gravity increases there, too. In contrast, if the groundwater bodies are filled to a lesser degree, the force of gravity decreases there.

Figure 2 shows a massive and large-scale decline of the water table in the catchment area of the Euphrates and Tigris in the Middle East. The epicentre of the decline is in Syria, Turkey, and Iraq, where it amounts to approximately 150 mm across a large area. The only place in the world where the water table is declining more rapidly is northern India. Nonetheless, 150 mm does not appear to be very much at first glance, but in many parts of this arid region, this amount corresponds to about one-third of annual precipitation.

On the left of Figure 3 is shown the mean groundwater level of the Middle Eastern region indicated in Figure 2 over time, and on the right, the changes in the water level of the Qadisiyah reservoir, which backs up the Euphrates in Iraq with a dam 9 kilometres long. These measurements were also made by satellites. The groundwater level first shows the normal annual cycle, characterised by seasonal winter rains and melting snow. From 2007 on, a distinct drop in the water table is overlaid over this cycle. A similar image of the water level of the Qadisiyah reservoir emerges, initially with seasonal withdrawals, followed by a strong decline of the water level from 2007 on.

What happened in Syria? Is the civil war raging in Syria since 2011 ultimately linked to this water scarcity and thus a regional expression of the global water crisis? Did the satellite with its measurements of the gravitational force witness the roots of the civil war long before it broke out?

As so often, it will not be possible to create a direct and compelling causal chain between the water loss measured by the global observation systems and the outbreak of the civil war. Yet five factors provide an explanation of the course of events. They sound almost like a blueprint for other potential regional water conflicts in other places on Earth.

First, the Southeastern Anatolia Project (GAP), whose influence on the regional water resources increased during the time period observed: GAP consists of a total of 22 reservoirs that store

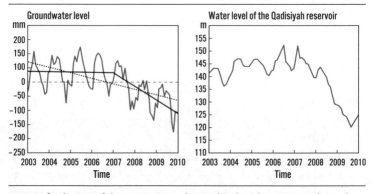

Fig. 3: Left: change of the mean groundwater level in the region indicated in Fig. 2, determined from measurements of the gravitational force by the GRACE satellite; right: water level [metres above sea level] of the Qadisiyah reservoir in Iraq, measured with satellite altimeters (changed, from Voss et al., 2013)

the water of the Upper Euphrates and Tigris and make it available for electricity generation and irrigation in Turkey. The increase in the usage of the water from these reservoirs for irrigation took place in the first decade of this century. Turkey is now diverting large amounts of river water to agriculture and is using it as green water. This has reduced the flow of Euphrates and Tigris water to Syria by 40% and to Iraq by 80%.[1] If the agricultural systems in Syria and Iraq are to be maintained even without this flow of river water, which has been available for millennia, then there is no alternative to increasing withdrawal of groundwater in this arid region.

Second, since the beginning of the century, Syria has been experiencing a prolonged drought, which is, however, not exceptional in historical terms. Before the beginning of the civil war,

---

1   Hammer (2013)

the lack of water already forced almost one million farmers to give up their farms, their heritage, and their way of life and to migrate to the cities (Arnold, 2013). Forced inactivity and unemployment brought about an atmosphere of desperation and lack of prospects.

Third, government agencies have been and still are largely unaware of the actual extent of the scarcity of water. In desperation, the remaining farmers have dug more and more wells and withdrawn water from ever greater depths in order to maintain food production to some extent. This was mostly illegal. As a result, nobody knew how many wells there were, how much water was withdrawn, and from which point on manageable water scarcity would become an out-of-control water crisis.

Fourth, many of the remaining farmers had the impression that Syrian President Assad had no interest in their plight and that the government was failing to do anything to stabilise their situation. This thereby gave the farmers all the more reason to become more aggressive.

Fifth, this region has seen a 4,500-year history of tensions and conflicts about the control of water resources. Historically, it has not been uncommon in this region to resolve conflicts by violent means, so it is difficult not to fall back into this pattern. As this example and its consequences, which reach all the way to Europe, show, the global water crisis is anything but over. It is only just developing a face. This face is characterised by multiple failures in handling regional and supraregional water scarcity, resulting in the complete collapse of the affected society's resilience. Key factors are a lack of communication and cooperation as well as a failure to understand that everyone is a loser in such a water crisis. Presumably, none of these factors alone could trigger a regional water crisis. On the other hand, if the population were smaller, if irrigation in the upstream regions did not excessively and massively reduce the amount of available river water, and if public administration were intact and ethical, even a combination of the other factors could not have had such a negative impact.

What can we learn from this example describing the most terrible civil war of this century and the water crisis that triggered it? Two insights appear important to me: first, the key role of the new sensory organs and social networks of the emerging global information society, which, taken to its logical end, will make all information available to everyone and thus immediately place every regional water crisis in a continental, if not global context. As we can see from the example of Syria, every regional crisis will be at least a supraregional crisis in the future. In a transparent world based on information, flows of refugees and movements of migrants will be the logical consequence of the information available as long as efforts to prevent desperation – for example, such as that emerging in a water crisis – are unsuccessful. On the other hand, this development towards an open, global information society holds practically unlimited opportunities to solving the water crisis, since the global community has the resources and instruments that individual countries or regions cannot muster. Secondly, we know today that the water crisis in the Euphrates and Tigris region was not unforeseeable, and we are beginning to understand that we could have seen it coming, although we were unable to interpret the signs properly. And even if we had been able to, what would we have had to do and what could we have done to prevent the water crisis and the following civil war? Herein lies a major task for the future: the development of systems for detecting and handling problems early on to enable timely diagnosis and minimally invasive therapy of future regional water crises.

The Euphrates and Tigris region is not a solitary case, even if the consequences of increasingly scarce water resources are currently extreme there. Other global water crisis hot spots are on the Nile with upstream-downstream conflicts between Ethiopia and Egypt (FT, 2013) as well as the increasing exploitation of the groundwater resources in India, among other places. In 2015, I had the opportunity to learn about the situation in southern India on the ground. Farmers there receive electricity free of charge and large subsidies for pumps and irrigation pipes, which practically creates competition to increase food production and pump India dry. The country seems incapable of identifying rules and incentives that prompt the farmers to use the water more sparingly, for example requiring them to pay for electricity or irrigation water, but such efforts have been politically infeasible to date. Instead, there are attempts to regulate irrigation water consumption in many places by means of (intentional or unavoidable) outages of the ramshackle power plants for some hours during the day. This neither gets to the root of the problem nor does it build trust in the government and public administration on the part of the population.

Will there be enough water to feed the global population?

Agriculture is responsible for an estimated 92–99% of the global consumption of green and blue water.[2] Two-thirds of the blue water used is for irrigation purposes. Because of the increasing global population, its increasing prosperity, and the resulting changes in consumption patterns as well as the rising demand for renewable resources for industry, the demand for biomass is expected to double by 2050.[3] This postulated doubling is to take place against the background of global warming, which will change the regional climatic conditions for agriculture (for good and for bad) by 2050. The end of unsustainable irrigation from fossil groundwater in many places because of empty aquifers will additionally and

2   Mekkonen and Hoekstra (2013); Hoekstra and Mekkonen (2012)
3   Bruinsma (2011); Alexandratos and Bruinsma (2012)

necessarily bring about a reduction of the use of blue water in agriculture. This will mean that a smaller amount of water will have to generate twice as much harvest on today's agricultural land in a changed climate ('more crop per drop'). The question of whether water will become scarce is thus directly linked to the future use of green and blue water for food production. This was already known in 2007, but the prospects were generally grim. At the time, it was already clear that on the one hand, 'business as usual' in food production would double the amount of water needed for agriculture by 2050, and on the other hand, the Earth could not supply these amounts of water sustainably and in the long term.

A massive expansion of agricultural land is not an option, either. It would come at the expense of the natural ecosystems. They in turn are urgently needed for maintaining the functioning of the Earth's life-support systems, naturally cleaning air and water, and as a gene pool to prevent unchecked species extinction.

The only remaining alternative is to increase water productivity by using water more efficiently in agriculture. This appears imaginable in principle, but beyond this simple statement it was still mostly unclear in 2007 how this could be achieved. More irrigation and expansion of agricultural land are unsuitable for the reasons mentioned above, so the options of improved cultivation practices, improved seed, and trade with virtual water remain. How has the perspective on these options changed over the past ten years?

By now, we have a better understanding of what is happening. Figure 4 shows one of the key diagrams for assessing water productivity in agriculture.

Using the example of wheat, Figure 4 shows the relationship between green water consumption in the form of evapotranspiration – that is, the evaporation from plants and the soil in millimetres – and the yield in t/ha. What stands out immediately? The ascending line obviously shows that there is an upper limit to water productivity for wheat, independent of the region observed.

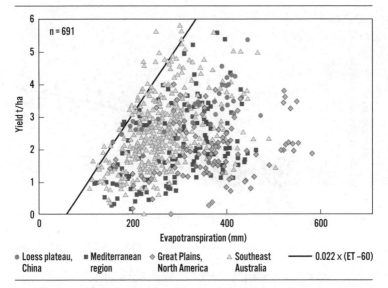

Fig. 4: The relationship between green water consumption through evapotranspiration and yield (t/ha) for wheat in various regions of the world (changed, following Sadras and Angus, 2006)

At most, approximately 1 t/ha of wheat can be produced with 100 mm evapotranspiration; at most, 5 t/ha with 300 mm. So that is the minimum amount of water needed in each case to generate this yield. But in addition, there is a large cloud of plot-dots that makes clear that enormous amounts of water can be wasted in wheat cultivation. Water consumption for a yield of 2 t/ha ranges from just 150 mm all the way to over 500 mm evapotranspiration. The reasons for this wastage are many and varied. They range from selecting the wrong variety of wheat to low fertilisation and thus insufficient growth. This leaves the soil exposed and increases unproductive water evaporation. Farmers doing everything right will move along the ascending line, thus making optimal use of the available water resources.

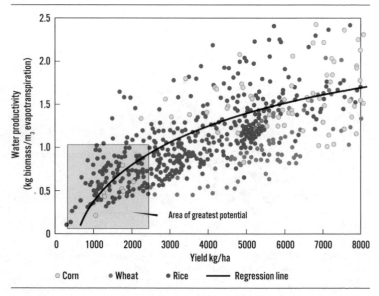

Fig. 5: Water productivity as a function of the yield of corn, wheat, and rice (changed, from IAASTD, 2009)

Figure 5 shows another key diagram for understanding water productivity in agriculture. For the three important crops – corn, wheat, and rice – it shows water productivity and thus the yield that can be produced with 1 m^3 of evapotranspiration. In Figure 5, water productivity of 1 means that production of 1 kg of yield requires 1 m^3 (1,000 litres) water evaporation. A value of 2 means that 1 kg of yield requires just 500 litres of water. In Figure 5, water productivity is represented as a function of yield in kg/ha.

Figure 5 makes obvious that water productivity increases with increasing yield. In other words, the greater the agricultural yield on a piece of land, the more productive water consumption is, and therefore the smaller the amount of water wasted. This is astonishing and remarkable in two respects. For one thing, it says that high-yield agriculture is most efficient in its use of water, and for another, that efficient water use simultaneously increases yields and thus contributes to satisfying the globally increasing demand for food and biomass. That sounds like a golden solution. But there is a catch, and that lies in increasing the yield. If this increase is achieved in an unsustainable way, then little is gained, as the soils and agricultural production systems are destroyed in the longer term. I will come back to this below, but would first like to consider the question of whether this simultaneous increase of yield and water productivity is enough to satisfy the rising demand for food. Or are we forced to breed new, significantly more productive plants through massive genetic engineering interventions, e.g., in the photosynthesis mechanism?

So the question is whether – if they are used optimally – the existing ways to increase yields on today's agricultural land with today's precipitation, today's irrigation, and today's crop plants can even satisfy the future demand for food and biomass. I recently conducted a study with colleagues[4] whose results astounded us in the positive sense of the word. The results of the simulations for the globe are presented in Figure 6.

A simulation model combining plant physiology and macro-economics determined the highest possible yield of 18 crops for the irrigated and unirrigated portions of all of today's cropland with the climate from 1980 to 2010 (results shown in Fig. 6). The economic aspects of the yield potentials were taken into account as well. In many regions, mostly in Africa, our investigations show that the selection of local crops, which is often determined by colonial traditions even to this day, means that yields are significantly lower than they would be if crops were grown there that would achieve the highest profits at current market prices. The findings were compared with the FAO's yield statistics, and increase rates in per cent

---

4   Mauser et al. (2015)

Fig. 6: Global potential to increase yields on today's cropland with the plants and the water from precipitation and irrigation available today (from Mauser et al., 2015)

were calculated (see Fig. 6). There were no surprises for large parts of the Earth. In Western Europe, the US, Canada, and southern Brazil, the actual harvests are already close to the maximum achievable, i.e., water productivity is very high. Further yield increases of around 20–40% are possible there, but would likely have negative impacts on sustainability. All of sub-Saharan Africa as well as India are at the other end of the spectrum. Enormous yield increases can be achieved there. They amount to more than 500% across the board, with maximums of up to 800%. So this is where the Earth's wasted water resources are to be found. This is where the reserves are that permit substantial increases in food production. But will these increases be enough to satisfy demand in 2050, which will be twice as high as it is today? The answer is given by a global averaging of the potentials in Figure 6. It enables a possible increase of global food production by a factor of 2.5. Thus, the potentials are 20% higher than the demand expected for 2050.

What does that mean? Today's cropland can provide enough green and blue water, and today's crops can therefore produce enough yield to feed future generations as well. This makes it abundantly clear that the demand for food in the future is unsuitable as a justification for expanding cropland and thus for the destruction of natural ecosystems, much less as a rationale for genetically modifying crops in order to increase yield and water productivity.

The 20% reserve in the potential is reassuring. But it is necessary as well, for one thing because potentials can hardly be exploited to their full extent in practice, and for another, because the required intensification of cultivation must be sustainable. Therefore, it is better to forego the last few percentage points of yield increases in favour of sustainability. How large this difference between potential and sustainable intensification must be in the various regions of the Earth is a complex question that more and more scientists are studying.

So a small light at the end of a long tunnel is just becoming visible in the tension between water and food. Yet two questions remain to be answered: (1) is it possible to exploit the existing potential to increase water productivity and food production in the various regions quickly enough to keep up with the increasing demand for food? And (2) are the impacts of greenhouse gases and climate change cancelling out the positive prospects?

Both questions are being examined closely. The first is particularly controversial, as the highly volatile food prices of recent years have shown. In light of the sharply downsized state food reserves, even short-term food scarcity brings about nervous price fluctuations and speculation, with dramatic consequences for the poorest segment of the global population. If we are unable to have food production keep up with demand, that will hardly have any direct impacts on us in Europe, but it will have incalculable consequences for large parts of the population in Africa, for example. But as we have seen in the example of the Syrian civil war, it will certainly come back to haunt us.

We are currently increasing yields much too slowly. If we continue to increase yields at the same leisurely pace as today, we will add 67% for corn, 42% for rice, 38% for wheat, and 55% for soy by 2050.[5] That is a far cry from doubling yields. So how can we accelerate unlocking these potentials?

In my opinion, there is reason for hope, namely the dynamic development of the digitalisation of all areas of society – social networks, the internet, and smartphones mentioned at the outset. This also opens up entirely new opportunities for digital agriculture. The system is fed by the stream of data from the environmental satellites that constantly observe, for example, plant growth, pest infestations, and unsustainable and unnecessarily high fertilisation and irrigation, as well as the state of maturity for every point on any individual field on Earth. The data stream feeds simulation models like the one introduced above. On the basis of current weather forecasts, they simulate vast numbers of alternatives to determine the most sustainable, water-productive, and yield-increasing option for every point in time throughout the agricultural calendar for every field on the planet. Farmers on every continent receive this option (and perhaps also the second- and third-best alternatives) on their smartphones and decide to put the most appropriate option into practice precisely with a data-driven tractor. Science fiction? At the threshold of the self-driving car? No!

This is a description of a new 'digital green revolution', this time not driven by the belief in new turbo seed and the infinite utility of infinite fertiliser use, but by the idea of sustainable intensification. In comparison with the alternatives (expansion of agricultural land and genetic engineering), I consider this 'digital green revolution' to be worth every effort. The burgeoning expansion of smartphones and social networks to the remotest corners of the world shows the extraordinary dynamics the digital revolution can

---

5   Ray et al. (2013)

achieve. It would be unconscionable not to harness these dynamics for the necessary acceleration of the sustainable intensification of agriculture out of misunderstood scepticism of technology.

What will the impacts of climate change be?

Solutions can be arrived at at the time of writing that we were not aware of in 2007. But what about greenhouse gas emissions and climate change? Major research projects have shed light on these matters in recent years, so it is now possible to better estimate the consequences of global climate change for water scarcity in agriculture. Two results are becoming apparent. For one thing, climate change will produce identifiable winners and losers: regions such as the Mediterranean and the Middle East will experience increasing drought, whereas agriculture will become possible in vast areas of Canada, Russia, and northern China only because of climate change. The positive and negative regional effects of climate change on food production, which will manifest themselves particularly through a combination of changes in local temperatures and precipitation, are likely to roughly balance each other out globally.[6] To prevent misunderstanding: this means that even though the global impacts of climate change will be more or less balanced, they can be very serious at the regional level. In some regions, they certainly have the potential (together with other factors) to trigger a regional water crisis.

Another factor mostly neglected to date in the discussion will contribute to the fact that, as far as we know today, foreseeable climate change will not limit global food production to a substantial extent. We now have very robust insights into the CO_2 fertilisation effect in agriculture. It has long been known from

---

6   Zabel et al. (2014)

laboratory studies that artificially raising the atmospheric CO_2 concentration simultaneously increases the growth of C3 plants such as cereals, rice, sugar beets, and potatoes and enhances water productivity. This is because of the interchange of gases between the atmosphere and the plant. The plant absorbs CO_2 through stomata, small openings in the leaves, and, in combination with water and light, it transforms it into sugar in the process of photosynthesis. At the same time, the plant evaporates water through the same stomata. If the atmospheric CO_2 concentration increases, the plant can absorb more CO_2, produce more sugar, and thus grow more quickly, provided sufficient light is available. If the additional light is not available, the plant makes the stomata smaller. Because of the higher CO_2 concentration, the smaller stomata are sufficient for absorbing the original amount of CO_2. But because the stomata are smaller, less water can evaporate from the leaf. Absorption of the same amount of CO_2 with simultaneously reduced evaporation means higher water productivity. If these laboratory findings prove to be valid in the field, too, this would mean that increasing the atmospheric CO_2 concentration not only causes climate change, but also increases the water productivity and yields of C3 plants. During the past ten years, major research projects financed by Germany, the EU, and the US National Science Foundation have pursued the question of whether this relationship, which is valid in the lab, is also valid in practical agriculture. And now it is clear: it is![7] Increasing the atmospheric CO_2 concentration enhances the water productivity of the C3 plants, and not only in the lab. This effect will become increasingly noticeable as the CO_2 concentration rises, and it will also significantly decrease the water consumption of agricultural C3 plants, which means that the impacts of climate change on global agriculture overall should remain manageable. However,

---

7   Kimball (2011); Fleisher et al. (2011)

this does not include C4 plants such as corn and sugarcane. They can actively store CO_2 themselves. Their growth is largely independent of the atmospheric CO_2 concentration.

What is the role of virtual water for reducing water scarcity?

Global trade makes food available even in places where nothing can grow, thereby overcoming local water scarcity. If the traded goods were produced with sustainably available water resources at their places of origin, then trade with virtual water makes sustainable water use substitutable across space. If the underlying conditions are suitable, trade with virtual water can thereby create incentives to shift the production of water-intensive goods to those areas of the globe where the required water resources are available sustainably, and to import such goods to places where water resources are insufficient. Theoretically speaking, this would make it possible to save green water overall. Highly intensive rain-fed agriculture of the moist middle latitudes with its high water productivity saves large amounts of green water compared with inefficient water-wasting irrigated farming in arid areas. If the decision were made to terminate irrigated farming in arid areas and to import food from the moist middle latitudes instead, this would save real blue and green water.

As indicated above, Saudi Arabia has reoriented its agricultural production in recent years on the basis of these deliberations. One of the most arid countries in the world, Saudi Arabia advanced to become one of the leading wheat producers and a veritable wheat exporter in the early 1990s by overusing its groundwater resources and desalinating sea water, using cheap oil as the energy source. Against the background of the rapid depletion of its underground aquifers, Saudi Arabia decided in 2016 to end its own wheat production, to refill its groundwater bodies with desalinated water for future generations, and to purchase the wheat required to feed its population on the global market. Thus, the country is following the policy of many of its neighbours: 'sell hydrocarbons to buy carbohydrates'. This will reduce global water consumption and increase sustainability in managing regional water resources. According to the Saudi assessment, the global trade in food now provides sufficient security to relinquish self-sufficiency in favour of more sustainable development.

Can this easy-to-understand example catch on? In many regions of the world, the state of affairs is not so simple. By now, we know quite a lot about the virtual water concentration of almost all traded goods. We even know that charging an iPhone once requires 0.5 litres of water and doing a Google search 0.5 millilitres.[8] We also have a good idea about how much water from the Ogallala aquifer in the Midwest US, for example, is exported to Japan as virtual water in wheat.[9] The great achievement of this type of statistical research was to raise consumers' awareness of how they could change the pressure they exert on water resources by varying their consumption habits. Beyond the example of Saudi Arabia, however, the concept of virtual water has not yet had any demonstrable impact on agricultural trade.

Why is that? An astounding body of figures has been gathered which at times begins to weary the reader. On the other hand, efforts to assign a value to virtual water (except for its quantity), thus making it possible to valuate it, have not been successful. What is decisive for valuating the virtual flows of water is water productivity and water resource scarcity in the place where the water is used, and therefore sustainability in that place. If water is available sustainably there, why not use it to farm cattle? The resulting large flow of virtual water would be exported to other

---

8   IEEE (2010)
9   Mekkonen and Hoekstra (2010)

places with the beef. What does 'unsustainable use of water' actually mean, how can it be proven, and where on Earth is water used unsustainably? As long as there are no satisfying answers to these reasonable questions, it will not be possible to formulate sustainability goals for agriculture concerning the use of blue and green water and to introduce financial mechanisms supporting them.

How has the situation of global and regional water governance changed?

Good water governance means successful collaboration of the responsible levels of government toward just, sustainable, and efficient use of water resources. The guiding principles laid down in the Dublin Statement on Water and Sustainable Development, which was adopted as early as 1992, have provided the basis for this. They are founded on the notion that water use worldwide must employ a holistic approach and include humans, nature, water, and land resources. The Dublin Statement formulates the basic human right to water and sanitation and rightly emphasises the key role of women for improving the situation. At least formal progress can be reported in recent years. For example, the United Nations General Assembly recognised the right of access to clean water as a human right in 2010. Unfortunately, General Assembly resolutions are not binding, unlike those of the UN Security Council. Therefore, the status of the 'human right of access to clean water' is still unclear. In 2015, the UN General Assembly adopted a resolution that expanded the right of access to clean water to include the right to sanitation. The Federal Foreign Office of the Federal Republic of Germany states:

'Guaranteeing the human rights to water and sanitation is an individual right and creates no claims between states. Whilst the right to water and sanitation is primarily a matter for governments, there is no reason why the supply should not be privatised and appropriate charges levied.'[10]

The fact that governments are named as those primarily responsible for fulfilling the human right of access to clean water and sanitation is not surprising, as it is primarily the task of states to formulate and implement legislation. This concerns the very important points of supplying clean water to the population and managing wastewater. A change in the assessment of the specific situation of water and sanitation has been visible in this respect since 2007. 663 million people still do not have access to more or less healthy drinking water, and 2.5 billion people have no appropriate sanitation. Even if it is difficult to define precisely what that means, the fact remains that these figures have been stagnating at a high level for decades. So, have developments with regard to this question, which is so important for health, education, and development, come to a standstill? In my opinion, by no means. Although the number of people affected has remained constant during this period, the global population has more than doubled. So the fraction of people affected has been cut in half. In other words, there has been success, but we are moving too slowly here as well. As in fighting hunger, a major initiative is necessary. It is more than likely that both initiatives will very quickly find that they are addressing the same people, namely the poorest people on Earth.

What is more astounding is the fact that the privatising of water supplies has been mentioned explicitly. In the tangle of political and administrative levels and economic actors, who is actually responsible for high-performance and reliable water supply and sanitation services? At the beginning of the century, the answer was clear, following the spirit of the times: whoever performs most efficiently. At the time, the general assessment was that that meant the private sector. The private sector, it was assumed, had

---

10 German Federal Foreign Office (2015)

efficiency in its DNA; the public sector, in contrast, was not even remotely capable of achieving the same quality in performing this complex task at the same cost. Municipalities were to grant private businesses the concession, in a public-private partnership (PPP), to operate all the necessary structures for water supply and sanitation services for the entire population for a limited period of time, generally 10–20 years. Thus the private companies would mostly determine the prices for water supply and sanitation services themselves.

Today, the answer to the question is still: whoever performs the tasks of water supply and sanitation services most efficiently should be responsible for them. But today, this usually no longer means the private sector, but the public sector. What went wrong with private-sector provision of water supply and sanitation services? The experiences with PPP in the water sector are clear and comprehensible, and they induced cities such as Berlin and Stuttgart in Germany to put the waterworks back in municipal hands. Three reasons support the change of opinion on the part of the municipalities and the population:

(1) Water is a common good, and although it has a value as a raw material, it has no market price. Water costs are service costs and arise for the establishment and maintenance of the extensive infrastructure required. It includes wells, pipes, storage facilities and above-ground reservoirs, purification and treatment plants, pumping stations, household connections, consumption measurement devices, a sewerage system, wastewater treatment plants, and more. Establishing and maintaining this infrastructure is complex and expensive and requires time and effort. Because of this, only large firms can generally provide successful system solutions for water supply and sanitation services. What is more, the annual investment costs decline the longer the time horizon is for which the infrastructure is designed. The construction of a water infrastructure that will last for 100 years is less than 5 times as costly

as construction of water infrastructure that will last for 20 years. If a private company has a contract over 20 years, it would not be rational for it to establish and operate the infrastructure to last 100 years. On the other hand, no municipality wants to make a 100-year commitment to a single company. That would contradict the idea of increasing efficiency through competition. This first point makes clear that private companies have difficulties establishing and especially operating water supply and sanitation infrastructure, which is designed for sustainability and long-term utility.

(2) In order to guarantee the functioning of a market-based solution to water supply and sanitation services, there must be competition between various companies. Paradoxically, though, private-sector competition must often first be organised by the public sector. For an efficient market-based solution can emerge only if the public-sector clients generate sufficient orders and thus long-term profits to guarantee that at least two larger, qualified companies can compete with each other. So the water price must secure the profits of at least two companies. Otherwise, a private monopoly emerges as a result of the public-private partnership, which in contrast to the municipally operated water supply pursues the goal of profit maximisation. This second point makes clear that the public sector should not permit overall profits that are too high in individual cases, especially if it also has to organise competition in the context of privatisation, as has often been the case – this in turn relativises efficiency.

(3) The practice of PPP in many municipalities gave the impression that water prices increased and service got worse when water supply and sanitation services were privatised – especially against the background that the quality demands made of drinking water are quite rightly high.

So the experiences from the past 15 years would tend to raise doubts as to whether water supply, with its high and long-term infrastructure costs and its complex tasks, is a suitable candidate for privatisation. In so-called Third World countries, which have seen themselves exposed to an unprecedented wave of privatisation of public water supply and sanitation services over the past 20 years, that wave is now subsiding. Both sides have learned that privatisation as such in the absence of good, corruption-free governance structures can guarantee neither a water supply affordable for all nor attractive profits that can be made in legal ways.

Conclusion

'How long will water resources last?' Ten years after I examined this question for the first time, it has lost none of its topicality. The perception of the world in transformation has changed substantially in recent years. What was then a mostly academic concern for the future has now become widespread everyday perplexity and anxiety. What if the phenomena we are seeing today – regional wars, migration, refugees, terror, water rationing in California and São Paolo and a long list of further symptoms – were actually the prognosticated global water crisis? If that should be true, then our experience with water marks a historical turning point brought about by the now globally recognisable limitations of the foundations on which our livelihoods depend. One thing can no longer be overlooked: this historical turning point has arrived in people's everyday lives. It is certainly perceived in different ways: many established people in the so-called developed world respond aggressively and try to shield themselves from it, whereas many young people in the developing countries are exuberant and euphoric because they see a real hope for a better life for their generation for the first time.

If the phenomena we are seeing really are symptoms of the global water (resource) crisis, and there are many reasons to believe that this is the case, then one question arises above all: how can we ever get out of this situation again?

Besides the perceived dangers of the global water crisis, developments and paths for solutions are becoming clear that actually should not give reason for pessimism. Stabilisation of the global population, increased literacy and improved health care, decline of the share of people going hungry and without access to clean drinking water, as well as dramatic increases in life expectancy in all regions of the Earth are just some examples. Other factors include the almost epidemic spreading of the Internet, social media, early warning systems, and new forms and means of communication. Just as the written word transcended borders and disseminated knowledge and capabilities around the world, these developments will also take hold of the entire globe and put us in a position to handle the upcoming resource scarcity in a completely different way, finally putting an end to the prevailing wastage. Efficiency and sufficiency in the way we deal with nature will become more widespread, just as will transparency and tolerance in the way we deal with each other.

Too optimistic? Certainly too optimistic for a pessimist. But not too optimistic if we succeed in practically implementing what we already know very well in theory: there is enough green and blue water even on the fraction of Earth that we use today, enough food can grow on it, and the sun and the wind are capable of providing the energy to use both water and food sustainably.

Bibliography

Alexandratos, N., Bruinsma, J. (2012), World Agriculture Towards 2030/2050: The 2012 Revision; Food and Agriculture Organisation of the United Nations (FAO), Rome 2012.

Arnold, D. (2013), Drought Called a Factor in Syria's Uprise, Voice of America, 20 August 2013. http://www.voanews.com/content/drought-called-factor-in-syria-uprising/1733068.html, last accessed: 7 June 2016.

German Federal Foreign Office (2015), Human right to water and sanitationhttp://www.auswaertigesamt.de/EN/Aussenpolitik/Menschenrechte/Wasser-Sanitaer_node.html, last accessed: 11 June 2016.

Bruinsma, J. (2011), The Resources Outlook: By How Much Do Land, Water and Crop Yields Need to Increase by 2050? In: Looking ahead in World Food and Agriculture: Perspectives 2050 (Conforti, P., ed.). Food and Agriculture Organization of the United Nations (FAO), Rome 2011.

Famiglietti, J.S. (2015), Water and the Roots of Violent Conflict in Syria. http://www.huffingtonpost.com/jay-famiglietti/water-and-the-roots-of-vi_b_3884175.html, last accessed: 7 May 2016.

Fleisher, D., Timlin, D., Reddy, K.R., Reddy, V.R., Yang, Y., Kim, S.-O. (2011), Effects of CO_2 and Temperature on Crops: Lessons from SPAR Growth Chambers. In: Handbook of Climate Change and Agroecosystems, ICP Series on Climate Change Impacts, Adaptation, and Mitigation (Hillel, D., Rosenzweig, C., eds), pp. 55–86. London: Imperial College Press.

FT (2013), Battle of the Nile. Financial Times, 20 June 2013, p. 7.

Hammer, J. (2013), Is Lack of Water to Blame for the Conflict in Syria?, http://www.smithsonianmag.com/innovation/is-a-lack-of-water-to-blame-for-the-conflict-in-syria-72513729/?no-ist, last accessed 7 June 2016.

Hoekstra, A.Y., Mekkonnen, M.M. (2012), The water footprint of humanity. Proceedings of the National Academy of Sciences of the United States of America (PNAS), Vol. 109, No. 9, 3232–3237. doi:10.1073/pnas.1109936109.

IAASTD (2009), Agriculture at a Crossroads. Global Report, International Assessment of Agricultural Knowledge, Science and Technology for Development (McIntyre, B.D., et al.). Washington, DC: Island Press.

IEEE (2010), IEEE Spectrum Special Report: Water vs. Energy. IEEE Spectrum, June 2010, pp. 18–23.

Kimball, B.A. (2011), Lessons from FACE: CO_2, Effects and Interactions with Water, Nitrogen and Temperature. In: Handbook of Climate Change and Agroecosystems, ICP Series on Climate Change Impacts, Adaptation, and Mitigation (Hillel, D., Rosenzweig, C., eds), pp. 87–108. London: Imperial College Press.

Marshall, T. (2015), Prisoners of Geography – Ten Maps That Explain Everything About the World. New York: Scribner.

Mauser, W., Klepper, G., Zabel, F., Delzeit, R., Hank, T., Calzadilla, A. (2015), Global biomass production potentials exceed expected future demand without the need for cropland expansion. Nature Communications, 6, 8946. doi:10.1038/ncomms9946.

Mekkonnen M.M., Hoekstra A.Y. (2010). A global and high-resolution assessment of the green, blue and greywater footprint of wheat. Hydrology and Earth System Sciences, 14, 1259–1276. doi:10.5194/hess-14-1259-2010.

Mekkonnen M.M., Hoekstra A.Y. (2013). Water footprint benchmarks for crop production: A first global assessment. Ecological Indicators 46, 214–223. doi:10.1016/j.ecolind.2014.06.013.

NASA (2013). NASA Satellite finds Freshwater Losses in the Middle East. http://www.nasa.gov/mission_pages/Grace/news/grace20130212.html; last accessed 7 June 2016.

Ray D. K., Mueller N. D., West P. C., Foley J. A. (2013), Yield trends are insufficient to double global crop production by 2050. PLoS ONE 8(6), e66428. doi:10.1371/journal.pone.0066428.

Sadras V. O., Angus J. F. (2006), Benchmarking water-use efficiency of rainfed wheat in dry environments. Australian Journal of Agricultural Research, 57, 847–856.

Voss K. A., Famiglietti J. S., Lo M., de Linage C., Rodell M., Swenson S. C. (2013), Groundwater depletion in the Middle East from GRACE with implications for transboundary water management in the Tigris-Euphrates-Western Iran region. Water Resources Research, 49, 904–914, doi:10.1002/wrcr.20078.

Zabel F., Putzenlechner B., Mauser W. (2014), Global agricultural land resources – A high resolution suitability evaluation and its perspectives until 2100 under climate change conditions. PLoS ONE 9(9), e107522. doi:10.1371/journal.pone.0107522.

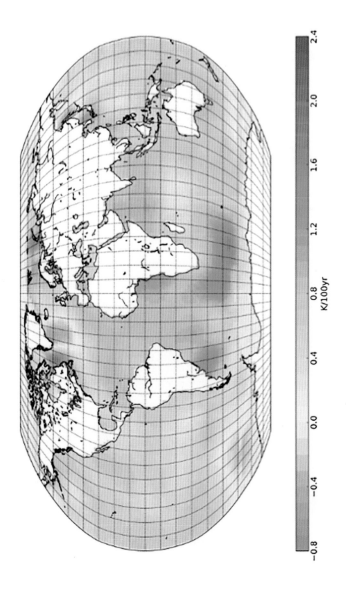

K/100yr

16
4.6
4.4
4.1
3.9
3.8
3.6
3.3
3
2.4
1.8
0

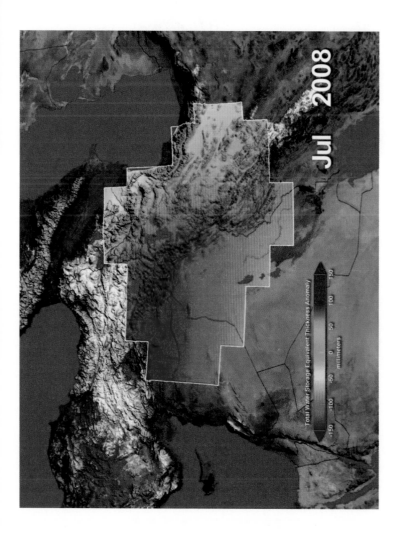

Total Water Storage Equivalent Thickness Anomaly

-150   -100   -50   0   50   100   150

millimeters

Jul 2008

Potential yield
increase in %

< 20
20 - 40
40 - 60
60 - 80
80 - 100
100 - 200
200 - 300
300 - 500
> 500

They can't put it back – Resource transition

F. Schmidt-Bleek

In the volume *The Earth: Natural Resources and Human Intervention* (originally published in German in 2006), I explained that the sustainable well-being of human society and the future viability of its industry on our planet are achievable only if technical energy, goods, and their use (services) are provided with resource productivity many times higher than today.

The present chapter summarises the origins and development of a resource transition that is still much too timid and lays out steps without which a society viable in the future is difficult to imagine.[1]

The greatest downside of science is that it cannot determine all side effects in advance.

1971

In 1971, I oversaw a team at the Appalachian Resources Project of the University of Tennessee System that was engaged in cost-benefit analyses of lignite mining in the nearby mountains in collaboration with colleagues from the Economics Department and the Oak Ridge National Laboratory. This seemed important to me in light of the large-scale devastation of the steep Appalachian hillsides and forests, not only because of the massive environmental damage, but also because impacts such as floods and extreme acidification of water bodies created dire circumstances

---

1   See also: Schmidt-Bleek, F. (2014), *Grüne Lügen*, Munich

for the population widely scattered across the valleys.[2] Our analyses showed that, using conservative assumptions, the cost of the damage was at least twice as high as the price of the coal.

With the support of the Tennessee Valley Authority and the university hospital, we were able to cut infant mortality in the mountains to one-third within a short time by using helicopters and achieve other improvements for the people affected. Our findings helped convince the then US Senator from Tennessee, Howard Baker, to initiate the US Surface Mining Control and Reclamation Act of 1977. This legislation also established the US Office of Surface Mining.

I realised during our work that, as a matter of principle, cost-benefit analyses can valuate only a lower limit of environmental damages. The true costs cannot be ascertained in full using this approach because we natural scientists are unable to determine all the ecological impacts of even a single substance released by human activity. This is also true of CO_2, even though billions have been spent on research into its paths and eco-toxicological impacts. Far more than 100,000 different substances and mixtures are emitted into the environment on a daily basis and in a vast number of places around the globe from myriads of anthropogenic sources. Many of these substances are manmade and have never been part of the development of our biosphere. Their consequences for the further evolution of human beings and other living things are mostly unknown.

Yet the Appalachian miners found an even deeper truth and expressed it in the song 'They can't put it back'.[3] At the time, I failed to realise this truth, namely that nobody can restore the devastated natural environment to its original form. Today we say that

2   Udall, S. (1967), *Surface Mining and Our Environment*, Washington, DC

3   Rich Kirby and Michael Kline, 'They can't put it back,' Label: June Appalachian Recordings

technology cannot replace services and functions of the ecosphere that humankind has disrupted and destroyed. In other words: not only the dwindling availability of natural resources is a geological-ecological barrier to the further development of the human economic system.[4] Even simply extracting natural resources and transporting them away from their original locations changes the foundations on which our lives depend on our planet.

1989

It was New Year's Eve 1989 in a snowy village south of Vienna. Stash Shatalin, then chief economic adviser to President Gorbachev, said 'nyet' when I asked him if it was time to establish our successful Western system of environmental protection in the Soviet Union as well. The Kremlin had asked us at the International Institute of Applied Systems Analysis (IIASA) to adapt a number of draft laws for Russia's economic future to Western conceptions.[5] Shatalin's reasoning: 'Only when we have become as rich as you are will we be able to afford your kind of environmental protection.'

That hit me hard and by surprise. After all, we had already initiated what we considered to be a substantial framework of well-conceived and effective environmental protection measures in Bonn, Brussels, and at the OECD in Paris.

I began to ponder how concepts for effective and affordable environmental protection could be designed in a different way. I wondered whether there was a way to fundamentally design and use goods, services, and the energy supply that would cause fewer problems with the environment, and also to stop using isolated solutions to individual problems at high cost after the damage

---

4   Donella and Dennis Meadows et al. (1972), *The Limits to Growth*
5   Aven, Shatalin, and Schmidt-Bleek (1990), *Economic Reform and Integration*, IIASA

had already been done. In other words, to take a precautionary approach to avoiding problems. The question was about the
deeper roots of the growing threats to the ecological foundations
of our lives. What is the path to protecting the environment in a
precautionary way without endangering our prosperity? And how
can success and failure be compared in ecological terms across the
globe? Of course, these questions also concern the future of the
EU as well as global developments such as trade[6], the refugee question, terrorism, and the digitalisation of society.

My eureka moment came when it struck me that the root cause
of the environmental damage caused by the human economy is the
wanton consumption of natural resources for creating a plethora
of products, services, shelter, automobiles, and infrastructure.

I became increasingly aware that it is impossible to secure a stable
environment by prosecuting individual failures after the damage to
the ecosphere has been done. Pesticides, CO_2, and CFCs come
to mind. The development goal of sustainability, which was proclaimed in Rio de Janeiro in 1992, cannot be achieved through
end-of-pipe policies. And this is true beyond the field of environmental protection.

It is beyond dispute today that resource productivity (often
called resource efficiency) is decisive for generating the sustainable well-being of human beings on the planet and for the future
viability of industry. What are at stake are the natural resources
water, land, and materials, including fossil fuels and biomass.

The final declaration of the 2015 G7 summit at Elmau stated:
'The protection and efficient use of natural resources is vital for
sustainable development. We strive to improve resource efficiency,
which we consider crucial for the competitiveness of industries,
for economic growth and employment, and for the protection of
the environment, climate and planet.'

---

6   Wohlmeyer and Schmidt-Bleek (1990), *Trade and the Environment*, IIASA

The importance of resource consumption for protecting the foundations of our ecological livelihoods has apparently dawned on the political community.

However, 'resource efficiency' is not a singular feature for regaining ecological sustainability. The statement at the 2015 G7 summit leaves open whether the desired improvement in resource efficiency refers to individual goods and services or to the economy as a whole.

An illustration of the ambivalent wording: the global airline industry predicts significant efficiency gains in terms of its fuel consumption per passenger kilometre.[7] At present, it is responsible for 11% of the emissions from the transportation sector with an impact on the climate. Yet the industry is also planning to expand its global fleet by more than 30,000 passenger aircraft in the coming years. That could amount to an additional investment (extraction, shipment, denaturing processing) of more than 500 million tons of natural resources and a significant rise in total fuel consumption. In other words, global resource consumption would increase. This is called the boomerang or rebound effect, and because of it, sustainability would become an increasingly distant goal.

Even today, unchecked consumption of natural resources is the most important reason for the escalating scarcity of water and clean air, for the massive erosion of topsoil, for the loss of species, for climate change, and even for the growing number of cases of Zika through the loss of rain forests and increasing global warming. Since every instance of natural resource extraction and shipping disrupts, changes, and also destroys the services and functions of the ecosphere, the limitation of resource use today is a sine qua non on the path to sustainability.

In 1990, I performed some rough calculations and found that reducing the absolute amount of damaging resource consumption

---

7   Perhaps also a more environmentally friendly fuel supply based on hydrogen and CO_2

by the West by a factor of 10 should suffice to stabilise the situation
and leave sufficient 'environmental space' for the growing needs of
poor countries.[8] That seemed to be an unimaginably high hurdle.

1992

In 1992, Ernst Ulrich von Weizsäcker gave me the opportunity
to measure my often-disparaged ideas against reality at the newly
established Wuppertal Institute with some intelligent and coura-
geous colleagues.[9]

We first turned our curiosity to the question: how high is the
real resource intensity of goods, calculated 'from the cradle'? For
commodities, we found values ranging from just over 1 kg/kg
(e.g., logs) to far more than 500,000/l (e.g., for precious metals
and rare earths).[10] Everyday products proved to have a surprisingly
large average 'rucksack' of 30 kg of material for every kg of final
product, which means that more than 90% of the transported
and denatured mass was lost on the way to the usable product. It
is hardly surprising that the specific amounts of water used[11] for
producing foods were often high, as were the erosion rates.[12] In
the area of information and communications technology (ICT),

---

8   Schmidt-Bleek (1994), *Wieviel Umwelt braucht der Mensch? MIPS, das ökologische
    Maß für die Wirtschaft*, Birkhäuser

9   Especially Prof. Dr. Stefan Bringezu, Dr. Fritz Hinterberger, Prof. Dr. Christa
    Liedtke, Christopher Manstein, Dr. Joachim Spangenberg, Prof. Ursula Tischner,
    and Dr. Jola Welfens. Other colleagues at the Institute also provided substantial
    support, e.g., Dr. Harry Lehmann and Dr. Willy Bierter

10 See appendix in Schmidt-Bleek (2014), *Grüne Lügen*; further sources: Dipl.-Ing.
    Holger Rohn, Faktor 10 Institut in Friedberg (Hesse, Germany), as well as M.
    Lettenmeier and Prof. Dr. Liedtke, Wuppertal Institute

11 The appendix in the book *Grüne Lügen* lists the rucksacks for many materials and
    products in the form of abiotic and biotic material, water, air, and moved soil

12 Bringezu (2004), *Erdlandung*, Stuttgart

the values were even 10 to 20 times higher.[13] For instance, today a smartphone 'costs' more than 70 kg of nature; in other words, it has a rucksack of about 600/1. These astoundingly large rucksacks could, however, provide the opportunity to reduce them in a targeted fashion using innovative technology, which would decisively improve their resource productivity. Obviously, the lifespan of goods also plays an important role. After all, the longer a resource investment which has already been made is used to produce utility, the better the 'return on nature' will be.

We also asked: can resource use be cut by a factor of 10 without losses of quality of life? We demonstrated in practice that dematerialisation of consumption goods by a factor of three to four was often attainable easily and without the output losing quality. One way to do this was by replacing materials with a large material rucksack with others that fulfilled the technical specifications with lower resource consumption. For example, replacing aluminium window and door frames with ones made of PVC amounts to enhancing resource productivity by a factor of 10. Yet increases in resource productivity through new paths to the desired utility are technically more interesting. A few examples: lotus-effect surfaces enable large savings in water and detergents; small stores in Berlin sell food without packaging; simple portable solar cookers in Africa help save large amounts of scarce firewood; when large airplanes are moved on the ground, the weight of the front of the plane is piggybacked onto the aircraft tug to achieve the necessary friction instead of increasing the weight of the aircraft tug many times over. An example worth special mention is the wooden skyscrapers with up to 30 stories built by the company Rhombergbau from Bregenz (Austria). Their rucksack is smaller than that of traditional buildings by a factor of 4; their MIPS is smaller by a

---

13 Kuhndt (2004) In: *Der ökologische Rucksack*, F. Schmidt-Bleek, ed., Stuttgart

factor of up to 10.[14] Roughly 40% of damaging material resource consumption occurs in the construction sector. In addition, this sector requires an enormous amount of land, as does agriculture. Reducing the consumption of natural resources in private households also yields astounding results.[15]

Then we had to answer the question: Which indicator is suitable for dematerialisation? MIPS (later also called 'material footprint'[16]) seemed to me to be the right answer. MIPS = MI/S, i.e., material input across the life cycle per unit of service or utility. After all, what matters is the utility that goods provide, not ownership of goods.[17] And since no service in our society is possible without using technology, this old truth also applies to services. MIPS also makes it possible to directly compare functionally equivalent goods of the most different kinds, e.g., a bicycle and an airplane.

In the MIPS concept, all material flows which occur during the entire life cycle of a product are documented and added up in order to create utility service as an output, including those induced by providing technically generated energy. MIPS is a quantitative measure for the consumption of mass to generate a defined amount of benefit or service. The material input is given in units conforming to SI, e.g., kilograms or tons, and is related to the service unit, e.g., provision of a cubic metre of building volume.

Resource productivity and resource intensity are key

---

14 Rhomberg (2015), *Bau 4.0*, Bregenz; see also http//www.maz-online.de/lokales/
    Potsdam/Fluechtlingsheim-in-Holzbauweise

15 http://www.sitra.fi/en/artikkelit/resource-wisdom/success-households-future,
    https://helda.helsinki.fi/handle/10138/38369, https//www.mdpi.com/2071-
    1050/4/7/1426, http://www.sitra.fi/en/artikkelit/resource-wisdom/success-
    households-future

16 Lettenmeier et al. (2009), *Resource Productivity in 7 Steps: How to develop eco-
    innovative products and services and improve their material footprint*

17 Aristoteles (ca. 300 BC): 'Riches in the true sense lie in the usefulness of things – not
    in owning them'

concepts when measuring sustainability because they represent the decoupling of resource consumption from direct and indirect environmental destruction. Their particular strength lies in the fact that they can be used as a yardstick both for economic and for ecological 'costs and benefits'. The goal of sustainability is to maximise resource productivity and to minimise resource intensity, i.e., MIPS.

Besides a large number of publications from the Wuppertal Institute, the economic policy statements of the International Factor 10 Club have received worldwide acclaim; Jim MacNeill, the recently deceased former Secretary General of the Brundtland Commission, was one of its members.[18]

Of course, the question of what adjustments had to be made in our economy in order to achieve a sufficient increase in resource productivity also arose. More on this below (see section 2015).

2006

As part of his initiative 'Encouraging Sustainability', Klaus Wiegandt invested major funds of his own to attract scientists to present 12 central themes of ecological sustainability.

I had the privilege to contribute a book dealing with resource transition,[19] which can be summarised as follows: (1) The services and functions of the ecosphere are necessary for our human life and survival. (2) They cannot be replaced by, but are damaged locally and globally or even destroyed irreversibly through, resource-intensive economic activity and lifestyles. (3) The consequences of this include enormous erosion of farmland around

---

18 See appendix in *Grüne Lügen*, 2014
19 Schmidt-Bleek (2009), *The Earth: Natural Resources and Human Intervention*, London

the world, climate change, water scarcity, and species extinction. (4) While people with a high standard of material prosperity are mostly responsible for the plight of the environment, *all* human beings suffer the consequences, especially the poor. (5) Since it would require more than two planet Earths as the resource base to globalise the Western level of prosperity, and since the ecological risk threshold has already been overstepped, the inevitable demand emerges to minimise technical interventions in the ecosphere and to comprehensively reduce the amounts of materials and water used to underpin prosperity. Technically speaking, this is possible in principle, and often without a loss of consumer satisfaction. However, the economic incentives and legal provisions to do so are lacking to this day. (6) The process of dematerialisation must commence at the beginning of the economic process; it has to take effect 'from the cradle to the cradle' and encompass all processes, products, infrastructures, and services, including the supply and consumption of technical energy (energy that is generated and applied in the technosphere). (7) Eco-innovation means creating novel and competitively priced goods, processes, systems, services, and procedures that can satisfy human needs and bring quality of life to all people with the lowest possible use of natural resources per unit of output and minimal release of toxic substances.[20] (8) Approaching sustainability and measuring progress requires goals, as well as directionally reliable and practically applicable indicators for the resource intensity of economic activities, of goods and services. 'Factor 10 in absolute terms' (by 2050) for Germany is a reasonable and attainable goal, and the specific material consumption per service generated (MIPS), the ecological rucksack, and total material flow (TMF) suggest themselves as

---

20 Reid and Miedzinski (2008), *EUROPE INNOVA, Final Report for the EU Sectoral Innovation Watch Panel on Eco-Innovation.*

globally applicable indicators.[21] It is estimated today that by the middle of the twenty-first century, the annual amount of material consumed per capita should not exceed 5 to 7 tons globally. (9) Neither economic nor ecological sustainability can be achieved in the absence of radical dematerialisation. And sufficient dematerialisation is possible only if the underlying conditions of the economic system offer sufficient incentives to this end instead of disregarding the laws of nature as is the case to date. Short-term profit maximisation, ecologically incorrect prices, and a lack of precautionary thinking are the reasons why approaching sustainable ecological conditions is still impossible. The government can change this. But acting sustainably and taking on real responsibility for our children and their descendants takes exceptional courage. (10) Planet Earth needs dedicated people participating and systemic, holistic policies. 'Policy by one hand', as Chancellor Merkel occasionally says. Only if committed citizens support such a policy and unwaveringly insist on adapting the economic system to nature's 'guide rails' will they be able to secure a future with a future for their grandchildren and their grandchildren's grandchildren. (11) Sustainable development must be the guiding principle for Europe in its global responsibility. Europe should design an eco-social market economy, put it into practice, and thus be a role model for the rest of the world. (12) It is time to act. Sweeping technical changes need 10 to 20 years for development and market penetration. For this reason, one must bear in mind that effective dematerialisation will take decades. In other words, we have no time to lose.

---

21 www.materialflows.net

2011 Energy

On 11 March 2011, the Tōhoku earthquake triggered a tsunami off Japan, which resulted in a meltdown in blocks 1–3 of the Japanese nuclear power plant Fukushima Daiichi in Ōkuma. Large amounts of radioactive Xe-133, Cs-137, and other long-lived isotopes were released. To this day, their contamination of soils, water, and food is life threatening.

As a consequence of this catastrophe, the German federal government decided that year to close down some nuclear power plants immediately and the rest within a few years. The energy transition decided on was set in motion with the goal of 'decarbonising' the energy supply within a few decades, i.e., eliminating CO_2 emissions with the expectation that this would make an appropriate national contribution to decelerating climate change.

This energy transition is a classic example of tackling an isolated environmental problem after the fact, as mentioned above. Dealing with individual existing problems in an isolated way, however, cannot bring about system-oriented precautionary action and thus cannot achieve sustainability, either. In addition, this way of proceeding always interferes with established interests, structures, procedures, and investments. Thus, it often defeats its own purpose. How difficult and time-consuming this path truly is is demonstrated by the negotiations about the definition and fulfilment of commitments in the Kyoto Protocol of 1997, which have been going on for 20 years. One should not be surprised if larger and poorer nations do not fulfil the pledges they made in Paris in December 2015 to decelerate climate change in the future, either. It should always be remembered that, at some point, it will be too late to solve environmental problems. For a long time, I have proposed expanding or even replacing the enormous efforts to enforce global measures against climate change with a dialogue about a global resource transition. Climate change is also, and primarily, a consequence of our unchecked consumption of natural resources.

In the course of the energy transition, it has become common to use the intensity of CO_2 emissions as the predominant indicator for the environmental quality of products, vehicles, processes, facilities, services, investments, even entire cities ('carbon footprint'). Among other reasons, this is incorrect because (1) CO_2 is just one of the emissions damaging to the climate (others include nitrous oxide and methane), (2) emitting CO_2 is not a function of the resource intensity of products and facilities (e.g., the resource intensity of electricity generated by nuclear power plants is very high, even though the CO_2 emissions of nuclear power plants are relatively modest), (3) 'carbon-dioxide-free' does not mean 'sustainable', and (4) advice for reducing CO_2 emissions often entails increasing resource intensity through resource-intensive technical countermeasures such as use of the dual-engine car.

One might comment that the general and singular use of CO_2 as an indicator has succeeded in classifying nuclear power plants in the same environmental threat category as Stradivaris and paintings by Rembrandt or Miotte. Yet musical instruments, paintings, and many antiques are among the ecologically most valuable achievements of humankind, not least because they frequently have a long life.

Many years ago, I proposed in jest to BMW's Head of Development that his company could make a major contribution to sustainability if it built cars for a very, very long lifespan, roughly like airplane manufacturers whose products travel over 1,000 times as many kilometres as his cars. The Chief Financial Officer was not amused.

The ongoing hype of calling electric vehicles, in particular hybrid vehicles, environmentally friendly, and even offering impressive incentives for purchasing them, is absurd from a resource perspective. Whereas a normal gasoline-powered mid-range car has a material footprint of approximately 450 grams per kilometre (!), comparable electric cars are in the same category at best.[22] No sign of factor 10. The figure for the hybrid Prius: more than 700 grams. Both types of vehicle are the result of tackling the environmental problem of climate change in isolation, without attention to the overall environmental problem. Yet it would be possible today to use existing technology to dematerialise urban automobile traffic (which accounts for more than 85% of all automobile traffic) by a factor of 10 or more, using traditional engines and significantly reducing fuel consumption.[23] A *Washington Post* article worth reading and dated 29 February 2016 states: 'The car century was a mistake. It's time to move on.'[24]

To avoid misunderstanding, I would like emphasise explicitly that climate change must be decelerated with all available eco-logical, political, economic, financial, and technically reasonable measures. But as long as the energy transition is not embedded in a resource transition, it will fail in ecological terms.

Sustainable energy supply must involve transformation of natu-rally existing energy sources into the technically required form, and to distribute and use the energy with radically lower natural resource consumption than before.

2015 The Economic System

In preparation for the G7 summit in 2015, State Secretary Mat-thias Machnig of the German Federal Ministry for Economic

---

22 http://www.electrive.net/2015/01/25/bewertung, https://www.adelphi.de/en/
    employee/lukas-rüttinger, http://www.lbp-gabi.de/107-1-Roberta-Graf.html,
    http://www.emobil-umwelt.de/index.php/kontakt-impressum

23 *Grüne Lügen*, Munich, Ludwig Buchverlag, 2014

24 https://www.washingtonpost.com/news/in-theory/wp/2016/02/29/the-car-century-
    was-a-mistake-its-time-to-move-on/?postshare3101456817934445&tids=ss tw

Affairs said: 'Material and commodity costs account for 45% of the costs in manufacturing industry and are thus the greatest cost factor by far. Resource efficiency as a driver of innovation in businesses is thus of central importance for more competitiveness, employment, and environmental protection.'

I consider this insight to be a noteworthy and highly welcome step in the right direction from this traditionally conservative ministry.

Yet despite numerous warnings, the governments in Germany and other countries have failed to recognise future opportunities and threats in time,[25] design new solutions that do justice to our natural support system, and make socially acceptable and preferably crisis-free restructuring a reality, or at least to tackle it.

In the 2014 book *Green Lies*,[26] I described once again the reasons why our economic system is still not developing toward ecologically sustainable conditions as well as paths out of the plight. Labels such as 'green', 'eco', and even 'sustainable' have increasingly become buzzwords in political and commercial advertising and have degenerated into unintentional and also intentional deception. By now, most consumers have also understood that 'bio' on the packaging does not necessarily mean that the contents are wholesome. And neither 'regenerative' nor 'renewable' is the same as 'sustainable' or 'viable in the future'. Serious labels should reliably support customers when they seek to select ecologically advantageous products on the market. But consumers today are faced not only with the price, but also with a vast number of different, often incomprehensible 'green' labels, each of which concerns only a segment of the danger to the environment. And many are not even about the stability of the ecosystem, but about human

---

25 The German Greens' call to opt out of the nuclear industry may be considered an exception.

26 *Grüne Lügen*, 2014

health. It is as if different goods were labelled with prices in different currencies. A gigantic, confusing game that brings profits to the business community but tends to harm the stability of our support system. How can one seriously expect such labelling to help the average consumer make purchasing decisions that buttress the stability of the support system Earth? I learned long ago that the market can function only if the demand side is sufficiently informed.[27]

We are still a long way from effective resource protection, particularly because usage of nature is still permitted practically free of charge and is therefore commonplace. And as long as people can continue to waste nature at practically zero cost and with life-threatening consequences, we will remain prisoners of a civilisation that more or less forces us to destroy the environment. Never before has humankind been further away from sustainability than today – and the problem is becoming more severe.

It is true that we could get a handle on this fairly quickly in the area of technology without diminishing well-being significantly. But saving nature would have to pay off. The prices for usage of nature would have to be adapted to the true costs. From a market-economy perspective, full-cost pricing of natural capital is the precondition for sustainability.

Growth and economic success are still measured by the growing number of goods produced and consumed, and thus by growing resource consumption. As long as the desire for progress, the willingness to take risks, and success are guided by the growth rate of the gross domestic product (GDP) with the present price architecture, the chances for a sustainable society are virtually zero. We can liberate ourselves from this dilemma only by

---

27 Perhaps the following book will be able to help a bit: F. Schmidt-Bleek (2016), *Die 10 Gebote der Ökologie*, Munich

means of a comprehensive resource transition. According to the world-famous economist Pavan Sukhdev, many entrepreneurs are seeking new investment opportunities today, and for this reason '... it is essential that market signals and market governance decouple profit maximisation from resource consumption if we are to transition to a "green economy" and aim for sustainable development'. For governments, this points toward a transformation in the tax system, taking the burden of taxation away from profits and toward resource use. For corporations, this places emphasis on the most progressive source of consumer surplus and customer satisfaction: innovation.'[28] A decisive step in this direction should succeed by increasing the benefits (services)[29] from the usage of 'low-MIPS' and high water-productivity goods with long life spans.

The resource transition requires more than individual measures in environmental, economic, and social policy, launched separately by the individual ministries. 'Across the board, naive trust in apparently incontrovertible facts and authorities in the world and the business community, the state and society, is a thing of the past,' wrote the editor-in-chief of *Handelsblatt* on 12 March 2008, referring to the financial crisis of the time. The environmental situation could not be described better, either. The resource transition requires efforts from all of society that must be harmonised and bundled at the highest level. 'Policy by one hand' at the decision level is urgently required.

The fact that manufacturers could improve resource productivity in a targeted fashion and save money even today was published by economists as early as 2004. According to them, Germany's SMEs could save roughly 20% of the costs for the resources they

---

28 Sukhdev (2012), *Corporation 2020. Tranforming business for tomorrow's world*, Washington, DC, page 171.

29 Article 20a in conjunction with Article 56 of the German Basic Law.

use, without compromising the quality of their output. This amounts to more than 150 billion euros per year.[30]

2016 Environmental policy

Current reporting on environmental policy and politics currently seems to have an overly strong focus on just a single important topic: climate change. And it seems that only a single cause is taken seriously: industrially produced CO_2 emissions. Other impacts of today's form of economic activity on the ecosphere are mostly blocked out. The resource transition, a targeted increase in resource productivity, is not part of parliamentary debates nor is it present in the media.

The campaign for the German Bundestag in 2013 made the continuing limitations of systemic thinking in many policy fields disturbingly clear. Even the German Green Party, who started out as a party for ecological competence, apparently still do not think it advisable to tackle other comparably serious environmental problems besides climate change. Just three of the 320 pages of their 2013 election platform deal with the problem of the disastrously low 'resource efficiency' of our economic system. But the platform also underlines the importance of major subsidies for electric cars.

While seeking to cope with a large number of 'epochal' problems, society seems to have no time today to avoid ecological decline. Little attention is paid to the protection of the ecosphere in the vehement struggles for solutions, even though the protection of the natural foundations of our livelihoods is the only task for which an inevitable 'too late' exists!

---

30 Fischer et al. (2004), 'Wachstum und Beschäftigungsimpulse rentabler Materialeinsparungen', *Wirtschaftsdienst*, 4 April

The simultaneous existence of so many 'epochal' problems is depressing and, in many cases, it is unfortunately due to a lack of strategic foresight on the part of governments and the lack of systemic, intelligent precautions. Examples include climate change itself, which was already predicted more than 100 years ago; the hasty expansion of the EU to the east; the failure of bad loans in the US and the global consequences; the financial collapse of Greece; and the arrival of vast streams of refugees at Europe's borders. All of them were foreseeable, and prudent, holistic policy would have prevented much human suffering, saved money, and avoided the destruction of irretrievable treasures and the environment. It seems as though we have simply been overwhelmed by the large number of threats. 'Where everything turns into a hazard, somehow nothing is dangerous anymore,' sociologist Ulrich Beck wrote more than 25 years ago.

We will pay a bitter price if we continue to be hesitant in securing the ecological foundations of our livelihoods and take a short-term view in the absence of a longer-term programme. It is not enough to describe reality. We must finally place the creation of prosperity and security between the 'guard rails' of the laws of nature.

In this context, it is important to mention that the oft-cited equilateral and equally weighted triangle of sustainability, *ecology –economy–social issues*, is questionable because we cannot change the limits of what the ecosphere can bear, but we certainly can change the conditions of social and economic policy.

VW may serve as an example to illustrate the lack of concern in the business community with respect to its own future viability. The automaker demonstrated how seriously the claims of some companies are to be taken that sustainability must not be neglected. Not only did VW (and other carmakers) intentionally violate the law in millions of cases; VW is also, like the other producers, seeking to increase sales of SUVs as quickly as possible

– SUVs being cars with an especially large rucksack that mainly serve to increase automakers' profits and the egos of the high earners. It will be up to mid-sized companies to restore the reliability of 'Made in Germany'. Follow-on financial costs will be left to taxpayers, as frequent experience shows. K+S Deutschland is also indicted for pumping millions of litres of salt solution underground and thus endangering the drinking water supply. Every reader could continue this list of developments driven by greed.

In his encyclical letter *Laudato si* ('On Care for Our Common Home'), published on 25 May 2015, Pope Francis wrote in section 139: 'Given the scale of change, it is no longer possible to find a specific, discrete answer for each part of the problem. It is essential to seek comprehensive solutions that consider the interactions within natural systems themselves and with social systems. We are faced not with two separate crises, one environmental and the other social, but rather with one complex crisis which is both social and environmental.'

On the basis of everything we know today, the window of opportunity for a paradigm shift toward an eco-social society viable in the future should not be measured in centuries, but in decades.

The Future: New business models

We should rediscover not only how to save natural resources. It is just as important to generate a maximum of utility from resources already in hand. The business model prevailing today is focused on growth, economies of scale, core business, and core competence, and it favours specialisation and concentration on selected markets. Business successes are valuated in cash and market share, and precisely not according to their suitability for creating sustainable utility for consumers. The decoupling of profit and resource consumption, which is essential for survival, is still alien to the prevailing business model.

It is evident that we need a new business model. A model that supports approaching viability in the future. The key precondition is that people's basic needs for food, services, and resources are met to the greatest extent possible from nearby areas and under their own responsibility. A disquieting example: Hawaii was able to provide its population of almost 1 million with all the food, water, and energy required through the late nineteenth century. In contrast, it imports 98% of its food and 95% of its energy today. The billions required to do this are earned mostly through tourism; from an ecological perspective a schizophrenic triple-lose situation.

An example from Gunter Pauli's *Blue Economy* collection illustrates how ten or one hundred times more value than is common today can be created from available resources: only some 0.2% of the weight of the coffee bean contributes to the drink. In other words, 99.8% of the bean mass used must be 'disposed of'. (One should note that coffee beans have already amassed a large ecological rucksack before being placed on the market.) The Nestlé corporation and others realised that the mass to be disposed of is suitable for generating economically inexpensive energy. Nestlé did not pursue other options for economic reasons; for example, use as animal feed or as substrate for growing mushrooms or as a component of potting soil. In other words, the company removed 99.8% of the biomass used for coffee from the biosphere's material cycles and transformed it into greenhouse gases even though, for example, mushrooms grown on coffee grounds in Berlin, Amsterdam, Madrid, San Francisco, and Sydney are already competing with mushrooms from China. Because of the business model adopted, Nestlé intentionally omitted the possibility of value creation that would be hundreds of times better in ecological terms. Apparently, coffee grounds are not yet considered operating capital. The glossy, colourful annual 'sustainability reports' published by major companies take the utmost care to avoid even hinting at the resource intensity of their products.

So much for the ecological side of the story.

Now to financial value creation: Starbucks earns roughly 3,000 times as much on a cup of coffee as the farmer producing the coffee beans. If ecological value creation, which is technically possible but mostly unused for economic reasons, is combined with the difference of a factor of 3,000 in financial value creation, then the mismanagement of the globalised world becomes embarrassingly obvious, not least because the opportunity to create new jobs that will be secure in the future is squandered. This path is unsuitable for achieving sustainability in the social as well as in the ecological sense. It is due to an unsustainable price architecture that renders labour and innovative activities expensive while inviting business to waste natural resources.

In the case described here, the mainstream business model also has an additional disconcerting dimension. While Starbucks's commercially produced and practically tax-free profits remain untouched, private donations and taxpayers' billions in development aid contribute to enhancing low incomes in the developing countries. Accordingly, one could consider the Starbucks business model as a pump enabling the enrichment of a few at the expense of the general public, without taxation or liability.

The know-how for creating value from locally available resources has a historico-cultural tradition reaching back millions of years. It was pushed aside on a wide front only in the past two centuries by admirable inventions such as those of James Watt, Rudolf Diesel, and Carl Benz as well as by 'cheap' fossil fuels. However, the trend toward resource-efficient value creation has quietly gained momentum. Gunter Pauli's Blue Economy programme has already put many commercially interesting examples into practice. The growing sharing economy in rich countries is a further sign of people's sense that being rich does not necessarily mean owning and consuming lots of objects.

The Future: A community of the 'willing and able'?

> The thought process advanced by the West drew the world into a crisis from which it must emerge by a radical break: 'always more,' in the financial domain but also in the fields of science and technology. It's high time that concerns about ethics, justice, and lasting equilibrium (economic and environmental) prevail. Because the most serious risks threaten us. They can put an end to the human adventure on the planet, which they can make unfit for habitation by man.[31]

We must give up the dream of limitless material growth as fast as possible. It makes no sense on a finite planet. The future viability of society and industry are imaginable only if we learn how to create more prosperity for more and more people with radically smaller amounts of natural resources.

What is to be done?

It seems to me that replacing unchecked material economic growth by increases in utility (services) is a promising path. This notion is already laid out in the German Basic Law. This Constitution does not speak of material growth. The oath of office sworn by the Chancellor and her ministers says (Article 56): 'I swear that I will ... enhance the benefits ... of the German people ...'[32] Enhancing benefits is not necessarily a question of increasing material growth. From an ecological stability point of view, it means extracting maximum benefits from a minimum of natural

---

31 Stéphane Hessel, 2011
32 ... seinen Nutzen mehren ... werde.

resources. Technically speaking that translates into using goods with resource footprints (MIPS) that are as small as possible, consuming as little low-MIPS technical energy as possible from cradle to grave, and goods with the longest achievable lifespan.

In other words, this would be about goods requiring a minimum of material, technical energy, water, and land for providing the desired benefit or service lifecycle-wide.

Only the state can enable the underlying conditions for a sustainable future. As free and responsible citizens, we should contribute to this future wherever we can.[33] But we should also use every opportunity to remind decision-makers in industry and politics of their responsibility to act – because time is running out.

I propose the following key points to pave the way to a future with a cohesive society:[34]

1. 'Taking a chance on more democracy' (Willy Brandt) – Public discourse about opportunities, priorities, and paths to preserving the ecological foundations on which our lives depend, about peace and freedom, about the kind of democracy, economy, and technology that we would like in order to support our goals.
2. Development of a comprehensive strategic plan to achieve and secure the future viability of Europe.
3. Clarifying the question whether Germany should favour establishing and participating in a new eco-socially oriented community of willing and able countries in Europe – including Norway and Switzerland – in light of EU member states' increasingly nationalistic behaviour.

33 Schmidt-Bleek (2016), *Die 10 Gebote der Ökologie*, Munich
34 A number of goals worth considering were presented in the 'European Roadmap to a Resource Efficient Europe'. European Commission, Brussels, 20 September 2011, COM (2011) 571. Little has been heard about these goals since Jean-Claude Juncker took office as President of the European Commission.

4. Creation of and participation in such a community must be founded upon a joint precautionary policy.[35] And only those countries should have the prospect of participating that are prepared to enforce precautionary protection of the foundations of our livelihoods, that take human rights, freedom, and self-determination of their citizens seriously, and that practice freedom of expression and freedom of the press. Of course, this community should be open for suitable countries to join later.

5. The following points should be taken into account when establishing the community:
   - creation of a common constitution;
   - the duty of all to respect the foundations of our ecological livelihood and the dignity of all living creatures and to promote their protection;
   - the duty of all political and business decision-makers to enhance the benefits enjoyed by people;
   - the duty of the governments to inform society regularly and in a timely manner about threats to security and the foundations of our ecological livelihood, as well as about planned measures to counter such threats;
   - consideration that at some point, it will be too late to protect the ecosphere;
   - joint development and application of precautionary solutions to problems and developments taking a systems/holistic approach to policy;
   - consideration of the paramount importance of ecological threats through unchecked consumption of the natural resources materials, water, and land;

---

35 Declaration 2010 of the International Factor 10 Club: *A Coalition of Willing States Needed to Catalyze a Ten-Fold Leap in Energy and Resource Efficiency*

- establishment of a circular economy with the goal of minimising the total consumption of natural resources;
- increasing incentives to save natural resources, especially cost-neutral adaptation of their prices to ecological reality;
- observation of possible 'boomerang effects' and preventing them;
- definition of indicators in all policy areas related to the stability of the environment;
- adaptation of all legal provisions, norms, and standards to ecological requirements;
- joint discussion, definition, and publication of political and business goals, with deadlines;
- improvement of the resource productivity of technical energy, and all goods, processes, infrastructures (systems), services, and courses of action with the goal of achieving annual consumption of 5 to 7 tons of material per person by 2050;
- labelling all goods and services – also in advertising – with their specific and lifecycle-wide resource intensity (material footprint MIPS), as well as with additional characteristics that enable end users to make directionally reliable decisions;
- prevention, as far as possible and in a precautionary manner, of introducing hazardous materials into the ecosphere, the work environment, and foodstuffs;
- prevention of health-threatening noise;
- establishment of an independent, publicly accessible resource information centre that collects, develops, reviews, and evaluates data and information about the global consumption of natural resources, relating them to changes in the environment, tracks the pledges made

by members of the business and political communities, and routinely reports on their fulfilment;
- optimising the resource productivity of all purchases and leases by the public sector;
- adaptation of all norms and standards, and laws and regulations that contradict the common goals and agreements.

The following developments should be advanced as accompanying measures:

- effective liability for decisions made in the political and business communities;
- improvement of the balance between rich and poor;
- limitation of subsidies promoting resource consumption;
- priority for research, development, and innovation that support the community's goals;
- avoidance of 'toxic products' (Stiglitz);
- avoidance of excessive incomes (including bonuses) for top functionaries in the business and political communities;
- provision of regular information about the global consumption of natural resources and its consequences, in the style of weather reports and business news;
- restricting and controlling technical developments that can threaten ecological stability.

I am firmly convinced that only a common and successful eco-social policy can secure Europe's global significance into the future.

How can we observe the planetary boundaries? Findings from the research project POLFREE

Bernd Meyer

The problem

Our form of economic activity involves both removing resources from the environment and emitting harmful substances into the environment. Both processes damage nature in a way that entails major dangers for humanity.

If the existing structures are not changed, anthropogenic emissions of CO_2 and other greenhouse gases will bring about approximately 5–6°C global warming by the end of the century. We know that this development alone will destroy the livelihoods of many people: the frequency and intensity of storms will increase, the sea level is rising, catastrophic floods are becoming more frequent and more severe, harvest yields are expected to decline in many regions, and the oceans are becoming more acidic, which will have significant consequences for fish stocks. Also, we cannot rule out that climate change will cause additional disturbances of nature's equilibrium that could have far more serious impacts.

Abiotic raw materials can often be removed from nature only with mining technologies that devastate vast areas, destroy the habitats of local plant and animal species, and introduce toxins into the cycles of nature. Since abiotic raw materials are also non-renewable, every removal is at the expense of future generations who cannot make use of this natural capital later on. Even today, the exploitation of non-renewable resources also brings about turbulences in general economic development as well as international conflicts. Considerable stocks of metals, oil, and natural gas in particular exist in politically unstable countries. Therefore, it is tempting for resource users to develop market power there, ranging from political interference to military intervention. In addition, processing raw materials, for example in the cement and steel industries, is energy-intensive, resulting in further CO_2 emissions if fossil fuels are used for such processing.

According to the medium-variant projection of the UN World Population Prospects, the global population will grow to approximately 9.5 billion people by 2050, which is roughly 30% higher than the current figure. The increase in developing countries will be about 50%. Population growth will increase resource consumption and emissions of harmful substances. But there is also another problem: how can we feed this population? It must be taken into account that unchecked expansion of agricultural land at the expense of forests is not a practicable solution since the forest ecosystems play an important role for maintaining biodiversity and are also needed for storing CO_2 and supplying oxygen. In addition, there are limits to increasing agricultural productivity by using chemicals and breeding new resistant and higher-yield varieties. There is also reason to fear that water scarcity due to climate change will result in steppe formation and declining harvest yields in many regions. Another problem is the competition between using agricultural land to produce food and using it to grow plants to be burned as fuels.

Yet how can we change the economic structures to prevent these developments from coming about? First, it is to be hoped that consumers, producers, and investors change their behaviour because they understand that this is necessary, even without state intervention. But can we really expect intrinsic motivation to be so strong that the dangers described above can be prevented? Scepticism is warranted because the behaviour modifications required are dramatic and because use of nature has generally been free of charge so far, or at least it does not reflect the 'true' costs. It is always tempting for people to retain their previous behaviour – and to soothe their conscience by believing that their own contribution to solving the environmental problem is minuscule in any case. That is why the state is needed as an actor: to support civil society's intrinsic motivation through information tools, to provide incentives to change behaviour by means of economic instruments, or even to force the necessary changes using regulation.

The global dimension of the problem is evident, and its solution has also been discussed for more than 30 years by the United Nations as a key question of international policy: as early as 1983, the UN General Assembly commissioned the former Norwegian Prime Minister Gro Harlem Brundtland to formulate a global programme for transformation as well as ambitious goals for the global community. The global commission she directed presented its findings in a report in 1987. It designated a type of development as sustainable if it 'meets the needs of the present without compromising the ability of future generations to meet their own needs'. The Brundtland Report was the focus of the United Nations Conference on Environment and Development (UNCED), which took place in Rio de Janeiro in 1992. The key result of this conference was the Rio Declaration, which was adopted by all 179 countries on Earth as a kind of constitution for environmental and development policy. Its most important points: human well-being is at the centre of all policies (anthropocentric approach), and environmental policy must always be seen in connection with development policy. The goal is an open global economic system. Environmental policy is to be oriented toward the precautionary approach, which calls for action even if ultimate certainty about serious environmental damage has not yet been achieved. The Rio Declaration mentions various environmental policy tools, explicitly including economic instruments, which introduce incentives to change behaviour through taxes, subsidies, etc. Agenda 21, a 359-page action programme, was also adopted at the Rio Conference.

A quarter of a century has now passed since the legendary Rio Conference, but the decisions have yet to be implemented even though numerous international conferences have taken place since then. On the contrary, environmental burdens have intensified dramatically, as the example of CO_2 emissions shows: global CO_2 emissions are more than 50% higher today that in 1992, the year of the Rio Conference.

Nonetheless, there is reason to hope for a turnaround: it was decided at the 21st UN Climate Conference in Paris in 2015 to limit global warming to well below 2°C, and if possible, 1.5°C. Another important outcome was that the developing countries are to receive 100 billion US dollars per year from 2020 to 2025 to support their measures, and additional funding after that. But no binding goals were stated for the individual countries, and no particular instruments were required. In this respect, the result of the conference must be considered a statement of intent. The greatest success of the conference was probably heightened public awareness of the problem. The German Environment Minister Barbara Hendricks aptly commented that Paris was not the end, but the beginning of a long journey.

But what comes next? The example of climate policy shows that defining individual country goals that are binding under international law was not feasible. Adopted on 11 December 1997, the Kyoto Protocol provided for reducing annual industrialised-country greenhouse gas emissions by an average of 5.2% compared with 1990 levels during the first commitment period (2008–2012). No reduction goals were agreed for emerging economies and developing countries. By the beginning of December 2011, 191 countries as well as the EU had ratified the Kyoto Protocol. The US rejected it as early as 2001; in 2011, Canada also withdrew from the treaty. No agreement about a second commitment period has been reached.

The parties to the Kyoto Protocol failed to reach agreement both in Bali (2007) and in Copenhagen (2009). Only at the Conference of the Parties in Qatar in 2012 was it decided that the Kyoto Protocol was to be extended through 2020 (Kyoto II). The contentious issues are the definition of the reduction goals and especially their distribution among industrialised and developing countries. In light of this history, skepticism is warranted whether it will ever be possible to define concrete goals for individual countries.

A different approach for making climate and resource policy concrete is to forge an agreement, based on scientific findings on the planet's environmental carrying capacity, about global goals for the emission of harmful substances and for the extraction of resources. In other words, an agreement to observe the planet's boundaries. A longer-term perspective until at least 2050 is necessary. In a second step, one would have to agree on the use of instruments for reaching these goals, which are then applied in all participating countries – ideally in all countries of the Earth. At first, the instruments would be utilised with a low intensity, which would then be gradually increased. The targets would be pursued in this way year by year; this approach would then enable any necessary corrections of the time schedule for utilising the instruments.

Of course it is questionable whether it is possible to get all countries of the world on board for such an agreement. If a group of industrialised countries takes the lead, it will be very important to select a combination of policy tools that does not put their competitiveness at risk. Then, there are many indications that the other countries will follow suit sooner or later.

The concept of solving environmental problems by means of an international agreement about measures to be taken was examined in the POLFREE research project, which was supported by the EU. The key questions were: which measures make it possible to observe the Earth's boundaries through 2050, and what impacts on social and economic development would they entail? The linkages between economic development and environmental burdens are so complex that the answers cannot be provided simply by contemplation. For this reason, computer models were used in the POLFREE project that model the necessary interdependencies in great detail according to countries, groups of goods, types of raw materials, and harmful substances, without losing sight of the big picture. The present contribution is an attempt to make the insights gained in the POLFREE project available to a larger audience and focuses on the results of the computer simulations.[1] Interested readers may also refer to the POLFREE summary page (http://polfree.seri.at/), which provides additional material, including videos on the topic.

The POLFREE project: An overview

Under the coordination of Paul Ekins (UCL), the following research institutes responded to the question posed: University College London (UCL), the Wuppertal Institute (WI), the Netherlands Organisation for Applied Scientific Research (TNO), the International Centre for Integrated Assessment and Sustainable Development of the University of Maastricht (ICIS), the Sustainable Europe Research Institute (SERI), and the Potsdam Institute for Climate Impact Research (PIK), as well as the Institute of Economic Structures Research (GWS).

The first task was, of course, to clarify what quantity of human usage of the environment would not violate the planetary boundaries. Jill Jäger summarised the results of the discussions among the experts involved by formulating four headline targets which must be reached by 2050 in the EU or globally:[2]

---

1   cf. Meyer et al. (2015)
2   Jäger (2014)

- CO_2 emissions in the EU must be 80% lower than in 1990. Globally, the level of emissions is to be cut by about half compared with current levels.
- A region's 'cropland footprint' must be 30% lower than in 2005. It designates how much agricultural land is used around the globe for domestic consumption of food and feedstuffs as well as for the consumption of agricultural products in industrial processes, for instance production of agrofuels.
- A region's consumption of abiotic raw materials must not exceed 5 tons per capita (2011: EU 12.5 tons; global 7.5 tons). This refers to the raw materials (coal, oil, natural gas, metals, as well as construction and industrial minerals) incorporated in manufactured and imported goods, minus those in exported goods.
- The water abstraction index must be lower than 20%. This refers to a country's abstraction of surface water.

Comparisons with current figures demonstrate that these goals are evidently very ambitious in light of global economic and population growth. Which policy tools must be used to reach these goals? Under the leadership of Henning Wilts, a large number of the tools discussed and/or tested around the world were identified, data compiled thereon, and assessed as to their suitability (cf. Wilts et al., 2014). But the review was not limited to the possibilities for government interventions to make a difference; societal processes with respect to heightened intrinsic motivation of civil society to observe the Earth's boundaries were discussed as well.

In a next step, it was clarified how much international participation was to be assumed in the various scenarios of the future. The question to what extent the necessary transformation was to be modelled by top-down state and political action or by civil society's bottom-up insight into the necessity for transformation was also clarified. Jill Jäger and Karin Schanes (2014) coordinated the discussion between SERI, UCL, and GWS and presented the following result:

- The scenario 'Global Cooperation' assumes that all countries of the Earth agree to a package of measures to reach the stated goals (including 2°C global warming) that is characterised by state and political action.
- In the scenario 'EU Goes Ahead', the EU strives to reach the environmental-policy goals without waiting for globally coordinated treaties, whereas the other countries limit their activities to moderate climate policy.
- The scenario 'Civil Society Leads' also assumes that the EU goes it alone, whereby more of the impulses for change derive from civil society.
- The 'Business-as-Usual' scenario serves as a reference scenario which assumes that neither civil society nor the state provide impulses for solving the environmental problems above and beyond current activities.

The computer models for analysing these scenarios for the future were developed by GWS (GINFORS),[3] TNO (EXIOMOD),[4] and PIK (LPJmL).[5] LPJmL is a global vegetation model that explains the development of yields for 13 different plant species which are important foods and/or feed for animal farming at the detailed level of a 10 × 10 km spatial resolution. Besides other factors, the availability of water and climatic developments are highly relevant. The LPJmL model was coupled with the two economic environmental models EXIOMOD and GINFORS,

---

3   Meyer et al. (2015)
4   Hu et al. (2015)
5   Beringer et al. (2011)

which determine the demand for the 13 plant species and the land available for each one in each country. Plant production can be calculated on the basis of the land areas and the yields per unit of land. Dividing demand (in monetary units) by production figures for each plant species yields their prices.

The EXIOMOD and GINFORS models are global economic environmental models. GINFORS models the economic development of 38 countries and one 'rest of the world' region (ROW), each broken down into 59 goods markets, the labour market, and the capital market. International trade is explained bilaterally between the 38 countries and the ROW at the level of the 59 groups of goods. The countries are the 28 EU countries, Turkey, Russia, the US, Canada, Mexico, Brazil, Australia, Japan, South Korea, China, and India. The region ROW mainly includes developing countries.

GINFORS models the decisions of producers, investors, and consumers, whereby the relative price ratios of goods and production factors play key roles. The wage rate and the prices of all goods are determined in the context of the model. The extraction of raw materials and agricultural land use are determined by the output of the mining and agricultural sectors in the various countries. Emissions of harmful substances can be allocated in particular to the use of fossil fuels in certain sectors' production and private consumer demand. Water abstraction can also be explained using production figures in the various sectors and private consumption. It is important to state that modelling the interlinked production of goods and representing international trade in terms of goods and countries permits calculation of the indirect resource consumption incorporated in a country's imports of goods. Since this is of course also possible for exports, direct and indirect resource consumption can be determined for each country.

Even if major differences exist between GINFORS and EXIOMOD concerning details, the models do agree for the most part with respect to the characteristics described. There are, however, two fundamental differences between the models with significant impacts on their characteristics: EXIOMOD assumes neoclassical modelling in which the conditions of perfect competition are fulfilled in all markets: all actors have complete information about their alternative options for action, which permits them to make optimising decisions every time. Prices are determined so that supply and demand correspond in a market. The GINFORS model, in contrast, is neo-Keynesian: actors do not have perfect information and are therefore limited in their rationality. Also, suppliers set prices in relation to their unit costs. Then, demanders make their decisions, and suppliers produce the amount demanded.

The second difference concerns the way in which the parameters of the equations are determined. EXIOMOD sets price elasticities[6] on the basis of assumptions – as do most neoclassical models – and the other parameters of the model are determined in such a way that the model variables fit the data of an observation point (generally one year). GINFORS, on the other hand, determines all elasticities and other behavioural parameters by applying statistical procedures from historical time series observations. The result of the calculations automatically provides a measure for how well the equation fits reality. The behavioural hypotheses that pass this empirical test are the only ones to be included in the model.

The results of the simulation calculations with GINFORS/LPJmL show that the environmental goals for the EU can be achieved using the assumed policy measures in all alternative scenarios,[7] whereas this is not the case with the combination of the EXIOMOD and LPJmL models. (cf. Hu et al. 2015). This

---

6   How much a quantity of demand or supply reacts, in per cent, to a 1% change in a price ratio

7   Meyer et al. (2015)

discrepancy can be explained by differences in the parameters of the behavioural equations.[8] In this case, we tend to place more trust in the empirically validated model and decide to base the following discussion of the scenarios on the results of the GINFORS/LPJmL model combination alone.

Business-as-Usual

What kind of economic development is to be expected through 2050, and which violations of the environmental goals must we endure if environmental policy is not decisively developed further worldwide? This is the key question that is to be answered first. In order to do so, the model requires some assumptions concerning the development of the global market prices of fossil fuels (coal, natural gas, oil), the prices of metals, and population development. Also, it must be put in concrete terms what we consider to be 'business as usual' in terms of policy.

The assumptions

With respect to the development of global market prices for coal, oil, and natural gas, we follow the assessment of the IEA[9] for its 'Business-as-Usual' scenario: the continuing increase in demand and the rising costs of producing fossil fuels are reason to expect a price increase in real terms (price in relation to the development of prices of US gross domestic product) by 2050 of approximately 50%, compared with 2012. This amounts to an approximately 1.1% average increase per year. The current drops in prices are the consequence of predatory competition on the supply side that will

---

8   Distelkamp et al. (2015)
9   International Energy Agency. We call the IEA's '6-degree' scenario its 'Business-as-Usual' scenario

not continue long-term according to this assessment. No reference is available for metals. The real price of metals increased by an average of 5.6% per year from 2000 to 2015, with strong fluctuations. Sizeable increases in demand through 2050 are to be assumed for this category of raw materials as well, yet the development should not be quite as turbulent as in the first decade of the century. We assume an average real price increase of 4.0% per year. Our population development figures are taken from the medium-variant projection of the UN World Population Prospects (UN, 2013).

In its climate policy, the EU has committed to reducing CO_2 emissions by 20%, increasing energy productivity by 20%, and having renewables account for 20% of electricity generation by 2020. We assume that the trade in CO_2 emission rights, which has collapsed in recent years, will become effective again; a flexible supply will absorb the demand fluctuations and enable a stable price for emission rights. Renewable and nuclear energy's shares of electricity generation will follow the reference scenario through to 2020 (European Commission, 2013). After 2020, however, there will be no further increase in renewables' share of electricity generation. The share of nuclear energy will follow the IEA's 'Business-as-Usual' scenario through to 2020 (IEA, 2015). Countries such as Germany, which have committed to phasing out nuclear energy, are exceptions. This type of political agreement is accounted for in the 'Business-as-Usual' scenario. In the non-European countries, the shares of renewables and nuclear energy also follow the 'Business-as-Usual' scenario. Tax rates and all other climate-policy tools remain at their 2012 levels.

In recent years, many countries allowed public budget deficits to grow so large in some EU countries that they brought about a crisis of the euro. In order to be able to rule out such developments for the simulation period, we introduced the following budget rules which correspond to the prevailing neoliberal paradigm of financial policy: if the new net debt level of an EU country is greater than 3% of GDP (gross domestic product), or if the ratio between government debt and GDP exceeds a threshold value of 1.3, then income taxes will be raised and/or government spending will be reduced. For the non-European countries with government debt problems (esp. the US and Japan), a similar paradigm is assumed, although it has higher limit values.

The results (of the model)

How is the global economy expected to develop under these conditions? Figure 1 shows the growth rates of real global GDP (US dollars in constant prices from 1995 to 2050). The average annual growth rate from 1995 to 2015 was 2.6%; it will decrease to 2.2% from 2015 to 2050, whereby growth will weaken especially after 2030. This global development can be explained by declining population growth. The average growth rate of global GDP per capita from 2015 to 2050 will be 1.3%, the same as in the period from 1995 to 2015. In the EU, the average annual growth rate of 1.6 % (1995 to 2015) will decline to 0.9% (2015 to 2050), in Germany from 1.4% to 0.8%. The developments in the EU and Germany are due only in part to population growth: in the EU, the average GDP growth rate of 1.3% (1995 to 2015) will decline to 0.9% (2015 to 2050), in Germany from 1.3% to 1.1%.

Figure 1 shows that this development will involve significant structural transformation: in 2015, the EU and the US together still accounted for almost half of global GDP; in 2050, this value will have declined to just under one-third. At the same time, the share of the emerging economies of China and India, plus that of the developing countries, will increase to almost half of global GDP.

In the EU, the number of persons employed will decline by 32.6 million from 2015 to 2050 (−14.9%). Since the number of 15 to 64-year-olds in the EU population will decrease at the same time,

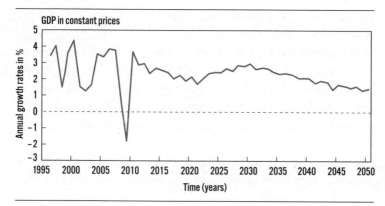

Fig. 1: Development of the global economy in the Business-as-Usual scenario

the proportion of persons employed in that age group, 64.6%, will remain only slightly below the level of 2015 (65.5%). But since this initial level entails high unemployment in many EU countries, the situation on the EU labour market will by no means be acceptable on average in 2050. In Germany, the number of persons employed will decrease by 5.8 million by 2050, but at the same time, the age group of 15-to-64-year-olds will decline by 13 million, so that the

	2015	2016
EU	25,7 %	16,5 %
USA	23,0 %	15,5 %
China	9,1 %	18,2 %
India	2,7 %	5,5 %
Developing countries	15,1 %	25,0 %
Other countries	24,4 %	19,3 %

Table 1: Selected countries'/regions' shares of global GDP in constant prices in 2015 and 2050 in the Business as Usual scenario (in per cent)

proportion of persons employed in this age group will increase
from 74.3% (2015) to 83.8%.[10]

Explaining the EU's weak growth compared with the development of the past 20 years involves many factors. For example, the
normalisation of growth dynamics in emerging economies such as
China and India, whose productivity increases will gradually come
in line with those of the industrialised countries by 2050, plays
an important role. Its effect of slowing down economic development in the EU cannot be compensated for by promoting growth
dynamics in the developing countries, either.

Yet two factors do appear to be particularly important. First,
it must be stated that from 1995 to 2008, growth was promoted
in many industrialised countries by increasing government debt.
The neoclassical notion that new government debt has a negative effect on GDP because private investors' investments in the
capital market are reduced by the new government debt can
be refuted easily with reference to the above-average growth of
investments in the EU[11] and the US during this period. The
global economic crisis, which began in 2008, then required additional increases in government debt in industrialised countries
to prevent the collapse of the economy. For this reason, government debt is already very high at the beginning of our simulation
period and must be stabilised. If this is done by budget consolidation – as assumed in the 'Business as Usual' scenario – then
growth will be slowed.

A second obstacle to growth could lie in the strong increase
in commodity prices for fossil fuels and metals. In the past 20
years we experienced such a phenomenon only during the brief

---

10 When interpreting these figures, one should keep in mind that the models do not
    take adaptations of intra-European immigration and emigration resulting from
    diverging labour market developments into account.

11 In Germany, however, investments developed at a below-average rate because many
    companies increased their capacities abroad.

phase from 2002 to 2008. The question also arises how food prices will develop; over the past 20 years, they have not increased in real terms. But globally, real food prices will increase on average by 2.1% per year through to 2050 (in relation to the GDP price index). This means that food prices will increase nominally by 320% through to 2050, whereas general price levels will rise by only 158%. This creates major problems for emerging economies and developing countries because food consumption can hardly be reduced and increasing proportions of disposable income must be spent on food; this will occur at the expense of other goods and will therefore also lower demand for imported industrial products. In India, for example, food expenditure's share of private households' disposable income was 47.4% in 1995, then dropped to 39.7% at the time of writing in the course of the growth process, but will rise again to 46.8%, the 1995 level, by 2050. In the industrialised countries, the extreme increases in food prices will of course directly bring about considerable social problems as well.

By why will food prices increase so dramatically? The reasons include, firstly, increasing demand, which is a result of continuing economic and population growth, especially in the developing countries and emerging markets. Also, global per capita meat consumption can be expected to increase despite an expected increasing proportion of people opting for an entirely or partly vegetarian diet in many European countries. This entails increasing demand for feed crops and pastureland.

Yet the supply cannot keep up; one reason is the limitations on expanding agricultural land use. GINFORS calculates the various crops' demand for land, which can be derived from economic development, for each country; determines the overall extension of land use required; and compares it with the maximum extension of agricultural land use measured historically in that country. This historically maximum extension of agricultural land use is the upper limit for future extensions of agricultural land use. Over the past 20 years, global agricultural land for crop plants has increased on average by 0.1% per year; by 2050, this rate will increase to 0.2% per year because of increasing demand, which expands global agricultural land overall through to 2050 by 6.7%, compared with 2015. The second component is soil productivity. In the past, global soil productivity was increased by 2% per year on average, mostly by increasing fertiliser use and by breeding more resistant varieties with higher yields. But we are reaching the limits of these options, and, at the same time, adverse climate impacts will increase as we approach 2050.[12] Global average soil productivity across all countries and crops is increasing by only 0.3% per year, and this is achieved by more irrigation of agricultural land in low-precipitation areas, among other things. But this also means that water abstraction will increase in these countries, significantly exceeding the acceptable figure of 20% of surface water. Average global agricultural productivity will rise by 12.3% over the course of the entire period from 2015 to 2050. Global plant production will thus increase in total by just 20%.

Global CO_2 emissions will increase by approximately 50% by 2050, compared with 2015, because of the continuing use of fossil fuels. Emissions will therefore be three times as high as the 15 Gt estimate corresponding to the 2°C goal.

The structural transformation this involves will be even more distinct than in the case of GDP, as shown in Table 2: even today, China, India, and the developing countries combined account for 42% of global emissions; by 2050, almost three-quarters of global emissions will come from this group of countries. It is obvious that any climate policy that does not include these countries is doomed to fail. The EU and the US together will cause only 16% of global CO_2 emissions in 2050.

Abiotic resources encompass coal, oil, natural gas, and ores, as

---

12 Hahlbrock (2009)

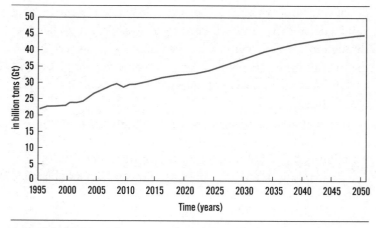

Fig. 2: Global CO_2 emissions in gigatons in the 'Business as Usual' scenario

well as construction and industrial minerals. In 2011, fossil fuels accounted for approximately one-quarter of all abiotic raw materials extraction; construction and industrial minerals for a good 60%; and ores for the rest (~14%). In the past 20 years, extraction of abiotic resources has increased from 29.4 Gt to 55.5 Gt, which corresponds to an average annual growth rate of 3.2%. This dynamic was accelerated, among other things, by the building

	2015	2050
EU	12,0 %	6,5 %
USA	15,6 %	9,7 %
China	13,7 %	29,9 %
India	5,6 %	10,7 %
Developing countries	22,4 %	32,1 %
Other countries	18,5 %	11,2 %

Table 2: Selected countries' and regions' shares of global CO_2 emissions in the 'Business as Usual' simulation (in per cent)

boom in China, which will, however, slow down in the coming years. Global extraction will grow by an average of 1.3% per year through to 2050 and will reach a level of 86.5 Gt that year. Nonetheless, this means that global extraction of abiotic resources will be 84% higher than the target value that is permissible if per capita use is limited to 5 tons.

The preliminary conclusion: if we continue with business as usual, global CO_2 emissions will reach a trajectory toward 5–6°C warming by the end of the century. Strong price increases for food will dramatically exacerbate social problems within and between countries. Extraction of abiotic resources will be 84% higher than the acceptable value by 2050. Water will be even more scarce than it is today in many countries. Economic growth in the EU will be curtailed by 30% compared with the development of the past 20 years. In the EU, it must be expected that the current unsatisfactory situation on the labour market will be exacerbated. Germany will avoid this fate only because of the numbers in the 15 to 64 age group, which will decline even more strongly than on average in the EU. Average public debt ratios (government debt in per cent of GDP) in the EU will increase from approximately 100% today to 130% by 2050.

The alternatives: the policy measures and other targets in the simulations

To indicate target prices for fossil fuels, we turn again to the IEA assessment for the various futures for orientation: for 'Global Cooperation' (2°C), this means that (because of the strong declines in demand for coal and oil), their real prices will drop by an average of −0.6% and −0.2% per year, respectively. The targets for 'EU Goes Ahead' and 'Civil Society Leads' (4°C) are between those for 'Business as Usual' (6°C) and 'Global Cooperation' (2°C), as expected: real price increases averaging 0.7% per year are anticipated.

The prices for metals are significantly lower in the 'Global Cooperation' scenario than in 'Business-as-Usual' because the demand for metals will decline drastically. The average real price increase is only 1.9% per year. In the scenarios 'EU Goes Ahead' and 'Civil Society Leads', in contrast, the real price increase is still 4.0% per year because the decline in demand is limited to the EU, but this has only a minor effect on the global market.

Which measures are assumed? A total of approximately 30 different instruments are applied. The following overview assigns the most important measures of the 'Global Cooperation' scenario to the various policy fields.

Global Cooperation

Climate policy

- Carbon tax
- Quota for using renewables for electricity generation
- Regulations and economic instruments for promoting electric mobility
- Support for investments in the energy efficiency of buildings
- Elimination of subsidies for transport by air and water and for using fossil fuels
- Air transport tax

If the goals are to be attained by 2050, the means used must gradually be made more stringent over the approximately 35 years through to 2050 and must achieve the following levels: the carbon tax increases purchaser prices for coal (+60%), oil, and natural gas (+40%). This makes all goods produced with these fossil fuels more expensive.

All electricity suppliers must prove that they fulfil the renewables quota for electricity generation. Such a quota makes sense even if renewables are uncompetitive with fossil fuels. Otherwise, there is the danger that operators of depreciated conventional power plants will continue to operate them. The quota must increase gradually from today's levels to 90% by 2050. The type of renewable technology – wind, solar, hydropower, etc. – is not regulated; it will be determined by the market.

Electric mobility must be supported if it is to prevail. Part of the revenue from the carbon tax must be used to subsidise the purchase of electric vehicles. In addition, traffic regulations (concerning parking, use of bus lanes, etc.) favouring electric vehicles should be introduced in cities. These measures should be expanded until fossil fuels' share of total energy consumption by road traffic has dropped to only 20%.

Investments in the energy efficiency of the building stock are to be supported in such a way that 2% of the stock is retrofitted annually from 2020 on. Retrofitting concerns heating systems, but also insulation.

By 2030, all subsidies for the use of fossil fuels and for transport by water and air must be eliminated. Since according to current knowledge, the carbon tax cannot achieve a technology change in air transport, a tax is to be introduced here with a tax rate rising to 50% by 2050.

Resource efficiency in abiotic materials
- Regulation of recycling of metals and other minerals
- Taxation of the use of metals and other minerals
- Programme to support innovations in materials use

Metal recycling is already a reality in individual countries and for individual types of metals, but to highly varying degrees. In the 'Global Cooperation' scenario, it is assumed that new legal requirements will raise each of these quotas by 50% by 2050. In recycling of non-metallic minerals, Germany has already reached the technically possible maximum, whereas other countries are still quite some distance from achieving this. In the 'Global Cooperation' scenario, it is assumed that the gap between the German recycling rate and that of other countries is cut by half.

The declining demand for ores and non-metallic mineral products because of recycling lowers the price of the raw material and thus the production costs and the price of metals and construction materials. To prevent this from increasing demand, a tax on ores and non-metallic mineral products will be introduced with a tax rate reaching 70% and 50%, respectively, by 2050.

The German materials efficiency agency DEMEA focuses on consulting small and medium-sized enterprises in terms of technological options to increase the efficiency of their use of materials. It is assumed that such agencies will be established in the other countries, too. Half of the consulting costs will be borne by public funding. Based on the German experience, it is assumed that efforts to reduce materials use in all companies by 10% by 2050 will succeed.

Sustainable use of land and water
- Regulation of water abstraction for agriculture
- Information programme to prevent waste in food production and consumption
- Information programme to support land use productivity
- Taxation of meat consumption

It is assumed that water abstraction for agriculture will be regulated so that it remains below 20% of surface water in all countries.

It is also assumed that an information programme reduces waste by 10% in food production and by 20% in hotels, restaurants, and private consumption.

Differences in soil productivity are caused by variations in soil quality, climatic factors, and the availability of water, but also by differences in management. The latter causes can be influenced through an information programme. It is assumed that efforts to eliminate 20% of the negative deviations from the average in the individual countries by 2050 will succeed.

A tax on meat consumption, which will double the price of meat by 2050, will be introduced.

Ecological tax reform
- Reduction of taxes on goods and services with low emissions of harmful substances and low resource consumption
- Reduction of business taxes depending on emissions of harmful substances and resource consumption

Ecological tax reform will be introduced in all countries which feeds the revenues from the newly introduced taxes and the lowered subsidies back into the economy so that tax burdens are not increased. Taxes on goods and services as well as business taxes are reduced depending on the environmental burdens they cause.

EU Goes Ahead

In this scenario, the non-EU countries pursue only moderate climate policies and no further environmental policy measures. They introduce the measures for electric mobility and the quota for renewables in electricity generation, as in the 'Global Cooperation' scenario, but the quota is only 70% for 2050.

The EU countries basically introduce the same measures as in the 'Global Cooperation' scenario; however, they must be designed in such a way that no disadvantages for international competitiveness arise. This will result in the following two changes:

(1) The general carbon tax is replaced by two tools: an emissions trading system is installed for the extractive industries and electricity generation, which, in contrast to the existing ETS, features a flexible amount of emission rights; this makes it possible to bring the price of the rights to a desired level. The other industries are subject to a carbon tax with direct compensation. This means that the tax revenues of a particular industry are paid back in full to the businesses in that industry, depending on their shares of turnover. Consequently, the tax is a burden only on those businesses that emit above-average amounts of CO_2, whereas the other businesses enjoy advantages and the industry in total is not subject to additional burdens.

(2) The tax on the use of ores is replaced by taxation of final demand for goods, whereby the tax rate depends on the ores incorporated directly and indirectly in the goods (RMC-based tax; RMC: raw material consumption). Exports are excluded as a matter of principle. This tax is also neutral in its effect on competition since exports are excluded and imports are taxed exactly like goods from domestic production.

Civil Society Leads

The measures in the non-EU countries are identical to those in 'EU Goes Ahead'.

For the EU countries, there are differences to 'EU Goes Ahead' since economic instruments are now replaced, at least in part, by autonomous behaviour changes on the part of consumers who are driven by the insight that they are necessary. All of the measures in 'EU Goes Ahead' not explicitly mentioned here also apply in 'Civil Society Leads'. The following list mentions only the changes compared with 'EU Goes Ahead'.

- Taxation on air transport is replaced by an autonomous reduction in the consumption of air transport services, reaching 25% of the level of the 'Business as Usual' scenario in 2050.
- There is no support for investment in the energy efficiency of buildings. People need less and less living space, as they live together with others and also increasingly live under the same roof with other generations. This makes it possible to reduce approximately 50% of living space per person involved. It is assumed that 20% of the population will take this path by 2050.
- There is no taxation of final demand for goods in terms of their metal content. Instead, it is assumed that the operating life of durable goods can be increased by ecodesign standards. This enables a 5% reduction of expenditures for electric household appliances. At the same time, expenditures for repair services double. It is also assumed that car sharing expands, so household demand for cars drops by 15% compared with the 'Business as Usual' scenario.
- Instead of taxing meat consumption, an autonomous reduction of meat demand per capita is assumed, reaching 50% of the level of the 'Business as Usual' scenario by 2050.
- Prevention of food waste reaches 40% by 2050, significantly more than in the 'EU Goes Ahead' scenario.

Of course, the scenario 'Civil Society Leads' also assumes that private households desire more leisure time and less work and are also willing to limit their overall consumption to achieve this goal. It is assumed that weekly working hours are reduced by 20% by 2050 and that households autonomously reduce their entire consumption spending by 0.3% per year at the same time. The latter induces strong endogenous contractions in the economy because the decline in consumption reduces aggregate production, households' disposable income, and thus also consumption. The extent to which this occurs will be discussed later.

The alternatives: results of the simulations

Of course, the global goals are attained only in the scenario 'Global Cooperation' because in the other scenarios, the non-EU-countries pursue only limited climate policies. Figure 2 illustrates that the 2°C goal is very ambitious: CO_2 emissions are reduced by more than 60% compared with the 'Business as Usual' scenario. Global extraction of abiotic resources is 56% lower in the 'Global Cooperation' scenario in 2050 than in the 'Business as Usual' scenario, and at 4 tons per capita, it is even significantly below the goal of 5 tons per capita. Use of agricultural land corresponds to that in the 'Business as Usual' scenario, but lower meat consumption and reduction of waste now diminish the demand for food. At the same time, efforts to increase land productivity somewhat are successful. As a result, the average price of crops in 2050 in the 'Global Cooperation' scenario is 32% lower than in the 'Business as Usual' scenario. Water abstraction remains below 20% of available surface water in all countries.

Since the revenue from environmental taxes is always paid back to the economy, the overall tax burden remains unchanged overall, with no strong economic effects resulting. The economic impacts are based above all on three effects: the various environmental policy measures – especially climate policy – trigger investment in new technologies, which stimulates the economy. Costly inputs (fossil fuels) are substituted by capital (renewables). In addition, the increase in resource efficiency generally also implies an increase in economic efficiency for the producers of end products; but turnover, value creation, and employment decline for the producers of inputs and raw materials. The same is true for the producers of fossil fuels.

In other words, decarbonisation and dematerialisation have both positive and negative economic effects. Since the world is not a spaceless economy, but is spread across many countries with highly divergent production structures, the net effects differ, of course. If a country does not have a high-performance capital goods sector, then the investment boom triggered by decarbonisation and dematerialisation will not occur there, but, rather, in other countries. If a country is mostly a producer of raw materials and has little production in the final parts of the value-added chain, then it will be negatively impacted by these measures. Conversely, a region with strong production of finished products and insignificant raw materials production – like the EU – will clearly be a beneficiary.

The situation is different in typical countries supplying raw materials: Russia loses 27.7 % of its GDP in 'Global Cooperation', but only 11.3% in 'EU Goes Ahead'; Canada loses 7% in 'Global Cooperation', but gains 2% of its GDP in 'EU Goes Ahead'; the corresponding figures for Brazil are −7.5% and −0.8%. In this respect, it is not surprising that, as shown in Figure 3, global GDP per capita in 'EU Goes Ahead' deviates more strongly from 'Business as Usual', namely by +8%, than from 'Global Cooperation'.

The environmental goals for the EU are reached almost in full in all scenarios, for which reason they are not described in detail here. Figure 4 shows how important economic indicators for the EU deviate from the 'Business as Usual' scenario in respect of the alternative scenarios. The first striking point is that in 'Global Cooperation', overall investment is 17% higher in 2050 than in the 'Business as Usual' scenario, whereas it is only 6.5% in 'EU Goes Ahead', even though the two scenarios assume very similar policies in the EU. The explanation is that, in 'EU Goes Ahead', taxation of the use of ores is replaced by taxation of final consumption, whereby the tax rate depends on the goods' direct and indirect metal content. Of course, this has a particular impact

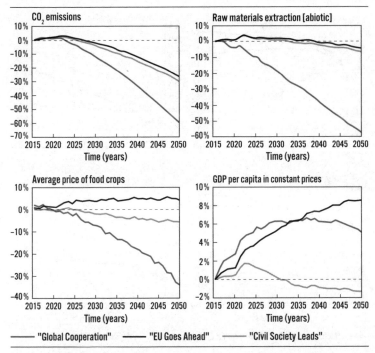

Fig. 3: The effects on selected global indicators. Deviations from the 'Business as Usual' scenario in per cent

on investment goods. In contrast, taxation of ores – as in 'Global Cooperation' – reduces the use of metals at all stages of production. This reduces the weight of investment goods, but demand for them does not necessarily drop. The strong decline of investments in 'Civil Society Leads' is the consequence of general consumer abstinence, which reduces production, income, and consumption by a total of 21% in a multiplicative process, thus also bringing down investment, of course.

The external trade balance (exports minus imports) has a much stronger positive development in 'EU Goes Ahead', compared with

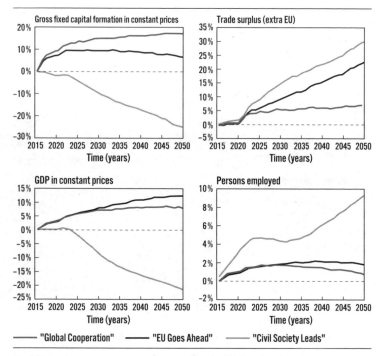

Fig. 4: Important economic indicators for the EU in the alternative
scenarios. Deviations from the 'Business-as-Usual' scenario in per cent

'Global Cooperation'. The reason for this is the EU's first mover
advantage in 'EU Goes Ahead'. As a region whose production is
mostly in the final phases of the value-added chains, the EU enjoys
considerable cost advantages arising from its ambitious environmental policy; those cost advantages increase the less the EU's
international competitors engage in decarbonisation and dematerialisation: in 'EU Goes Ahead', exports increase by 10.3% and
in 'Global Cooperation' by only 6.3%, whereas the imports even
drop by 2.3% despite increasing production in 'EU Goes Ahead'
and rise by 5.4% in 'Global Cooperation'. The strong increase of

the external trade balance in 'Civil Society Leads' is explained by the fact that the exports in this scenario are not affected by the measures, whereas the imports decline sharply because of consumer abstinence.

Because of the strong increase of exports and decrease of imports, GDP increases by 12% in 'EU Goes Ahead', even though investments increase less than in 'Global Cooperation', where GDP rises by only 8%. In 'Civil Society Leads', GDP remains constant, which is shown as a strong negative deviation from the 'Business as Usual' scenario in Figure 3.

The employment effects are positive in all the alternative scenarios. In 'EU Goes Ahead' and 'Global Cooperation', they are weaker than the corresponding changes in GDP because for one thing, the elasticity of demand for labour in relation to production is smaller than 1, and for another, an increase in real wages diminishes the positive employment effect to a certain extent. The strong increase in employment in 'Civil Society Leads', despite GDP remaining constant, is the consequence of reducing working hours and lower real wages, compared with the 'Business as Usual' scenario.

In 'Global Cooperation', net new government debt in the EU is 32% lower than in the 'Business-as-Usual' scenario in 2050; in 'EU Goes Ahead', it is 10% lower.

Germany benefits more strongly than the EU average from the effects described: in 'Global Cooperation', Germany's GDP increases by 10.6%, and in 'EU Goes Ahead' even by 14.4%, and the employment effects are correspondingly greater here as well: 'Global Cooperation': 1.2 %, 'EU Goes Ahead': 2.8%. In 'Global Cooperation', net new government debt in Germany is 20% lower in 2050; in 'EU Goes Ahead', it is no less than 40% lower.

Conclusions

If we do not succeed in establishing ambitious climate and resource policies, the planetary boundaries will be far exceeded. In the EU, this development, which entails major risks, will involve weakening economic growth, worsening social conditions, and increasing risks in the financial markets.

Yet the other messages that can be derived from the simulation calculations of the GINFORS model in the POLFREE project are extraordinarily positive. The second message is that ambitious global environmental goals are achievable and that positive effects for income, employment, and government debt can be realised at the same time. However, this requires an international accord regarding a comprehensive package of measures encompassing information instruments, economic instruments, and regulations. The measures must be targeted directly at keeping the consequences of economic and population growth for greenhouse gas emissions, the extraction of abiotic raw materials, and usage of land and water within the limits of what our planet can bear.

One may doubt whether such an agreement can be reached. If this does not succeed, then the EU could still go it alone. In this case, the third message of the modelling results comes into effect: the EU can reach its environmental goals, even if we fail to meet the global goals, because the EU is simply too insignificant at the global scale. But in this case, the EU would achieve major economic successes. For this reason, it can be argued that over time, these economic benefits would induce other countries to follow the EU's good example (corresponding effects are not shown endogenously in the model simulations). So if the international accord fails, the global goals may yet be reached, with delays and through gentle competitive pressure.

The fourth message concerns the role of civil society in this process. It was demonstrated that changes in consumption structures and consumption levels driven by insights into their necessity can make decisive contributions to reaching the goals. If society tends toward a 'beyond GDP' value system, people will accept income losses and appreciate more free time and leisure, which will then also guarantee a high level of employment.

Last, but not least, it should be mentioned that variations of the policy mix will surely enable further improvement of the results in all scenarios. In particular, preparation of country-specific analyses and policy mixes hold considerable potential for new insights.

References

Beringer, T., Lucht, W., and Schaphoff, S. (2011), Bioenergy production potential of global biomass plantations under environmental and agricultural constraints. Global Change Biology Bioenergy 3(4), 299–312.

European Commission (2013), EU energy, transport and GHG emissions: Trends to 2050: Reference Scenario 2013.

Hahlbrock, K. (2009), Feeding the Planet. Environmental Protection through Sustainable Agriculture. London: Haus Publishing.

Hu, J., Moghayer, S., Reynes, F. (2015), Report about integrated scenario interpretation. EXIOMOD/LPJmL results. Deliverable 3.7b of the POLFREE project.

IEA (2015), Energy Technology Perspectives 2015: Mobilising Innovation to Accelerate Climate Action. Paris: OECD/IEA.

Jäger, J. (2014), A Vision for a Resource Efficient Economy. Deliverable D2.2, POLFREE project.

Jäger, J. and Schanes, K. (2014), Report on Scenario Formulation. Deliverable 3.5. POLFREE project.

Meyer, B. (2016), Die Modellierung der Großen Transformation. In: Jahrbuch Normative und institutionelle Grundfragen der Ökonomik, Vol. 15, Held, M., Kubon-Gilke, G., Sturn, R., eds. Politische Ökonomik großer Transformationen. Marburg: Metropolis Verlag.

Meyer, B., Distelkamp, M., Beringer, T. (2015), Report about integrated scenario interpretation. GINFORS/LPJmL results. Deliverable 3.7a of the POLFREE project.

United Nations (2013), World Population Prospects: The 2012 Revision, key
    findings and advance tables. UN Department of Economic and Social Affairs,
    Population Division: Working Paper, ESA/P/WP.227.
Wilts, H., v. Gries, N., Bahn-Walkowiak, B., O'Brien, M., Busemann, J., Domenech,
    T. (2014), Policy Mixes for Resource Efficiency. Deliverable 2.3 POLFREE
    project.

Energy: the world's race for resources in the twenty-first century

Hermann-Josef Wagner

Not a week passes without media reports on necessary changes to the energy supply, not least to reduce greenhouse gases. The international political community is undertaking efforts toward treaties and goals for the future orientation of energy policy. Germany in particular has been taking a leading role for years. That is why there have been a number of changes in the energy supply, the underlying conditions, and the goals of energy policy in the past five years. All this is an occasion to re-examine what the future goals are, the extent to which they can be reached, and where we stand today. These deliberations are founded upon the state of affairs as it has developed since the publication of the most recent edition of the book *Energy: The World's Race for Resources in the Twenty-first Century* in 2011. In this contribution, an attempt is made to present all the important developments and influences of recent years in their totality. But it is not possible to go into each and every technical or economic option or every alternative that might come about in the future or be imaginable, as that would go beyond the scope of this contribution.

The faces of energy

We are familiar with energy from our everyday lives: for example, solar energy, wind energy, electricity, and that derived from natural gas and gasoline. One can also differentiate the forms of energy as electrical, mechanical, thermal, kinetic, etc. They can be used in many ways. Most of humankind's energy needs are still met today by energy sources that are burned and generate heat (thermal energy). In many cases, however, kinetic energy is required (to operate machinery), and it cannot be obtained easily from thermal energy. For this reason, a large number of conversion technologies exist, and they are subject to various laws of physics and limits to energy conversion. Thermal energy that has not been converted, for example, must be discharged to the environment as waste heat. Burning fossil fuels – coal, oil, and gas – produces CO_2 emissions. They are the subject of international efforts to change the energy supply in the future to alleviate the climate problem.

The energies that humans use are derived from primary energy sources. They are transformed into secondary energy sources, which we are familiar with in our everyday lives as commercially available energy sources, for example natural gas, electricity, or gasoline. In official statistics, such energy sources purchased by

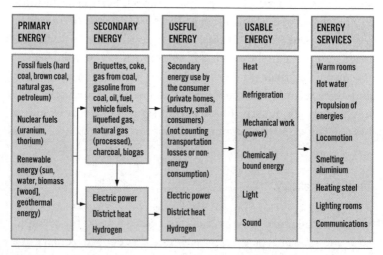

Fig. 1: Paths of energy: From primary energy to the factors determining energy demand

Prefixes for units and abbreviations			
kilo-	**K**	10^3	thousand
mega-	**M**	10^6	million
giga-	**G**	10^9	billion
tera-	**T**	10^{12}	trillion
peta-	**P**	10^{15}	quadrillion
exa-	**E**	10^{18}	quintillion

1 US (fluid) gallon = 3.79 litres
1 bbl (oil barrel) = 159 litres
1 million bbl/day = 50 million t/yr.
1 British thermal
unit = 1.055 kJ

Conversion factors				
Unit	MJ	kWh	TCE	TOE
1 megajoule (MJ)	—	0.000278	0.000034	0.000024
1 kilowatt hour (kWh)	3.6	—	0.000123	0.000086
1 ton coal unit (TCE)	29,308	8,140	—	0.7
1 ton crude oil unit (TOE)	41,868	11,630	1.429	—

Table 1: Conversion of energy units (see text for abbreviations)

consumers are called final energy. What people need, however, is usable energy, e.g., heat, refrigeration, mechanical energy, or chemically bound energy, as well as that relating to light and acoustics (sound). In addition, the concept of energy services has become common internationally. It expresses the desires of humans, which are fulfilled by consuming energy; for example, the desire to have warm living spaces or warm water, to be able to be mobile, or to heat and form steel in production processes (Fig. 1).

It is difficult to compare different figures because many different units are still in use worldwide in the energy sector and energy technology. Table 1 shows commonly used units, prefixes, and conversion factors.

Even though the joule (J) and the kilowatt-hour (kWh), which is derived from it, have been the legally binding units for energy in European countries since 1978, the coal unit and oil equivalent are still used quite frequently in practice because they are more easily accessible. These units are also used internationally in other countries. The global oil industry still uses oil barrels as a unit of volume (bbl – barrel [UK] or b – barrel [US]). Different units of energy are used in this chapter as well. The energy units J and kWh are not very easy to grasp, which is why amounts of energy are often indicated in tons of coal equivalent (TCE) or tons of oil equivalent (TOE). One TCE corresponds roughly to a three-axle truck transporting a load of about 15 tons, one TOE to a tank truck carrying about 21,000 litres or about 18 tons of oil. If the same amounts of energy were expressed in joules, it would be difficult to imagine how much that would be.

Population growth and energy consumption

Global primary energy consumption has grown considerably since 1950. Following the oil price increases in the 1970s, global energy consumption declined slightly for some years, but it has increased continually since the early 1980s. Even though it dropped somewhat because of the global economic crisis in 2009, it has been rising continuously again since then. In absolute numbers, and statistically speaking, this means that virtually all of Germany's energy consumption is added to global energy consumption every year. The fossil fuels oil, hard coal, and natural gas together still cover a good 80% of global primary energy consumption. Nuclear energy, hydropower, and renewables such as wind, solar, and biomass make up the remainder. Figure 2 shows more detail. Against this background in many countries and in global climate negotiations, a question is under discussion: to what extent can the energy supply be changed to reduce the amount of fossil fuels used?

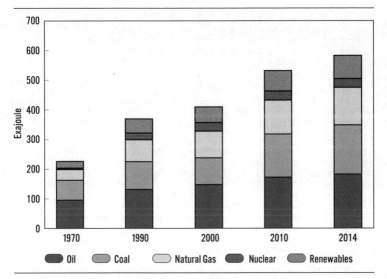

Fig. 2: Development of global primary energy consumption

The energy consumption and the related greenhouse gas emissions of the People's Republic of China, in particular, have substantially increased over the course of the past ten years because of economic growth. In contrast, the energy consumption of other important countries, for example India and the African nations, has not grown appreciably despite increased population growth. The European Union is aiming to reduce CO_2 emissions and energy consumption, which is stagnating or dropping slightly. Table 2 shows that energy consumption varies widely across the world. The European Union (EU-27) accounts for just under 22% of global energy consumption. Germany's share is declining and currently makes up approximately 2.4% of global energy consumption. Energy consumption per capita varies as well. If per capita consumption in Germany is normalised to 100, then the average citizen of the world consumes 46, or just under half that

Share of global primary energy consumption as of 2014		Relative primary consumption per capita as of 2014	
USA	17,8 %	Germany	100
EU - 27 total	21,9 %	World	46
Germany	2,4 %	USA	191
China	23,0 %	Japan	95
India	4,9 %	China	57
Japan	3,5 %	India	14
African countries	2,2 %	Ethiopia	1

Table 2: Selected countries' and country groups' shares of global primary energy consumption and selected countries' per capita consumption

amount; the average US citizen consumes more, namely a good 190, and the average Indian only about 14. This also demonstrates that energy consumption overall will continue to rise considerably in the coming decades, with global economic growth increasing and living conditions improving. India's population, for example, is almost the same as China's, namely 1.3 billion, but consumes only roughly one-quarter as much energy per capita.

The statistics regarding electricity consumption are comparable. The most recent global data available show that, statistically speaking, the average US citizen consumed approximately 12,000 kWh per year at the end of 2012. By comparison, the figure for Germany was 6,700 kWh, and for Ethiopia only a mere 50 kWh. In 2015, Ethiopia had a population of 100 million, and its population growth rate was 2.9% per year, the highest in the world. It must be taken into account that these figures include a country's entire electricity consumption (homes, transportation, industry), which is then divided by the population number. According to a study by the OECD and the IEA, roughly 1.4 billion people globally had no access to electricity in 2008; about 580 million lived in Africa and 610 million in India (i.e., roughly half of the Indian population had no electricity).

Energy as an economic good – significant changes

Since 2010, the world has seen appreciable changes in energy sources and their prices. Oil is still a major factor determining the price of natural gas. Besides the oil sands (tar sands), which have been exploited for a long time – for example in Alberta, Canada – a large number of new deposits in the form of light tight oil (shale oil) and oil shale (which is not be confused with shale oil) have been discovered and developed. Sometimes the two terms (shale oil and oil shale) are used differently in the relevant literature.

The light tight oils play the most important role. Light tight oil exists between layers of rock. It was unable to migrate from its bedrock because the surrounding rock is not sufficiently permeable, and for this reason it usually remains in carbonate or sandstone formations. In contrast to oil shale, light tight oil does not have to be upgraded in a complex process to produce crude oil. It is produced by hydraulic fracturing (fracking), which involves pumping water and other materials into the layers containing oil, thus making the oil flow out. It is now possible to obtain oil from a deposit twice (refracking) at a substantially lower cost than for fracking.

In the future, it may also be possible to produce oil shale. There are large areas of rock containing kerogen (oil shale), for example the Green River Formation in Utah, Wyoming, and Colorado in the US. However, no economically viable technology for its production has been developed to date.

The US have increased domestic oil production and become less dependent on the global oil and gas markets and are even aiming to export natural gas and oil medium term. Because of the

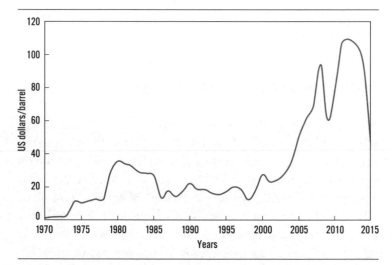

Fig. 3: Development of crude oil prices in recent years

increasing supply, crude oil prices have dropped considerably, as Figure 3 shows. It must be taken into account, however, that Saudi Arabia in particular is trying to keep crude oil prices low in order to make it less attractive for other countries to access additional oil reserves through oil-sharing. In recent years, Saudi Arabia has been marketing considerable amounts of conventional oil in an attempt to keep world market oil prices so low that accessing additional new deposits would not be economically feasible. Germans have benefited from this policy since 2015 as gasoline and oil prices have fallen. It is an open question how long this policy can be maintained. The significantly lower crude oil prices have also meant increasing foreign exchange losses for Russia and the resulting economic consequences in 2015 and 2016.

Besides light tight oil (shale oil), shale gas is also being produced in appreciable amounts in the US (Texas). Shale gas consists of natural mixtures of gases in shale. It can be produced by frack-ing (hydraulic fracturing), that is, by pumping sand, water, and chemicals into the deposit to create artificial fractures and increase permeability. Shale gas is a mixture whose largest component is methane (which is also the main component of natural gas), but it also contains ethane, butane, and propane.

Shale gas also exists in Germany, e.g., in Lower Saxony, and it was discussed at length whether or not to permit its production. The German Bundestag banned unconventional fracking as prac-tised in the US in the summer of 2016, but with the consent of the federal states, four exploratory holes remain permissible.

In recent years, it has been debated time and again whether it will be possible to use methane hydrate in the future. This is frozen natural gas lying at the margins of the oceans, for example off the coasts of India, China, Japan, and the US. It was formed by the decomposition of organic material in the ocean by living organisms. The deposits are in the continental slopes beneath roughly 500 to 5,000 metres of water. To date, neither mining technology for this methane hydrate nor knowledge about the geological consequences of such mining exists – might avalanches destroy the coasts after some years?

The US, Canada, and China also exploit coalbed methane, natural mixtures of gases occurring with coal deposits, where the water pressure pushes the methane to the surface of the coal seam, so it can then be brought to the surface with a suction bore. A study was prepared on the economic feasibility of such coalbed methane production in Lorraine, France.

With respect to natural gas, a new political analysis of security of supply resulted in the commissioning of a natural gas pipeline from Russia through the Baltic Sea directly to Germany; another one is under construction. For this reason, less natural gas des-tined for Western Europe needs to be piped through Ukraine and Poland. Since Ukraine and Poland have been receiving fees for this service, they have expressed their political opposition to the construction of the Baltic Sea pipelines several times.

In light of the fact that hard coal production in Germany is very expensive, the decision was made to end it; the last ton of hard coal intended for production in December 2017. Intensive discussions are currently underway in the political community and the energy sector regarding whether the amount of lignite produced can be reduced in the future to advance toward the stated CO_2 reduction goal. For this reason, an agreement was reached in 2015 to decommission older lignite power plants and to keep them ready for operation as power plant reserves, but for a certain transition period. On the other hand, lignite power plants with roughly 45% net efficiency (i.e., 45% of the chemical energy input in the form of lignite is transformed into electrical energy – electricity – and provided to consumers) have also been put into operation in Germany in recent years. They have the highest levels of efficiency of any lignite power plants in the world.

Following the nuclear accident in Fukushima, Japan, in 2011, the German Bundestag decided to phase out nuclear power in Germany by 2022. It cannot be ruled out that the phaseout will be completed more quickly because of the economic situation. The German Federal Network Agency (Bundesnetzagentur) must, however, agree to earlier shutdowns in order to guarantee security of supply.

The output of power plants previously running at base load, i.e., feeding the same amount of power into the grid year-round, must today be increased or decreased quickly, up to 100 times per year, depending on the weather and the resulting generation of wind and solar power. This requires retrofitting, some of which has been completed. This different way of operating the plants also increases wear and tear.

In 2015, generating one kWh of electricity in Germany gave rise to just under 0.6 kg of CO_2 emissions. One kWh of electricity generated in a lignite power plant creates just under 1 kg CO_2, and in a very efficient combined cycle power plant roughly 0.45 kg CO_2. Combined cycle power plants are the most progressive power plants in the world in terms of their efficiency. They use natural gas to generate electricity and operate with a gas turbine and a steam turbine.

Energy efficiency – the basis of the energy concept

One major goal around the world is to use energy as efficiently as possible. For about ten years, the German government has been pursuing an energy concept (Fig. 4) that aims, by 2050, to reduce greenhouse gas emissions to 20%, to increase renewables to roughly 60% of final energy consumption, and to lower primary energy consumption to 55% of the respective 1990 totals. In particular, less oil and natural gas are to be used, and hardly any coal. The concept includes the introduction of measures to this end, for example increasing efficiency in buildings. The political community is striving to increase the rate of energy retrofitting of buildings to 2% of all buildings per year. Taking the rates of demolition and new construction into account, energy retrofitting of all buildings would be completed in about 30 years. However, the 2% rate has not been achieved over the past ten years; the actual rate has been far below 1%. In contrast, renewable energy has been expanded considerably.

The goal of more electromobility has not been reached, either; the aim was to enable independence from oil in the transportation sector by using environmentally friendly electricity. The number of electric vehicles is still far behind the political expectations, partly owing to problems with batteries and with the expansion of the rail network. Nonetheless, the political community is pursuing these goals with appropriate means, for example by increasing funding for research on batteries in recent years.

The increasing stringency of the requirements of the German

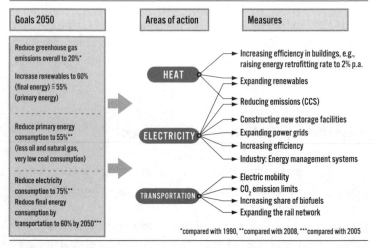

Fig. 4: The German federal government's energy concept

Thermal Insulation Ordinance for new buildings and buildings with substantial renovations is a step toward reducing CO_2 emissions. For example, it includes equipping buildings with solar collectors and/or heat pumps.

Renewables – significant progress

Particularly since 2010, renewables have been expanded in the form of solar and wind-powered electricity generation in Germany and worldwide. Nonetheless, one must take into account that these sources still make up only less than 5.5% of total electricity generation.

Figures 5 (photovoltaics; Germany and worldwide) and Table 3 (wind power; worldwide) show the currently available figures. For reasons of comparability, the output of photovoltaic systems is set in relation to a certain solar radiation value and a certain

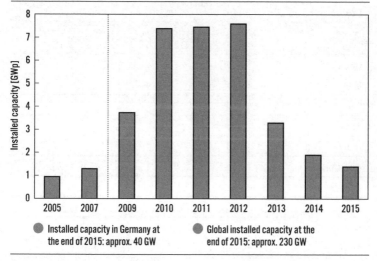

Fig. 5: Expansion of photovoltaics in Germany and globally installed capacity at the end of 2015

temperature, or so-called peak output. In connection with the increasing share of electricity generation from renewables, the Renewable Energy Sources Act was changed several times to fulfil the political and financial conditions pertaining to the support and expansion of renewables. While German wind energy systems are sold around the world, the production capacity in Germany for photovoltaic systems has been cut back significantly. One reason for this is that new production capacities have been established with the support of government subsidies, for example in China, that were able to compete with German companies.

The price per kWh of photovoltaic electricity has dropped substantially since 2010. Depending on the size of the installation, it is now lower than 12 ct/kWh, even down to approximately 8 ct/kWh. This is a significant advantage for market introduction. Historically speaking, it was up to 45 ct/kWh in 2005.

Global wind energy use (rounded)		
	Total capacity [GW], 2015	Global share [%], 2015
China	145	34
USA	74	17
Germany	45	11
Spain	25	6
India	23	5
Great Britain	14	3
Canada	11	3
France	10	2
Italy	9	2
Brazil	9	2
Other countries	65	15
Total	430	100

Table 3: Globally installed wind energy capacity at the end of 2015

The problem of cost-effective storage of the electricity generated by wind and solar is yet to be solved.

The overview of the installed and available capacity in Germany on 18 December 2013 (Fig. 6) shows that hardly any renewables were available on the day requiring the highest power plant output, namely a good 80 GW. This means that conventional power plant capacity must still be kept available, with the costs that entails. In recent years, for example, the shorter operating time of these power plant capacities has meant that the combined cycle power plant Irsching in Bavaria, which began operation in 2011, could no longer be operated profitably since it is not yet written off. It is the power plant with the second highest efficiency in terms of electricity generation worldwide, namely 60.4%. Since the beginning

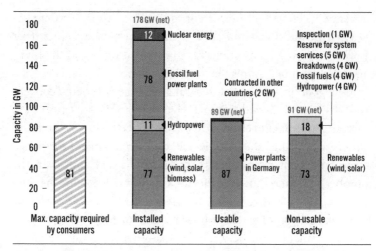

Fig. 6: Overview of the installed and available power plant capacity in Germany on 18 December 2013

of 2016 the combined cycle power plant Fortuna in Düsseldorf, Germany, has been the plant with the highest efficiency of 61.5%. Some other power plants around the world are still operating at less than 30% efficiency.

Conversely, there are summer weekends with plenty of wind and sunshine where almost all the electricity generated is from renewables. This was also the case, for example, for some hours at Christmas 2014. At the time, the provisions of the Renewable Energy Sources Act (EEG) required that the surplus electricity generated from renewables in Germany be transmitted to neighbouring countries and the recipients be paid to use the surplus electricity from Germany.

The role of new pumped-storage hydropower plants is increasingly under discussion. When wind or solar energy is over-abundant, it is used to pump water into the reservoir of such a plant; when more electricity is needed, that water is used to generate it. However, the current market prices for electricity do not permit additional profitable expansion of such capacities. That is why no permit applications have been filed for any of the envisaged new pumped-storage hydropower plants.

One goal of the German federal government's energy concept is to store surplus wind and solar electricity in the batteries of the increasing number of electric cars. Then, when little wind and sunshine are available, the batteries can discharge some of the stored electricity from renewables to the grid. To date, however, the number of battery-powered electric cars is much too low because they are too expensive.

Construction of a subsea power cable for high-voltage direct current transmission between Germany and Norway has been started in order to bring about a balance between Norwegian pumped-storage hydropower plants and German wind and solar energy. This 'NordLink' connection will have a transmission capacity of 1,400 MW (which corresponds roughly to the capacity of a nuclear power plant) and will be completed by 2019. Under average meteorological conditions, Norway produces 90% of its electricity from hydropower.

Changes in the electricity market

In 2015, renewables (wind, solar, biomass, and waste) already accounted for 30% of the electricity generated in Germany (Fig. 7). In Germany, electricity generation from waste incineration is statistically included in renewables since waste is always available anew. In 2010, just 17% of electricity was derived from renewable energy sources. The share of renewable energy is to be increased further. According to the provisions of the Renewable Energy Sources Act, green electricity is to account for 50% of electricity consumption by 2030. Offshore wind farms are to be expanded to a total of 17 GW installed capacity. For comparison: according to the German Federal Network Agency, Germany requires roughly 84 GW of secure power plant capacity plus a reserve in case of technical breakdowns on the coldest day of the year. The expansion of solar and wind energy is limited to a certain amount per year to cap the financial burden on consumers. The goal for photovoltaics is 2.5 GW/a. At its peak in 2012 and 2013, it was 7 GW/a.

In addition, new underlying conditions have been created for marketing so-called green electricity. Producers with new installations of a certain output can market the electricity themselves. There were attempts to determine the total amount of the feed-in compensation for new wind turbines through a competitive procedure during 2017. This has already been the case for new larger photovoltaic installations since 2015. While in the past, the additional costs for renewables had to be paid mostly by private consumers and smaller businesses, a change was introduced which

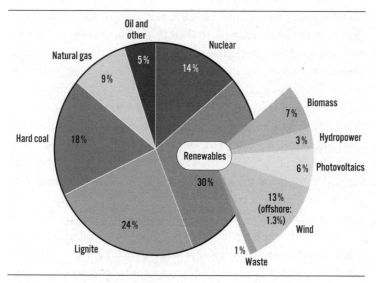

Fig. 7: Electricity generation in Germany, 2015

means that larger companies must also bear a certain part of the Renewable Energy Sources Act surcharge. This includes Deutsche Bahn, the German rail service, so train passengers are now making a small contribution toward the expansion of renewables by purchasing tickets.

The relevant provisions of the Renewable Energy Sources Act must be harmonised with the EU. The 2017 version was approved in October 2016 and focuses, among other topics, on more market economy aspects for renewables.

Furthermore, the increasing introduction of photovoltaics in rural areas, especially in Bavaria, means that in sunny weather the transmission capacities of the electric grids are not sufficient to transport the photovoltaic electricity. For this reason, a programme was introduced to fund battery storage devices that can store the electricity from renewables for several hours before discharging it to the grid.

Because of the increasing share of renewables and their priority, conventional power plants have been retrofitted so that it is possible to make larger changes to their level of output more quickly.

Since wind energy will increasingly be concentrated on offshore plants in the future and nuclear power plants in Southern Germany will be decomissioned, it will be necessary to build new high-voltage power lines in Germany in the next few years. Depending on the scenario and location of the expansion of electricity sourced from photovoltaics and wind, construction of 2,000 to 2,500 km of new high-voltage power lines along with additional strengthening and equipment for approximately 2,000 km of existing lines will be required by 2025, with priority over the construction of new lines. Because of the large distances across which electrical energy must be transported from northern to southern Germany, it will be necessary to build high-voltage direct current transmission lines to keep losses low. In late 2015, the federal government decided to lay the new lines underground to the greatest extent

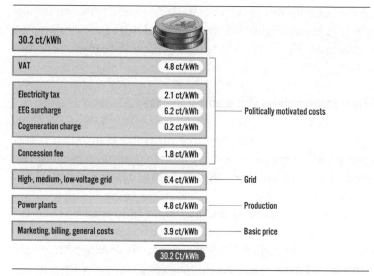

Fig. 8: Breakdown of the costs for a kilowatt-hour of electricity for a household consuming an average amount of electricity (approx. 4,000 kWh per year) (as of late 2015)

possible in order to enhance their acceptance by the population. However, this increases the costs by a factor of about three compared with overhead power lines. The first transmission routes are in the permission process.

Renewables' increasingly high share of the power plant capacity installed in the grid also means that a number of technical measures need to be taken to secure the electric grid. For example, it is necessary to guarantee electricity supply in the case of power plant failures, short circuits, etc. To this end, existing photovoltaic systems and wind turbines larger than a certain size are being retrofitted with electrotechnical equipment.

The element of private consumers' electricity bills corresponding to the Renewable Energy Sources Act (EEG) surcharge has grown significantly in recent years. It covers the costs of introducing renewables. Figure 8 shows the breakdown of costs for a typical household. The percentage of the surcharge is clearly to be seen.

Energy consumption – also an ethical question

The deliberations so far show that the global demand for energy sources will continue to exist in the future and will even grow. This fact, connected with the considerations of reaching a high global environmental standard and low greenhouse gas emissions, forms the ethical dimension of energy supply. Industrialised countries such as Germany have the advantage that many technical capabilities are available, which is not the case in less developed countries. This is also the reason given for changing German energy policy, which enjoys the support of a considerable fraction of the population. One can also observe that other countries around the globe are increasingly moving toward using renewables and saving energy because their motives to act are similar.

The largest numbers of births occur in countries that do not rank among the most highly developed countries in the world. For this reason, the industrialised countries must reflect from an ethical perspective how they can make energy supply as cheap, environmentally friendly, and climate-friendly as possible so that they can disseminate this knowledge and the corresponding technology around the world for the economic benefit of all.

The challenge of energy – using opportunities

Germany as a highly developed industrialised country and one of the technological leaders in energy production, has many opportunities and options for using energy sources, improving energy technologies, and reducing energy consumption. But it too is fully integrated into the global market since it still has to import significant amounts of fossil fuels.

Germany is pursuing a very ambitious schedule for its climate mitigation goals. Future energy supply must therefore balance the security of the energy supply, affordability, and climate-friendliness. In addition, one must take into account that such a change in energy supply across long time periods also requires acceptance and support on the part of the majority of the population.

Germany as one of the leading industrialised nations must also remain competitive in the global markets. A secure and low-cost energy supply contributes to this end.

The best energy, however, is the energy that is not needed. That is why saving energy and rational energy consumption continue to be important goals.

Supplying environmentally friendly and sustainable energy in the future remains a challenge – a challenge we cannot escape. Recent years have shown that we are well equipped to handle it.

But it must remain our priority.

The Demise of Diversity?

Josef H. Reichholf

Introduction

The passenger pigeon, the Carolina parakeet, the great auk, the dodo, and Steller's sea cow were all still thriving in the seventeenth and eighteenth century. They are no longer alive today. They were wiped out, as were numerous other animal species, and for no reason other than for greed and the thrill of shooting. No less than 130 bird and 86 mammal species or well-defined subspecies have died out since the Europeans began to sail the seven seas and conquer new (to them) continents and islands about 500 years ago. They continued the extermination of animals that other seafarers had started before them, but now on a far greater scale. Examples include the Arabs who had ravaged islands in the Indian Ocean or Polynesians when they reached New Zealand about three-quarters of a millennium ago and quickly wiped out the moas there, large ostrich-like birds. Wherever people arrived, they extinguished native species and spread whatever diseases they brought with them. This has been going on at least since the end of the last Ice Age 10 to 12 thousand years ago. Humans and nature do not seem to get along well. And the larger humanity grew and the more efficiently people intervened in nature, the more species fell victim. That is why it is justified to denote the geological era of the 'Human Age' as the Anthropocene. It signifies that humans now impact the Earth and life more strongly than natural processes such as alternating ice ages with interglacial periods, volcanic eruptions, and continental drift. Nature is exploited and changed as if it were inexhaustible and all enduring. Yet the biblical parable does not only command people to 'subdue the Earth', but also illustrates humans' expulsion from paradise as a consequence of misconduct. 'Thorns and thistles' shall the earth bring forth, and 'By the sweat of your brow you will eat your food'! The creation myths of many religions include concepts similar to Biblical ones. The so-called natural religions on the contrary already encompass the basic principle of sustainable, caring use of nature in the form of taboos and the veneration of the animals hunted and killed. This presumably developed originally as a consequence of exploitative behaviour and not as a precaution to protect nature from it.

After all, many large animal species were wiped out even in the millennia before the Europeans seized power around the globe. At first this happened unintentionally, because the Stone Age groups of hunters and gatherers, with their limited horizon, did not understand the links between population size and risk of extinction until it was too late. A new era of impacting nature on Earth began with the global expansion of the Europeans in the seventeenth and eighteenth centuries. Unbridled greed led to the unscrupulous annihilation of numerous species such as those mentioned earlier. As technology became more powerful, humans' direct dependency on nature diminished. Nature was now downgraded to a 'resource' and no longer considered the basis of life. The disconnection of humans from nature set in. We perceive 'nature' in contradistinction to us, as something external that must be kept under control so that it does not take on a free life of its own and become a threat. Nature is supposed to decorate the environment shaped by humans with pretty flowers, beautiful birds, and colourful butterflies. It is protected in special reserves. Good management is supposed to guarantee that the animals and plants there do not get out of control and potentially become pests that threaten crops or simply become 'too numerous' and therefore suspicious. We have a hard time dealing with nature, and an even harder time preserving its diversity. Yet there are many good reasons to do precisely that and to bridge the gap that has emerged between humans and nature. After all, we cannot live alone on Earth. Even with all the progress in science and technology, we remain integrated in the totality of life of the biosphere. Only slowly are we beginning to grasp how much we have in common with other forms of life. Without the bacteria that live in and on us, we would not even be able to survive.

Life on our planet exists in an immense abundance of different species, and we are only beginning to understand how great that abundance is. We know most about birds, of which there are approximately 10,000 different species. About one-fifth, almost 2,000 species, is considered to be in danger of extinction. To be precise: in danger of being wiped out, because their disappearance would not be natural extinction, which has accompanied the path on which life develops since time immemorial, but extinction caused by humans – extermination. We know quite accurately how dozens of bird species were annihilated. This was not merely a matter of remote islands species that were rare in any case, such as the dodo on Mauritius. The seafarers cruising around the southwest Indian Ocean, fetching water and hunting animals on the islands, beat the large defenceless birds to death and ate them or left them to rot when they had had enough. They also brought rats, which escaped from their ships and probably finished the dodo off.

The last dodos died out around 1690. One might attribute their annihilation to the brutal times in Europe in which tens of thousands of women were tortured and burned to death as witches, wars raged practically all the time, and many people simply struggled to survive. Such an excuse is surely inaccurate in the case of the annihilation of the passenger pigeon in the late nineteenth century. The numbers of this small North American pigeon were so large that their swarms darkened the sky when they flew around looking for forests where they could nest. Overall, they numbered in the tens or hundreds of millions. The passenger pigeon was one of the most common of all birds. And yet it was annihilated ruthlessly in a few decades by mass culling in none other than the US, at the time the up-and-coming land of unlimited opportunities. Large numbers were no insurance against greed and the thrill of shooting.

The extermination of species has been documented more precisely since about 1500. In terms of numbers, a negligible percentage of the diversity of life on Earth, of biodiversity, appears to have fallen victim to humans. After all, the losses may appear well balanced by the millions of species still living. So why should we be concerned? The answer is that we cannot bring back to life the species that were exterminated. And those currently threatened by extinction should be preserved through appropriate protective measures in their natural surroundings, perhaps in zoos and botanical gardens under the care of humans to guarantee their further existence. Two thousand species of birds that have become (too) rare and a few thousand more of mammals, frogs, lizards, fish, and other animals, as well as of the hundreds of endangered plants, cannot be too many for conservation breeding. There are numerous zoos and botanical gardens as well as organisations and private individuals who take care of rare species and keep them alive. After all, humanity's artistic treasures are also preserved in museums and countless private collections. Major ensembles are subject to protection by the state or even UNESCO as World Cultural Heritage sites. It should be possible to preserve biodiversity in the same way. One would think. But the fact that this is not the case becomes comprehensible when we examine biodiversity more closely. It consists not only of ten thousand species of birds, a little more than half as many species of mammals, and several thousand species of orchids that can be bred in greenhouses and of trees whose fruits or seeds we can easily keep stored and use as needed. Global biodiversity encompasses more, much more!

The origin and nature of biodiversity

How large is biodiversity?

The animals and plants we see in zoos and botanical gardens represent a very small selection of existing biodiversity. Even in the case of mammals and birds, which people are particularly interested in, the spectrum represented in zoos accounts for hardly more than one-tenth of all living species. We know this because practically all the existing species of mammals and birds have been documented scientifically. Real discoveries of new species have become the exception. The situation concerning insects, spiders, molluscs, and many groups of marine animals is entirely different. It takes specialists to identify them. But there is a severe lack of such specialists – and the research funding to pay them – as well as experts on lichens, fungi, and the diversity of life in soil. Species of these groups number in the millions, and we cannot estimate today how many there could be. To date, just under two million species have been scientifically documented sufficiently, i.e., verifiably in terms of their characteristics. Insects make up the greatest number of them by far. Vertebrates, which include fish, amphibians, reptiles, birds, mammals, and thus also us human beings, do not even amount to one-tenth of the diversity of beetles or one-third of that of butterflies. Mind you: of the known species. Even in these conspicuous groups of insects, new species are constantly being discovered and described.

One would think that this is good news. The abundance of living creatures is large, and there are always new forms to discover. A wonderful activity for specialists! After all, this is not about tiny little points of light far beyond our reach, as when we map the stars, but about tangible living things with different characteristics and ways of adapting to their environment. The new discoveries come from interesting regions, such as mountain forests in southwest China or the South American Andes, jungles in India, and rainforests in

Amazonia, by the Congo, and on Southeast Asian islands. Islands everywhere always prove to be particularly fruitful for discovering new species. The Southeast Asian islands exhibit biodiversity of a similarly high level as Amazonia and Central Africa with their tropical rainforests. In Europe, the islands and coasts of the Mediterranean are distinguished by their great biodiversity; in the Americas, those of the Caribbean. The most extensive island region, the Pacific islands of the South Sea, is one of the centres of biodiversity. This distribution indicates the main problem of threats to and preservation of global biodiversity. It is about the tropics and the islands. That is why we need to examine the issue more closely, particularly as we have disregarded life in the oceans so far. What is it, then, that determines the distribution and numbers of species?

How is biodiversity distributed across the globe?

Although the total amount of biodiversity is not yet known, the abundance of research from the past three centuries shows the basic patterns of its global distribution. Most species live in the tropics, to be specific, in the tropical rainforests, on tropical islands, and in the coral reefs of tropical oceans. The smallest numbers of species are to be found at the cold edges of the Polar Regions and on the high mountains. Low levels of biodiversity characterise the middle latitudes densely populated by human beings, but species numbers increase rapidly towards the tropics. Biodiversity is high in regions with geographically rich structures and many islands, as in the (European) Mediterranean. In this particular sense, the Caribbean is similar; however, it is significantly more species-rich than the European Mediterranean because it is located mostly in the tropics and its islands are larger. In other words, two factors contributing to growing biodiversity can overlap and reinforce each other, in this case islands and increasing proximity to the tropics. Large, uniform expanses in cold and temperate climate zones, in contrast, are poor in biodiversity – for example the Nordic coniferous forests, i.e., the taiga, or the high plateaus of Central Asia and the South American Andes or the vast agricultural areas of the US, Europe, and China.

This is not about value judgements, for instance that the taiga might be less important than the Amazonian rainforest. Instead, it is about the fundamental relationship between the distribution and the numbers of the diversity of life on land and in the ocean. In the global view, western and central Europe cover areas that are low in biodiversity by their nature. In Europe and northern Asia most species are very common. Is this because Europe has been subjected to agricultural production for centuries and semi-natural areas have become very scarce? The influence of land use will be discussed below. Let us first clarify why biodiversity increases as we approach the tropics and which conclusions have to be drawn from this phenomenon.

How did biodiversity arise?

Before we tackle this question, we must first clarify what 'species' are. Organisms are grouped as species if they form reproductive communities, i.e., if they mate with each other and produce offspring that are capable of doing so as well. It sounds complicated, but can easily be explained using us human beings as an example. We all belong to a species scientifically called *Homo sapiens*. *Homo* is the name of the genus of humans, a category which also includes the extinct Neanderthals and other former species of humans. *Sapiens* is the designation of the species. The goal of research is to use such distinct names to identify all kinds of animals, plants, and fungi. Based on superficial observation, humanity could be divided by appearance into a handful or more of different species. But that is not correct, as we know with a very high degree of certainty, and there is no biological justification for dividing humanity into races. There is only one human species, though it is characterised by extraordinarily large diversity. This variance resulted from prolonged isolation of tribes and groups enhanced by humans' adaptation to highly different living conditions. Human beings had understood how to live in all kinds of environments on land. The outstanding degree of all human beings' individual uniqueness is a consequence of this. For it is based on the characteristics stored in their genetic make-up and their adaptational diversity.

In general, new species emerge through isolation, especially following sufficiently large differentiation from each other. The more pronounced the isolation, the faster and stronger differences develop. In contrast, if some genetic exchange occurs time and again, then clines develop in bordering and overlapping zones. In biological terms, the results are considered to be (geographical) races, which still belong to the same species and can produce fertile offspring together. Only when this is no longer possible because the genetic differences have become too large is the state of a 'good' species attained, i.e., one that is firmly established. To summarise: Isolation and adaptation to different living conditions are the most important preconditions for the emergence of species. Isolation is mostly the result of geographical barriers such as mountains, deserts, large rivers and, in particular, islands. On islands, however, especially on small ones, living conditions are not very diverse. But when a few animals or some viable seeds of a plant species have reached an island, these 'starting populations' will by definition not comprise the entire spectrum of characteristics of the species to which they belong. They make a start and have to deal with the local conditions on the island. After just a few generations, the new island population may differ from its parent population and develop in a different direction influenced by the circumstances on the island. That happens especially quickly if no new animals or plants of the same species arrive on the island for a long time. For this reason, island populations almost always diverge to a greater or lesser extent from the original species on the mainland where they came from.

Over time, the differences become more distinct. The island population becomes a species of its own if it has been isolated long enough. Among humans, the aborigines in Australia represent the oldest population isolated from the rest of humanity. Only a good 300 years ago did they regain contact with other humans after their ancestors came to Australia from Southeast Asia 40,000 to 50,000 years ago. For us humans, such a seemingly long period of isolation was by far too short to transform the aborigines into a human species of their own. So when it comes to mammals, we must reckon with similar timeframes, and we cannot simply consider them entirely different species because of any particular striking external features. Nor can we expect that something new will develop 'soon' to replace the species that became extinct.

This glimpse at humans serves to explain that the emergence of a new species may take a very long time. Tens of thousands of years might not be enough to generate biologically significant differences. In the case of small species producing new generations in rapid succession, this might occur in a shorter period of time. In the 15 to 20 years that humans need to mature, mice can generate as many as 50 successive generations. Only animals as large as elephants develop as slowly as humans. In the case of bacteria, reproduction takes place in a matter of hours or days, provided conditions are reasonably favourable. Even pigs and horses develop more quickly than humans. So the speed of reproduction must be taken into account when assessing the period of time it takes for new species to emerge. For this reason, we cannot say that it takes 100,000 years or more simply because that was how long it took for humans to develop, or that it happens with lightning speed because that is true of bacteria. Each type of living organism has its own timescale in this respect. Thanks to modern research methods, especially in molecular genetics, we can now determine the 'age' of many species at least roughly. We assume that our species, *Homo sapiens*, separated approximately 200,000 years ago in Africa from the now long-extinct *Homo erectus*, but that the Neanderthals, *Homo neanderthalensis*, with whom our species lived together for some tens of thousands of years in Europe and the Middle East, developed as early as half a million years ago. Similar magnitudes result for the time many kinds of (larger) mammals and birds took to develop. That means that much of the biodiversity of larger animals existing today emerged during the Pleistocene. But this next-to-last period of the history of the Earth, colloquially called the Ice Age, saw cold periods, the actual ice ages, alternating with interglacial periods in which conditions were so warm that hippopotamuses lived on the Lower Rhine and in southern England, as in the last one a good 100,000 years ago.

During the roughly 2.5 million years' duration of the Pleistocene, there were four major ice ages with warm periods in between. The 'Ice Age' can be characterised as a time of strong climate fluctuations ('climate swings'). The last one ended about 12,000 to 15,000 years ago with the transition to our age, the Holocene. Since humans have left their mark on it to such an extent that it has become fundamentally different from all the other previous geologic eras, it is now called the Anthropocene, at least in its more recent part.

Now, the climate swings of the Pleistocene have special significance in terms of the Earth's biodiversity. Their effect was like a 'species pump' as cold periods with advancing ice alternated with warm periods like the present or with an even warmer climate. Why that was so becomes apparent when we view an atlas indicating ocean depths. The shelf area of the continents and islands currently extends to a depth of approximately 200 metres. Yet in times with massive glaciation, such a huge amount of water was held in the ice that the sea level had dropped by one hundred metres and more. Thus, many of today's islands were connected to the continents they are actually a part of. When the sea level rose again, they were separated from the continents once more.

These dynamics had a particularly strong impact on Southeast Asia, and most likely also on Africa and South America. Borneo, Sumatra, and other islands were not only connected to the mainland at times – as was England to Europe – but due to the major changes in temperature and precipitation in the cold and warm periods, the continents saw massive changes in the type and composition of habitats. Forests became forest islands, lakes dried out or were newly formed, the volumes and courses of rivers changed, and nature in the mountains was strongly impacted. As explained above, however, new species emerge mainly as a result of isolation. Therefore, the repeated isolation of islands and of habitats on the continents had the effect of driving the formation of species, as indicated by the term 'species pump'.

But this mechanism does not yet explain why there are so many more species in the tropics than in the temperate and cold climate zones. Understanding the reasons behind this phenomenon will prove particularly important with respect to the future of biodiversity. That is why we must again turn our attention to the ecology of the formation and preservation of species. When it comes to threats to species, their preservation, or their extinction, their actual or potential numbers are crucial.

How is biodiversity maintained?

The size of the population, i.e., the number of animals or plants belonging to a species, is decisive for survival. When the last specimen of the passenger pigeon died on 1 September, 1914, in the Cincinnati zoo, its species was already long 'dead'. Martha, as she had been named, could no longer reproduce. In terms of her species, she was akin to a living corpse. A small handful of specimens of a species are usually no longer sufficient to secure survival because they do not produce enough offspring for replacement and growth. Survival generally depends on the ratio of new offspring and deaths. Expressed in terms of generations, this is about rates: the birth rate and the death rate. Together, they yield the rate of reproduction. It must be positive across the length of the average life span otherwise the population will dwindle and die out sooner or later. If only this one population of the species in question exists, its status is called critically endangered. Minor things that would be completely unimportant for a sufficiently large population can cause sudden extinction. There is no general minimum size of a population that would guarantee its survival since the ability to reproduce varies immensely between species. In the case of animal species that (can) produce offspring only once a year and need several years to achieve sexual maturity, 500 to 1,000 individuals capable of reproduction are assumed to be the minimum. Most mammals, almost all birds, many reptiles, and some amphibians and large insects (very large beetles whose larvae take a long time to develop) belong to this group. In the case of smaller species that reproduce rapidly, even several times per year, 100 or 200 individuals are enough, but by no means in all cases. Their survival is secured only if several local populations of this minimum size exist which have at least occasional contact with each other.

That is a second important condition for survival. Most species do not live only in a single place, but in several or many places where they find suitable living conditions. Their total population is separated into local populations. If one, or some, are in trouble, but the other ones are doing better, then the losses usually balance out. Some parts of the total population generate surpluses, and others rely on being able to draw on them because their own losses are too high; such parts are called sources and sinks. The decisive balance between producing offspring and immigration on the one hand, and losses and emigration on the other, is the balance of these factors. Expressed in rates: reproduction and immigration rates must be greater than death and emigration rates. This is essential for the species to survive.

The ideal condition, with gains and losses balancing each other out perfectly, hardly ever occurs in nature; it does so only as a coincidence due to momentarily favourable conditions. Populations almost always fluctuate, and they do so around an average which expresses the existing living conditions for the species in question, which is also changing. This average is called environmental capacity. If it is high, then the species can live in large populations and easily replace major local losses. If the population is small and bound to a small area, as is the case on islands, then there is the risk of sudden extinction. Species that occur on small islands are therefore inherently more vulnerable than comparable species on continents, simply because their populations cannot grow large enough for them to survive long term. This is also true of habitat islands on the mainland as well as of real islands. Habitat islands are places in isolated locations with unique conditions different from those of their surroundings, such as smaller lakes, mountains distant from the nearest mountain ranges, or remnants of forests or steppes surrounded by intensively cultivated land. Fragmentation of special and species-rich habitats (biotopes) is playing an increasingly important role for nature conservation because the situation turns critical if habitat islands are surrounded by a vast expanse of cultivated land, a situation which cannot be overcome by the inhabitants of these habitat islands to enable them to reach other islands providing the conditions they need.

The smaller these islands, the smaller the populations of animals and plants that can live there – and the greater their danger of local extinction; that's the rule of thumb. Of the almost 2,000 globally endangered bird species, the vast majority live on islands and in the remaining fragments of their habitats on continents. And with a few exceptions, it was island species that were wiped out in the past centuries.

Conversely, almost all species occurring across large areas and in large numbers are not threatened by extinction. Almost – and this qualification must certainly be added here – because, in fact, several of these species have been wiped out in the more recent past. The worst example in this respect is the passenger pigeon mentioned above. The great auk of the North Atlantic islands and Steller's sea cow of the North Pacific were by no means few and far between. They, too, were wiped out completely. The bison of the North American prairie, the wisent of the eastern European forests, and the great whales of the seven seas only barely managed to survive. The quagga, a zebra in South Africa, did not. All rhinoceros species are in a highly precarious situation, and the same will soon be true of elephants, snow leopards, and tigers.

The four main components that determine the size of every population do not explain everything. Birth rate, death rate, immigration, and emigration occur within the scope of what is possible – the environmental capacity. But what does environmental capacity mean? By no means simply area alone, the size of a region, where the species in question can live. After all, no species, including humans, simply exists. Fundamentals for life such as food, water, places for reproduction and the like must be available. But infectious diseases, parasites, and enemies, which cause losses, are also part of the environment. More often than not, they are the main threat to the survival of small, weak populations. In larger ones, there is an additional factor limiting possible increases in numbers, namely competition with other species and with members of the same species. If several species use mostly the same resources, then each of them reduces the amounts of resources available to the other species, thus diminishing the environmental capacity available for each. The grass already eaten by buffalo cannot be used by gnus and zebras. The gazelle killed by lions or African hunting dogs can no longer be hunted by cheetahs. That is why many hunters do not want to lose any deer to predation by lynxes and wolves since they would prefer to hunt the game themselves. Yet, aside from humans as hunters, hardly any of whom depend on kill for their livelihoods today, animals' strongest foes and competitors are not other species, but members of their own species because their habitat needs are fundamentally the same. Therefore, competition between and within species creates additional limitations on the growth and size of a population. Interspecies competition determines the amount of environmental capacity, intraspecies competition the extent of emigration necessary.

All this is decisive for life and survival, but also mirrors the reasons why biodiversity came about. The 'paradox of tropical biodiversity' is an illuminating example. As already emphasised, the greatest diversity of species by far exists in the tropical rainforests and on tropical islands and coral reefs. Even though space is a very important factor for biodiversity, diversity increases by much more than can be attributed to the amount of space available. Habitat always means two- or three-dimensional space. Neither can be reduced indefinitely. As with population size, if the size of a habitat falls below certain marginal dimensions, then more and more species will disappear at an increasing pace. Size matters, as is rightly said in international conservation. But not size alone. How else could Costa Rica, which is only about two-thirds the size of Bavaria, boast more bird species and many more butterfly spieces than the entire North American continent? Roughly one in five of all bird species on Earth lives in Amazonia. Perhaps more than half of all insect species live in the South American rainforest alone. In light of the still existing gaps in our knowledge of global species richness, we can only speculate about the state of many groups of animals and about how much is lost as the tropical forests are annihilated. The plant kingdom, which we know relatively well, and for which we assume a good 300,000 species (excluding algae and the like), reaches peak values of biodiversity of several hundred tree species per hectare in Amazonia. The Southeast Asian islands are similarly species-rich.

Amazonia and Southeast Asia are located geographically in the inner, humid tropics and are by nature covered with tropical rainforest, as is the Congo Basin in Africa. This type of forest has existed for millions of years. Yet it has changed over time; today, there are vast expanses in Amazonia and the Congo Basin, and it is spread across islands in Southeast Asia. During the cold periods of the Ice Age, the sea level dropped, and precipitation declined. Many special features of the Amazonian species indicate that they emerged when habitats were fragmented. They form an enormous mosaic of adjacent areas, and many do not overlap, just as populations on different islands cannot overlap.

Now, populations on islands are small by nature if the island is not large. The same is true of populations in mountain valleys and at various altitudes on mountain slopes.

The more difficult it is to exchange with other populations, the more quickly individual species develop from deviations and special adaptation. Amazonia's history practically mirrored that of Southeast Asia. When connections to the mainland existed because the sea level had plummeted and Borneo, Sumatra, and other islands of the continental shelf had become part of Southeast Asia, there was a lack of precipitation in Amazonia, the mouth of the Amazon was lower, there was less river flooding, and the forests became fragmented. In the tens of thousands of years when these conditions persisted, differences developed in the isolated populations that acted either as subspecies (geographical races) or, in the case of repeated and longer isolation, as real species when encountering others later on.

Now, the climate dynamics of the ice ages affected the entire globe. Yet they had different effects in different places. The availability of minerals required for plant growth is the main factor explaining those differences. Amazonian soils are extremely poor in nutrients essential for plants, so poor that most of the Amazonian rainforest literally lives from the air, namely on the dusts transported from the Sahara across the south Atlantic by the trade winds. These dusts met the rainforest's mineral requirements and compensate for losses. In the ecological sense, the rainforest is a very tightly closed circulation system from which only very small amounts of plant nutrients leak out. They are available in much greater abundance in the Congo Basin to support plant growth. Winds transport minerals directly to the forest from the Sahara and the high plateaus and volcanoes of East Africa. In any case, volcanic soils are much more fertile than those in the Amazon that have been weathered and leached out for millions of years. The soils in Southeast Asia are particularly diverse. For thousands of years, a large human population has thrived on volcanic soils like those in Java, where high yields can be achieved without degrading the soil. The same is true in parts of China with fertile loessic soils and the soils washed ashore by the large rivers flowing down from the Himalayas. Below, the links between nutrient richness and bio-diversity will be explained as they apply in Europe, where we know far more about the soils, but still do not use them sustainably.

Where life-supporting resources are scarce, the populations using them cannot grow large. This is the most important fact concerning the future of species.

It explains a paradox: the extremely species-rich Amazonian rainforest, which looks so abundant, is so poor in animals that one might think they had all been mostly wiped out – except for ants and termites. But even if this is certainly true of jaguars and in large areas for caimans, it is not the case across the board. In fact, the overwhelming majority of the rain forest species are rare. How could it be otherwise if there are hundreds of different tree species per square kilometre? It would be impossible for any single species to be as common as spruces and pines or beeches and oaks in the northern hemisphere.

As early as the mid-nineteenth century, naturalists found that it was often easier to collect a dozen different species of butterflies in Amazonia than ten specimens of the same species. The reason for this shortage is the scarcity that is prevalent but concealed by the sheer plant mass of the forest. This plant mass generates no, or only little, surplus. The rainforest sustains itself by means of a circular economy with few losses; the same model is frequently promoted as the goal of sustainable economic activity. It is driven by the two actually super-abundant resources: water and solar energy. What is built up by photosynthesis in the annual cycle is used up again by degradation processes during the same period. In this mature natural state, the tropical forest does not grow any more. The many animals and plants living in it must remain rare. None of the species involved can become so common that it would crowd out others. Rarity means weak power to compete, but also protection. This diversity emerged through isolation. It stabilised by developing a large number of different, special adaptations and characteristics, as shown by orchids, the most species-rich plant family, which adapted to very specific pollinators and thus became more and more specialised.

Scarcity generated biodiversity, and it is scarcity that maintains it and distinguishes it from the conditions we are familiar with in Europe, North America, and East Asia, where far fewer species live, but mostly in large, vital populations.

Preserving biodiversity

The global threat

As pointed out above, biodiversity increases from the poles to the tropics. On land, it is the tropical forests where most species live; at sea, it is the tropical coral reefs. The greatest efforts toward preserving biodiversity must target these large regions as they are precisely the ones that are under extreme threat today. Tropical forests are currently being cut down on a practically unimaginable scale for oil palm plantations, soybean fields, or cattle grazing lands, or simply by overexploitation of valuable timber.

In Brazil alone, about 156,000 square kilometres of rainforest were lost between 2002 and 2012, and in 15 years, an area roughly the size of Germany. The products grown where the forest was cleared are marketed globally, and only a very small fraction remained for the poor rural people. The annual rates of destruction of the tropical forest reflect the fluctuating global prices for palm oil, soybeans, and beef. Destruction of the forest does not combat global hunger, but instead supports the production of surpluses in the rich industrialised countries whose highly subsidised agriculture not only competes massively with the poor in tropical countries, but also makes its own energy footprint appear smaller by externalising the primary production of animal feed, including its consequences for the global climate. Stabled livestock in Europe, and specifically in Germany, which produces the highest amount of meat per square kilometre of agricultural land, is therefore continually devouring diversity of life in the tropics. Since the end of direct colonialism, the industrial societies have continued to exploit the tropics in a colonialist way, and China, which is quantitatively highly significant, has joined them in doing so. As the country with the largest population – at the time of writing almost one and a half billion people – this giant carries special weight globally.

Current exploitation does not affect just the tropical forests. What is happening in the oceans is less visible and more difficult to document with satellite images. Overfishing impacts all parts of the oceans, but it too has particularly strong effects on the tropical oceans with coral reefs because the fish stocks there recover from disturbances much more slowly than in nutrient-rich, cold marine areas. In this respect, oceans and soils are similar. In the tropics, soils tend to lose their fertility rapidly because the layers of humus are thin, which makes sustainable use thereof difficult or impossible. Most tropical waters are also nutrient-poor and therefore particularly susceptible to overuse. Rare, highly specialised species on the coral reefs quickly become threatened by extinction. The example of the great whales shows how swiftly that can happen. A century ago, their situation was dire, and despite their being protected, several species are still struggling to survive, one reason being that human fishing is depleting the stocks which make up their food basis.

Connecting tropical and cold marine areas up to the edge of the polar ice as they wander, whales indicate that the non-tropical regions of the oceans are by no means on the safe side. Because of their higher productivity, they are hunted and exploited to an even greater degree than in the usually meagre tropical waters. This has consequences for the entire living environment in the oceans and on the coasts because birds such as the penguins of the Antarctic waters and the auks in the Arctic as well as many other animals also depend on finding and catching sufficient food. Again, the situation on land is similar. Many migratory birds rely on sufficient food being available, both in the breeding habitats – for example in our mid-latitude forests with their temperate climate and in the Nordic forests – and at resting places on their migration to the often tropical and subtropical wintering grounds, to feed their young. For instance, if there are not enough insects for our swallows there, then our protection for swallows will have little effect. And vice versa. If, as is currently the case, the numbers of pairs of most European and North American songbirds that spend winter in the tropics are decreasing, then this is not necessarily due to the tropics and the shrinking forests there. The cause may also be steep declines in the abundance of insects in the breeding areas. As is the case in Germany.

Regional threats: Germany as an example
Of the roughly 60,000 different animal and plant species occurring in Germany, stocks of at least half are declining and must be classified in the various categories of Red Lists. Up to 10% of species can be considered to be in acute danger of extinction, i.e., they

will no longer occur in Germany in the near future if the current situation continues. The extent of vulnerability differs by region. For example, the former Iron Curtain, the border running across Europe between the former East Bloc and the West, is still clearly visible in the sense of the distribution and numbers of endangered animal and plant species: more and better-protected stocks of rare species live in former East Germany than in former West Germany. The same is true along Austria's eastern border and less distinctly, but still clearly enough, between Bavaria and Austria.

The reason is the intensity of land use, which is the main threat to biodiversity in Central Europe. The decisive factor here is over-fertilisation. As already explained in the global context, scarcity and diversity go together. In the presence of an overabundance of nutrients, just a few species benefit and prosper. The large major-ity, however, fall by the wayside because they are too sensitive, too weak, and not adapted to the overabundance, unable to hold their ground against their competitors. It simply demonstrates a general principle: where nature is highly productive, it is species-poor. But that is precisely what agriculture seeks to achieve with massive fer-tilisation. It promotes crops and only crops. Corn, for example, is to grow from a small kernel to a huge plant two and a half to three metres high in a brief season of less than half a year in order to produce a maximum yield. Any competition developing in the realm of weeds is annihilated by massive use of poison. Invasive species multiply anyplace untouched by the poison because agri-culture has literally prepared fertile soil for them. They are then considered 'bad' species that crowd out the 'good' native ones. Yet they are doing exactly what crop weeds used to do; they had benefited from the new type of habitat in the fields and meadows before poison and modern tillage had, by and large, eliminated them. Now they enjoy protection as wild herbs, with millions invested in preserving them. Invasive species are the work of humans and not simply bad species because they benefit from the conditions created in our times. That is the principle. Biodiversity falls victim to land use, to over-fertilisation, poison, and large-scale operations that leave less and less land unused. That is why the big losers are the species of the open fields. Larks no longer sing in many places. Hares have become rare, butterflies fluttering above an abundance of colourful flowers are a thing of the past. And since agricultural land takes up approximately 55% of Germany's land area, the demise of biodiversity in the open fields weighs especially heavily on the overall figures. They would be even worse if not for a certain balance in a habitat that initially was not considered one for animal and plant species at all, but seemed reserved for human beings, namely the city. So many animal and plant species (this means those growing wild, not those planted!) live in the settled areas that take up approximately 10% of Central Europe's land area that major cities such as Berlin, Vienna, Hamburg, Cologne, and Munich would certainly qualify as nature reserves in terms of bio-diversity. For in contrast to open fields, they are rich in structures (biotopes), diverse in small areas, not fertilised, or only slightly burdened with plant nutrients. In addition, the animals are not hunted. Many species that are skittish in the wild are less so in the city and get along well with the world of human beings – because we let them.

In this respect, trees growing in the (big) cities are even doing better than in forests because in the wild they are used almost exclu-sively for producing wood and cannot simply grow undisturbed in urban parks. Urban water bodies are also subject to less usage (and disturbance) than the lakes and rivers in the 'great outdoors'.

The development of water bodies in recent decades points to the improvements made in agriculture. Lakes and rivers were at one time severely polluted with wastewater, however, since the 1970s, many billions have been spent on making bodies of water cleaner again. Regeneration consequently began, as did the rena-turation of watercourses. Wastewater from human activities is treated effectively in powerful sewage plants, and we pay high fees for this service. The open fields, however, are in dire need of similar treatment and cleansing. They are over-fertilised and polluted by poisons that percolate down to the groundwater, making it difficult and extremely expensive to supply clean drinking water. If we want to achieve a sustainable circular economy, then the amount of fertilisers applied to the fields must not be greater than the amount of nutrients removed through harvesting. Because of existing over-fertilisation, it would be necessary to refrain from fertilising entirely for years, if not decades, to reach balanced conditions that no longer pollute the groundwater and the environment. Then biodiversity would develop again by itself in the environment, and agriculture would have become sustainable as was called for at the 1992 Rio Earth Summit.

Germany, of all countries, is far away from sustainable use that preserves biodiversity; the actions of its former environment minister Klaus Töpfer had been decisive in bringing about the Rio Earth Summit and he had left his mark on its outcome. The fact that Germany's stabled livestock feeds on tropical biodiversity also means that we are wiping out species that we do not even know of yet. We can only speculate about the numbers of such species. We are willing to spend more on mapping the stars in the heavens than on preserving living creatures on Earth. Actually, Germany would have to export the amounts of wastewater (= slurry) that correspond to the imported masses of feed and oil palm products back to their areas of origin to achieve a global balance. Or – better – Germany should manage its economic activity in line with its ecosystem productivity and without such imports, which would certainly be the only strategy sustainable long term. Treatment of wastewater from human activities has shown the way. Agriculture produces three times that amount of slurry, and it floods the land year by year, yet it remains exempt from the wastewater laws. Like much else in agriculture. Which makes agriculture the main global as well as national exterminator of biodiversity and one of the main sources of air and climate pollutants. The unjustified and dangerous exemption of agriculture from environmental standards, which are otherwise so high in Germany and improving internationally, is the Achilles heel of environmental and conservation policy. Climate changes will not be able to shift or annihilate much more biodiversity here if they have the prognosticated impacts, because the majority of species will have been wiped out by agriculture long before – and also by the energy sector owing to its highly intensive biomass production on open fields, this being coupled with agriculture.

Encouraging prospects

Preserving the biodiversity of known species that still exists is not impossible or unrealistic. This optimistic assessment is justified by positive developments which species protection can point to as great national and international successes. For example, the number of species whose extinction has been proven has been declining for decades. Elaborate species protection programmes are securing the survival of the most severely endangered species, such as the Californian and the Andean condor and the unassuming Seychelles brush warbler. The giant panda has not become extinct in the wild because China is making intensive efforts to preserve it. The newest figures for the tiger showing a slight positive trend provide reason to hope that the Asian tiger will survive, as did the lion in Africa, and will not follow the path of the sabertooth tiger into the world of fossils. Measures are being taken against poaching, even if the situation of rhinoceroses in Africa is dire and they can only be rescued in captivity until the time when the black market in their pulverised horns no longer yields profits. Germany, too, is also home to major successes in species protection. For example, efforts to protect the golden eagle and the white-tailed eagle, the peregrine falcon and the goshawk from hunting and pursuit have been successful across most of Europe. Germany now has almost a thousand breeding pairs, making it one of the white-tailed eagle's most important breeding habitats across its entire geographic range. The populations of cranes have grown almost tenfold compared with the days preceding World War II. The black stork, the peregrine falcon, which was almost extinct, and several other large bird and mammal species are seeing positive developments. But the greatest success story in Europe is the return of the beaver. Its numbers are now larger than they have been for half a millennium.

Common to all these species is that they are minimally, or no longer, hunted and pursued. As a result, they have become less timid, which means that they can now also live and successfully reproduce in places where living conditions permit, but which their previous timidity had led them to avoid. For example, bee-eaters effected a comeback when they were no longer considered a danger to bees. The great white egret, which was almost wiped out a century ago because ladies loved decorating their hats with their courtship plumes, is doing even better. Otters, and even wolves, which were both almost gone in Central Europe through the late twentieth century, have also returned. The fact that wolves are living in Germany again and that the human population is getting accustomed to their existence is an expression of the fact that biodiversity certainly does have chances for survival, despite all the problems and hostile opposition. Biodiversity has a future. But people have to want it.

Why protect species?

Many reasons have been put forward to support protecting species, and only a few oppose it. The greatest misunderstanding is linking extinction due to human activities with natural extinction. Indeed, practically all species that ever lived succumbed to natural extinction; estimates speak of 95 to 99%. Yet this natural extinction occurred in the background, simultaneously with the emergence of new species, in time periods ranging from tens to hundreds of thousands of years. The result was a turnover of species keeping up the diversity of life or – very slowly – redeveloping it after truly catastrophic extinctions such as the one killing off the dinosaurs almost 66 million years ago. Several catastrophes of this kind took place in the history of the Earth, some or most of which were triggered by huge meteorite impacts or gigantic volcano eruptions. What is new, entirely new, about the current extinction, which many scientists call the sixth great extinction, is that it is not caused by a natural disaster, but by humans. We do not know how rapidly extinction is occurring in our time because hardly any thorough studies were conducted on the species-rich areas before their recent devastation. That is why estimates range from dozens of species being wiped out per year to tens of thousands. The numbers depend on which probable total number of still existing species is used as a benchmark. Now, is that really so dramatic in light of the (many) millions of species? Do we need all those critters? Wouldn't it be good enough if some of them, a representative sample, survived? If so, which ones? Which are the 'good ones' to be transported to the future as if in a new Noah's Ark, and which will be downgraded to 'life unworthy of life'?

Humankind should do everything in its power to renounce such differentiations, bearing in mind the events in Europe in the first half of the twentieth century and in numerous ethnic wars and attempts at annihilation which have taken place since then and to this day. Yet the question as to the 'value' of species somehow seems justified; after all, substantial utility is gained from a large number of animals, plants, and microbes. That is why the utility argument is usually the first reason given as to why we should preserve biodiversity. We should seek to preserve the Earth's treasure trove of species as completely as possible because we do not know in the here and now what this diversity is good for, and even less what it might be used for in the future. After all, species are carriers of genetic information having to do with problems of life and survival. For a long time, we have been using the capabilities of bacteria and yeasts to produce bread (e.g., sourdough bacteria), wine and beer, and other products of alcoholic fermentation, to make cheese and yogurt out of milk, and to treat injuries and illnesses with antibiotics. Countless plant materials and animal products are used in medicine, and new remedies and ways of using them are constantly being discovered. When it is brutal and behind the times, utility is also the target of controversy: for example, when people aim to outlaw extracting bile from living bears or grossly exaggerated forms of fattening animals that do not fulfil even minimum standards of animal welfare. Utility can also refer to beauty: for example, plants bred for this purpose and grown in gardens and greenhouses, or animals that become economic quantities because millions of people enjoy observing them. This includes nature tourism, which many national parks and other protected areas have to thank for their designation. Recreational value is almost always much higher in the medium and long term than the direct use of animals or forests, which yield short-term profit, but also death and destruction.

This utility argument also applies – or would also apply – to the genetic resources inherent in species; the possibilities they hold can hardly be imagined today, while genetic engineering is already being vehemently opposed. Here, nature conservation finds itself in a dilemma. Calling for the preservation of species, especially the small, unremarkable, and apparently useless ones, but rejecting the exploitation of their genetic resources, is not helpful for either side of the argument.

That is why the 'ecological argument' is almost always put forward instead: because of its very existence, every species has a function in the ecosystem. The vast majority of functions are still unknown, and for this reason, we should at all costs avoid losing potentially important parts of the fabric out of ignorance and superficiality. What is certain is that keystone species exist which actually and undoubtedly play very important roles in the ecological processes, such as earthworms for the fertility of the soil and bees, both wild bees and honeybees, for pollinating a very large number of flowering plants, or root fungi that live in symbiosis with trees, supporting their growth or making it possible in the first place. In light of the thousands upon thousands of species interacting in forests, water bodies, and even in urban nature, even the most powerful computers fail to accurately valuate the importance of the species involved.

Finally, a third main argument is about the higher level of responsibility toward other people and future generations. According to this view, we have no right to annihilate species for the sake of a short-term personal advantage. Instead, we have the duty to leave the Earth and all life on Earth to future generations in the best condition possible and without losses. Consequently, we must bring our actions in line with an orientation toward the future and across generations. This imperative of responsibility was and is a central concern of most religions and is a part of general ethics, as expressed by Albert Schweitzer's call for 'respect for life!' But today, particularly the well-off part of humankind, which is doing better than ever before, is acting in anything but a responsible and reverential way, but selfishly and short-sightedly. That is why we must fear that the sixth great extinction will occur.

Bibliography

Kolbert, E. (2014), The Sixth Extinction: An Unnatural History. New York: Henry Holt and Company.
Pearce, F. (2015), The New Wild: Why Invasive Species will be Nature's Salvation. Boston: Beacon Press.

Reichholf, J. H. (2009), The Demise of Diversity: Loss and Extinction. London: Haus Publishing.

Wilson, E. O. (1992), The Diversity of Life. Cambridge, Mass.: Belknap Press of Harvard University Press.

The New Plagues: Pandemics and Poverty in a Globalised World

Stefan H.E. Kaufmann

It is the microbes that will have the last word.

Louis Pasteur, 1822–1895

Introduction: new names, old problems – and a new perspective

Ebola, MERS, Zika: infectious diseases have plagued the global community in recent years multiple times – and this is not surprising. Some outbreaks commanded headlines for a longer period of time; others spread under the radar even of some health experts. Almost a decade has passed since the book *The New Plagues: Pandemics and Poverty in a Globalised World* was published. Looking back on the years that have passed since then, we can report positive developments for some diseases, but for others setbacks and changes for the worse. Drug-resistant problematic pathogens are causing increasing concern. For example, it is practically impossible to successfully treat extremely resistant tuberculosis (TB) in tens of thousands of patients. Drug-resistant nosocomial pathogens are causing serious infections more and more often, endangering the success of routine procedures in clinics.

Beyond these diagnoses of individual parts of the problem, the perspective on epidemics and their control has changed: today, the health-care sector is increasingly being viewed in economic terms and in the complex contexts of our networked world (see Fig. 1). For parallel to handling the global financial crisis and the crisis of the euro with their systemic risks, contagion scenarios,

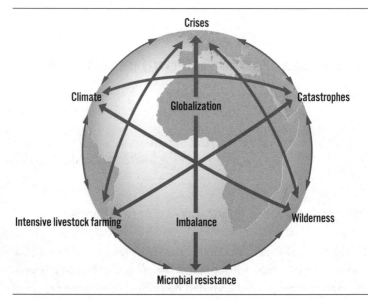

Fig. 1: The strong interlinkages between the various hot spots for new and existing pandemics are illustrated. The cornerstones are the hot spots of climate, crises, catastrophes, wilderness, microbial resistance, and intensive livestock farming, all of which are interlinked with one another. Increasing globalisation and urbanisation in the face of existing inequality and poverty serve to intensify the problems.

and domino effects, a similar type of risk analysis and assessment has become increasingly common for global disease outbreaks and their prevention. The Ebola crisis of 2014/15 induced a number of international organisations and coalitions, which had previously not been primarily concerned with health, to take up the topic: the World Bank (whose goal is to combat poverty by promoting economic development), the Organisation for Economic Co-operation and Development (OECD), the G7 as the association of the seven leading industrialised countries, the broader G20, and the World Economic Forum in Davos. These organisations generally cooperate with the World Health Organisation (WHO).

All analysts of the economic organisations are working against a background of the same basic assumption: the risk of a disease spreading quickly across many countries and continents is increasing. That is why the central goal is to find paths for reducing the risk of such a pandemic. It is generally agreed that an outbreak would not only be catastrophic for the poorer countries, but that it could also plunge emerging economies and industrialised nations into a serious crisis.

In the course of the expert groups' work, the costs of a disease outbreak were systematically calculated at the global scale. They included not only the direct health-care costs such as expenditures for medications, vaccines, and patient care, but also indirect losses due to absence from work, missing educational time, and lost years of life or early deaths. Disease-related drops in wholesaling and retailing, air travel, and tourism were added as well. All the new analyses come to the same conclusion: we simply cannot afford to ignore the risk of global pandemics. Active prevention is the most cost-effective way to intervene, not least from an economic perspective.

Let us look at the numbers: according to World Bank calculations, disease outbreaks cost the global community an average of 30 billion US dollars year on year. The figure given in other reports is twice that amount. The economic losses due to the SARS virus outbreak in 2003 alone, which was less severe than expected, are estimated at 54 billion US dollars. An outbreak of an influenza pandemic on the scale of the 1918/1919 Spanish flu (which claimed more than 50 million lives, with a global population of less than two billion at the time) would today induce more than 55 times the costs for SARS, the report says. The direct economic losses in such a scenario are calculated at four trillion US dollars. Gross world product would nosedive by almost 5%.

So how can the risk of pandemics be reduced in a globalised world? Strategic countermeasures have centred around the One Health approach, which aims to have human and veterinary medicine collaborate more closely. This is advisable for multiple reasons: today, more than 70% of all new human pathogens originate from animals. These microorganisms overcome the boundaries of species in the wild or in high-density urban spaces. At the same time, such pathogens can spread more and more swiftly in our increasingly interconnected world with its rapid urbanisation.

First, a number of minimum requirements were compiled. They are to be implemented by all countries of the world – whether rich or poor – and especially by crisis-ridden countries.

Minimum requirements for containing disease
- Equip countries with well-run clinics and implement adequate hygiene standards
- Secure functioning basic health services
- Create global organisations for fighting pathogens without borders
- Establish global monitoring structures that quickly identify new hot spots before a local outbreak develops into an epidemic, to the extent possible
- Establish an international centre for global emergency measures that guarantees effective interventions in dangerous situations
- Strengthen research and development for new medications, vaccines, diagnostics, medical devices, and equipment for protecting against infection

---

Another global health hazard is 'bad bugs' which antibiotics are hardly able or no longer able to fight. The danger posed by pathogens resistant to antibiotics continues to be underestimated by the general public. One reason is that the problem has been slowly getting worse over many years and that people seem to feel that antibiotics have somehow always been around and been effective. Infectious diseases that break out suddenly attract much more attention than well-known ones. Yet resistance is a serious threat for all people in developing, threshold, and industrialised countries.

New calculations also demonstrate the enormous financial dimension of antimicrobial resistance (AMR): the working group 'AMR Review', appointed by the British government, arrived at disturbing results. Significantly, a prominent economist was the chairperson of the working group: Jim O'Neill, former Chief Economist of the investment banking group Goldman Sachs. The working group's conclusions: if the increasing trend of antibiotic resistance were to continue unchecked, then in 2050, ten million people worldwide would die every year of infections that could no longer be treated. 390,000 of these deaths would occur in Western Europe alone.

The costs amount to losses of up to 210 trillion US dollars over the next 35 years. If we do not succeed in limiting the causes of the unchecked increase in drug resistance without simultaneously developing effective new antibiotics, then up to 7% of global gross domestic product could be lost by 2050. The costs arise from the consequences of resistant tuberculosis, resistant malaria, and resistant strains of the human immunodeficiency virus (HIV), as well as an increase in infections with resistant pathogens affecting patients undergoing routine operations, immunocompromised cancer patients, and organ transplant recipients.

Most importantly, the 'AMR Review' calls for the establishment of an innovation fund that secures long-term financing for research and development of new antibiotics, as well as alternative and complementary interventions such as vaccines and rapid diagnosis. It also calls for a global surveillance system for the development of drug resistance.

In the following, I discuss selected infectious diseases and problems stemming from microbes separately, and perform a reality check on the scenarios developed in the book *The New Plagues: Pandemics and Poverty in a Globalised World* using the knowledge available today. The purpose is to depict a brief, up-to-date status quo. It will refer in part to the United Nations Sustainable

Development Goals. After the time horizon of the Millennium Development Goals had been reached in 2015, their implementation was evaluated, and new goals – the Sustainable Development Goals – were formulated for the period until 2030. Some of them refer to the health issues relevant here.

Old pandemics in the new millennium

The HIV/AIDS pandemic: reined in, with localised exceptions

The immunodeficiency disease AIDS (acquired immunodeficiency syndrome) remains *the* tragic pandemic of the late twentieth century. Roughly 37 million people live with HIV, the virus that brings on AIDS, today. Many hundreds of thousands of people get infected with it every year, two million in 2014.

A closer examination of the numbers reveals three trends; we are far from having a handle on the disease. Globally speaking, however, we can report a positive development. The pandemic has been stopped, and its spreading has been slowed. Unfortunately, this is not true of Europe; infection rates are increasing in particular in Eastern Europe in the states of the former Soviet Union.

Let us take a look at the details: the total number of new HIV infections has dropped by one-third since the turn of the millennium (2000: 3.1 million, 2014: 2 million). The decline was even greater among children, namely by 58%. The global death rates have decreased sharply since their high point in 2004 (2004: 2 million deaths, 2014: 1.2 million). A more detailed breakdown of the numbers reveals that this is not true of two regions: North Africa with the Middle East and Eastern Europe with Central Asia. Let us turn to Europe and its neighbours; Eastern Europe and Russia in particular have seen a significant increase in HIV infections over the past 15 years. The WHO defines 53 countries as the European region, including the states of the former Soviet Union.

According to the WHO, up to 2.5 million people in the region lived with HIV in 2014 (only half of them being aware that they were infected). Over the course of the year, 140,000 people contracted the virus, more than half of them in Russia. There is no reason for complacency even in Germany, where more than 80,000 people are currently living with HIV. There were more than 3,500 new cases in 2014; thus, the rate of new infections is rising again in Germany, too.

We now have extensive knowledge about HIV/AIDS: never before has so much expertise been gathered in so little time about an individual pathogen and the syndrome it causes. With more than 30 approved medications available, AIDS can in principle be treated successfully today, but it is still incurable.

Antiretroviral combination therapy (ART), i.e., therapy with a combination of medications complementing each other, is becoming more widely available. The WHO recommends that all patients infected with HIV should now receive this therapy. We are approaching this goal, but are still far from reaching it: just under 17 million people received this effective therapy in 2015 (more than three-quarters of all infected pregnant women, just under half of the children affected, and 46% of infected adults). As late as 2000, this medication was not available to even one per cent of the people affected in poorer countries. Since the introduction of the first ART medications in 1995, roughly eight million human lives have been saved. Yet 22 million people – in other words, the majority of people infected – must manage without ART.

There is still no medication to cure HIV/AIDS and no vaccine that could prevent HIV infection. However, lifelong therapy puts enormous pressure on the pathogen to become resistant. Research has produced a number of promising findings in recent years. Among other things, it was shown that extremely early HIV therapy can eliminate the virus. For this to happen, therapy must begin immediately following infection, or better yet, preventively *before* a possible infection occurs. Approaches like this must definitely be pursued – above all because they help us gain a better understanding of the mechanism of action and open up new strategies for eliminating the virus with medications. Research into vaccines must also be actively advanced despite numerous setbacks. For only if we have an effective vaccine will there be a real hope for wiping out this pandemic or at least curbing it significantly.

If we review the data with respect to the United Nations Sustainable Development Goals, we can check some items off the list – namely the Millennium Development Goals that were in place through 2015: cases of illness and deaths were lowered significantly. Increasing numbers of people are receiving therapy. The new Sustainable Development Goals are somewhat more ambitious, but also quite vague: the goal is to 'end' the AIDS epidemic (better: pandemic) by 2030. If that is to mean eliminating it, then with a global population of an estimated 8.5 billion people in 2030, only 8,500 people per year would contract HIV per year if an incidence of less than one newly infected person per million is to be reached. The WHO did not set the bar quite so high. It aims to reduce deaths from currently roughly 1.2 million per year to 200,000 in 2030.

Tuberculosis: a serious pandemic faced with the problem of resistance

We must continue to focus all our attention on TB. It is the most persistent pandemic in the world, and the findings and data of recent years form a very mixed image overall. First the positive findings: the UN Millennium Development Goals were reached for TB, too. The spreading of the disease was not just stopped; its incidence was pushed back by almost half between 1995 and 2015.

But these figures do not reflect the entire truth. The number of deaths has recently increased. In 2015, the TB pathogen again received the inglorious distinction of being 'the number one killer'. 1.8 million people died of TB in 2015; no other pathogen was responsible for more deaths. The fraction of infected people among the global population has remained constant at almost one-third: roughly two billion people carry the germ, whereby the illness breaks out in only about one in ten infected people. The others remain healthy because their immune system successfully keeps the pathogen in check. However, if people are also infected with HIV, their immune response collapses. People infected with HIV have a ten times higher probability of TB breaking out than people without HIV. 15 million people around the world are affected by the dangerous co-infection. As a result, TB remains the most common cause of death among people with HIV.

It was true for a long time that it was HIV that enabled the resurgence of the 'white plague'. But by now, TB is taking on a life of its own again since hardly any effective protection exists against coughing family members and neighbours. It remains to be seen to what extent current crises will also impact pandemics. The millions of refugees are more highly susceptible to TB. The bacterium can spread easily in overcrowded camps and emergency shelters. Adequate treatment is barely possible considering the long period of therapy necessary. To date, no concrete data concerning this issue exists. Conservative estimates assume that of the one million people who fled to Germany in 2015, more than 1,250 had pulmonary tuberculosis. It will be critical that X-ray mass screening, which has been reintroduced, is followed up with a specific diagnosis and systematic therapy to prevent the disease from spreading further.

We are increasingly concerned about the unchecked rise in antibiotic resistance. Approximately half a million people are diagnosed every year with multi-resistant TB that no longer responds to first-line drugs, which means that their treatment takes two years or more rather than half a year. These patients must swallow more than 14,000 pills with the risk of serious side effects, along with only a 50% chance of recovery.

The rates of multi-resistant TB are alarmingly high in numerous Eastern European countries. More than one in three newly infected patients in Belarus is a carrier of such a superbug. In Kazakhstan, Kyrgyzstan, Moldova, and Uzbekistan, this is true of about one in four; in Russia and the EU Member State Estonia, one in five. Even more alarming is extensively drug-resistant TB, which hardly responds to any medication at all. Such cases have already been documented in more than 100 countries. Globally speaking, one in ten multi-resistant TB pathogens is de facto no longer treatable; this affects approximately 50,000 people year on year. The numbers of cases are highest in Ukraine, South Africa, and India. Concerned about this development, the US government published a National Action Plan for Combating Multidrug-Resistant Tuberculosis in 2015.

Analyses of the economic consequences have also been prepared for TB. In Germany alone, the disease is responsible for 50 million euros in losses year after year. The costs amount to more than 500 million euros per year for the entire EU. However, the total costs, consisting of all direct and indirect expenditures, are ten times that figure. The UK's All-Party Parliamentary Group on Global Tuberculosis published a report – which may be somewhat pessimistic – prognosticating 75 million additional deaths because of drug resistant TB by 2050 around the world, associated with 15 trillion euros in costs and a roughly 0.6% reduction in gross world product.

Astonishingly, the UN Sustainable Development Goals hardly touch on TB at all. The WHO proclaims that the number of TB deaths is to be reduced by 95% between 2015 and 2035. New cases are to be brought down by 90%. This is impossible to achieve with the existing intervention measures. The WHO is relying optimistically on better medications, diagnostics, and a new vaccine. As a sign of heightened alertness, the WHO held a 'Ministerial Conference on Ending TB' in November 2017 and the UN a 'High Level Meeting on Tuberculosis' in 2018 and the UN a 'High Level Meeting on Tuberculosis' in 2018.

Although progress has been made in this area, there is no cause for enthusiasm to date. We continue to lack an effective vaccine, even if some candidates are now undergoing clinical trials. Following a long hiatus, some new drugs have been approved in recent years. But they do not represent real breakthroughs in chemotherapy. Only diagnostics has made a major step forward: the GeneXpert rapid diagnostic test now makes it possible to determine both TB and potential drug resistance of the pathogen within a few hours. Unfortunately, the test is still quite expensive; it costs at least 10 US dollars even in poor countries.

New pandemics in the new millennium

SARS, MERS, influenza, EHEC: more frequent outbreaks in the globalised world

The year 2003 saw the first major pandemic of the twenty-first century: the rapid spread of Severe Acute Respiratory Syndrome (SARS). The pathogen had made the leap from animals to humans in connection with meat markets in China. It arrived on multiple continents with infected air travellers within a few days. The pandemic peaked in May 2003 with 7,000 cases in more than 30 countries. Subsequently, it faded away and disappeared. In total, more than 8,000 people had the disease, of whom roughly 750 died.

In 2012 we received the first information about a new corona virus similar to the SARS pathogen. It also caused severe respiratory illnesses and probably jumped from animals to humans for the same reasons as with SARS. It was named Middle East Respiratory

Syndrome (MERS) since it was probably in the Middle East where it managed to transfer from dromedaries to human beings. The outbreak was initially limited to countries in that region, for example Saudi Arabia, Qatar, and Kuwait. More and more cases were later documented in Europe, North Africa, the US, and Asia. South Korea saw a rash of infections in mid-2015 with 200 cases. The number reached almost 1,700 worldwide, and more than 600 patients died. The outbreak had already passed its peak by 2016. Intensive efforts to develop a vaccine are currently underway, with funding from some oil states. Initial reports about a vaccine that alleviates the progression of the disease in camels are reason for hope. A clinical study on its protective effect in humans is not possible at present since MERS has disappeared for the time being.

The risk of an influenza pandemic continues to be the subject of much discussion. In particular, the outbreaks of the influenza strains H5N1 – often called bird flu, and H1N1 – alias swine flu, caused alarm around the globe, but in retrospect, both were relatively harmless. Fortunately the upshot is that H5N1 has not (yet) succeeded in adapting to person-to-person transmission. Although the H1N1 swine flu spread around the globe rapidly in 2009, arriving in 48 countries in less than a month, its course was milder than had been feared. However, the threat due to a new influenza virus is anything but averted; new types of influenza virus are already close at hand. In several provinces of China, almost 700 people contracted the H7N9 virus by mid-2015; at least 275 of them died. This time, the Chinese authorities were better prepared and were largely able to contain the outbreak. This review permits only limited conclusions for the future. The risk continues to exist and close attention is being paid to the dynamics of influenza. An ideal form of prevention would be a universal vaccine also protective against newly developing types of influenza virus (see section on vaccines).

In Germany, another pathogen attracted attention in 2011:

EHEC. It was a strain of the intestinal bacterium *Escherichia coli* armed with special toxins. The bacterium itself was by no means unknown. Numerous strains of *E. coli* have toxins and other virulence factors at their command that they hijacked from related pathogens. In this case, there was an outbreak with 4,000 patients, with 3,000 cases of diarrheal disorder and 855 cases of serious kidney failure; 53 people died because of the infection. Although it would not be correct to speak of an epidemic, the outbreak did startle many people. Epidemiologists managed to track down its origins with their time-consuming detective work: the germs had reached German consumers' plates on fenugreek sprouts imported from Egypt. This highlighted once again how infectious diseases spread along our globally networked trade routes.

Ebola: major outbreak of the underestimated jungle pandemic
Images of physicians and nurses in white and yellow head-to-toe protective suits dominated the news for months in 2014. We witnessed a particularly dramatic outbreak of the Ebola virus. It mostly remained limited to three West African countries – Guinea, Sierra Leone, and Liberia – and the consequences there were catastrophic. By the end of the pandemic in 2016, almost 30,000 people had contracted the disease, and almost 12,000 had died. The already difficult economic and political situations in the affected countries were exacerbated dramatically. Their combined gross domestic product dropped by 12% in 2015.

Ebola is a typical zoonotic disease: the pathogen can make the leap from monkeys to humans. This time, bats were probably also carriers of the disease. As so often, the beginning of the epidemic was initially very slow: just a few Ebola infections were reported in late 2013. But then, the numbers of cases soared. The virus had travelled from sparsely populated rural areas to the cities where it caused havoc practically unchecked owing to the poor health-care system and close contact among humans. Because the people affected become seriously ill and often die after an extremely short time, the disease was fortunately unable to spread further. Only a few people with Ebola reached other countries, most of them infected or ill aid workers from the crisis areas.

Unfortunately, large parts of the global health institutions failed completely during this pandemic. Only in August 2014 did the WHO declare a global public health emergency. By that time, it was much too late to intervene in time and to rapidly put an end to the pandemic. The fight against the pandemic was too slow in building momentum. It was only thanks to the tireless, often life-threatened work of the staff members and aid workers of various nongovernmental organisations, especially Doctors Without Borders, that the virus did not wreak even more havoc. The WHO later admitted it had made mistakes.

The Ebola outbreak was a wake-up call for the world in many respects. It called attention to important weaknesses:

1. insufficient basic health care in poor countries
2. a lack of hygiene, medications, vaccines, and diagnostics
3. a lack of research for interventions against as yet unknown pathogens as well as underestimated ones.

The ideal means of intervention would have been a vaccine already available at the beginning of the outbreak. The world could be significantly closer to this goal for Ebola today, for a promising vaccine candidate was already available long before the Ebola outbreak. It had been developed as part of the US biological defence programme (National Biodefense Strategy), which had been initiated following the terrorist attacks of September 11, 2001. However, it had not been possible to test the vaccine's protective effect on human beings before. This was now possible near the end of the Ebola outbreak in Guinea in 2015. The results are promising, but not unambiguous. Some hundreds of thousands of doses are now being produced and put on shelf as a precaution in order to be better prepared in the event of a renewed outbreak. The vaccine has not yet been approved as it does not fulfil the strict approval criteria for vaccines.

Zika, dengue, chikungunya: neglected tropical diseases on the rise

A short time after Ebola, another new epidemic has now made headlines: Zika. It is a flavivirus transmitted by *Aedes* species mosquitoes (see box below: Pandemics piggybacking on mosquitoes). Most people infected with Zika experience only moderate discomfort, fever, and aching limbs. But if pregnant women contract the disease, it can have dramatic consequences for their children. It is assumed that the Zika virus induces microcephaly in fetuses, i.e., a permanent decrease in the size of parts of the brain. Guillain-Barré syndrome, which causes nerve damage resulting in facial paralysis, is also associated with Zika infections.

The Zika virus, which was first discovered in 1947 in rhesus monkeys in Uganda, was long considered harmless. Reports of it being transmitted did not trigger warnings. Between 2007 and 2016, Zika transmissions were reported from 75 countries around the globe. Physicians in Brazil first confirmed cases in May 2015. They raised the alarm there in late 2015, in early 2016 also in Colombia. This time, the WHO responded more quickly than in the Ebola crisis. In late January 2016, it stated the pathogen was 'spreading explosively' and declared a global public health emergency.

By early March 2016, the number of people infected had risen to 1.5 million in about 30 countries in Latin America. Zika has also been reported from regions in the southern US. It is important to note that the clinical picture is usually harmless. In the US, however, pregnant women have already been warned against travelling to Latin America. Men have been advised to use condoms as it is now considered certain that the virus can be transmitted sexually.

Pandemics piggybacking on mosquitoes

Aedes mosquitoes are carriers of other diseases besides the Zika virus, transmitting them from animals to humans and from humans to humans. The dengue virus, the chikungunya virus, and the yellow fever virus are transmitted in the same way. This list can very probably be expanded.

Aedes mosquitoes feel comfortable in standing water at temperatures around 30 °C. They multiply in puddles such as those forming in old car tyres after rainfall. Freighters often transport thousands of such tyres across the seven seas, and the mosquitoes travel comfortably in them from continent to continent – occasionally spreading one-time tropical diseases. Unlike *Anopheles* mosquitoes, which carry malaria, *Aedes* mosquitoes also manage to live in densely populated, highly polluted cities. They feel particularly comfortable in the townships of Africa, the slums of Southeast Asia, and the favelas of Latin America. Global warming is making it easier for the mosquitoes to spread.

Aedes mosquitoes have now arrived in the Middle East, India, the southern US, and southern Europe from their original habitats in the tropics and subtropics. They have also been spotted in Germany and the Netherlands, but so far free of pathogens.

Quite a number of other animal vectors besides mosquitoes are known as well, for example ticks, flies, fleas, and snails. They transmit almost 20% of all infectious diseases. The infections they bring about add up to more than one billion cases of illness with more than one million deaths every year.

Otherwise, however, our knowledge about Zika is marginal, which is why efforts are first focused on combating the *Aedes* mosquitoes. In the runup to the 2016 Olympic Games, Brazil mobilised more than 200,000 soldiers to take countermeasures against them using insecticides. In addition, there is a realistic hope that a vaccine against the Zika virus can be developed rapidly, since vaccines are already available for numerous other flaviviruses: yellow fever, tick-borne encephalitis, Japanese encephalitis, and now also dengue. In mid-November 2016, WHO declared an end to the global Zika emergency.

At the same time when Zika was spreading in Brazil, the numbers of people infected with two viruses transmitted by the same mosquito – known about for quite some time – skyrocketed:

those causing chikungunya and dengue. The former disease means 'becoming contorted' because it brings on strong severe joint pain; chikungunya may result in serious complications such as liver damage and meningitis. Dengue infections often cause similar symptoms at first – diffuse bleeding and circulatory failure – and are then often fatal. Dengue fever has long reached the status of a pandemic, though it continues to be widely ignored. The WHO reckons with 50 to 100 million cases and more than 20,000 deaths per year, but this estimate is probably significantly too low. There is, however, a flicker of hope: a new dengue vaccine was recently approved in Mexico, the Philippines, and Brazil. New biological methods for combating the *Aedes* mosquito are also currently being tested.

Remedies

Antibiotics: the resistance crisis is worsening

A terrible scenario became reality multiple times in recent years: newborns in hospitals got infected with dangerous bacteria that are resistant to a large number of antibiotics and therefore seldom respond to treatment. We have been warning of drug resistance for a long time. Today, we are increasingly seeing situations in which physicians and patients are slipping into an era without antibiotics.

What is this all about? MRSA and VRE are well-known strains of bacteria that have become resistant. The methicillin-resistant *Staphylococcus aureus* strains, called MRSA, are resistant not only to methicillin, which has been an important all-around antibiotic for treating numerous pathogens until now, but have also developed defence mechanisms against most other commonly used classes of antibiotics. While these pathogens already cause and complicate more than half of all staphylococcal infections in the US and some other countries, this figure is about 12% in Germany. They cause more than 40,000 cases of disease per year in Germany and presumably about 150,000 across the EU. VRE is the abbreviation for vancomycin-resistant enterococci. They, too, are resistant to most of the classes of antibiotics effective to date, but also to vancomycin, which was long used as an antibiotic of last resort to treat them.

We continue to be confronted with new bad bugs time and again: CRE, NDM-1, and CRKP must be added to the list. These three abbreviations stand for a group of highly dangerous pathogens. They have become resistant to carbapenem antibiotics, kinds of miracle drugs which have, so far, been available to treat a large number of bacteria as well as important nosocomial bacteria and pathogens causing septicaemia, commonly known as blood poisoning. CRE are carbapenem-resistant enterobacteria, among them *Klebsiella* and strains of *E. coli*. NDM stands for New Delhi metallo-beta-lactamase. This is a group of bacteria that have developed multiple resistance to carbapenems and other antibiotics. They were first discovered in New Delhi, India. From there, they piggybacked to other parts of the world, probably with the tens of thousands of tourists who had had low-cost cosmetic surgery in India. CRKP refers to highly resistant strains of the *Klebsiella pneumoniae* bacterium. They can cause pneumonia, septicemia, meningitis, or wound infections. CRE are already responsible for 4% of all nosocomial infections in US clinics. It was previously possible to treat these bad bugs with colistin and related antibiotics, which have been available for a long time, but were used rarely in the past because of their side effects. The first CRE pathogens have already become resistant to these antibiotics, so practically no treatment options remain.

Resistance is by no means a problem exclusive to bacteria in hospitals. But those bacteria that survive in hospitals cause the greatest concern; they have developed a large number of defence strategies against antibiotics because of both the persistent pressure of medications given there and their frequent contact with other pathogens. It is becoming more and more difficult to cure the resulting infections. Roughly one in 20 patients in a German hospital or doctor's surgery gets infected with a pathogen. This affects up to one million people in Germany every year. Septicaemia is one of the dreaded illnesses, where pathogens spread throughout the body via the bloodstream. Roughly half of these often life-threatening diseases contracted in hospitals are caused by nosocomials. And the numbers are increasing. Across the EU, at least four million nosocomial infections are reported per year, causing about 30,000 deaths. One-third of these deaths are due to resistant bacteria.

The reasons for this dramatic development are many and varied. They include overly lax use of antibiotics both in human and veterinary medicine, as well as excessive use of antibiotics in factory-like animal farming in many countries. A brief overview:

- In the first decade of this century, global antibiotic consumption increased by approximately 40%. Much of this was due to their increased use in the BRICS countries (Brazil, Russia, India, China, and South Africa). Fortunately, antibiotic consumption is decreasing slightly in Germany.
- Between 65,000 and 250,000 tons of antibiotics are used annually in animal farming worldwide. Just 15% serve to treat infectious diseases and 30% are used for prevention. Most antibiotics are used as growth promoters: by selectively suppressing certain bacteria in the digestive tract, antibiotics contribute to the creation of a microflora that helps animals make the best possible use of their food. In other words: to increase their muscle mass quickly.
- Because of strict regulations in Germany and the EU, among other things a ban on using antibiotics as growth promoters since 2006, there is reason to hope that

antibiotic use in animal farming and veterinary medicine will drop significantly here.

- In human medicine, significantly more than half of antibiotics are prescribed in doctors' surgeries – but they are often not useful in therapeutic terms.
- In many threshold countries such as India, antibiotics are sold over the counter.

At the same time as we are observing how more and more potent antibiotics are becoming ineffective, the development of novel antibiotics continues to plummet. Hardly any work is being conducted on new antibiotics in the research labs of academic institutes and the pharmaceutical industry. Between 1950 and 1980, 200 new antibiotics came onto the market; in the following 30 years, just 55. Most of them were approved before the year 2000. From 2003 to 2012, just seven new antibiotics reached the market. Only about 40 antimicrobials are currently in the development pipeline, just a few of which will be approved. Major pharmaceutical companies have largely abandoned the field of antibiotics. Less than 2% of all medications in research and development are antibiotics. Only five out of thirteen major manufacturers are still investing in this area. Although some companies have recently decided to reenter this field because of new incentives, the market for antibiotics remains a niche – which is unfortunate.

The prospects are grim and the consequences clear. We must understand antibiotics as constituting a non-renewable resource that must urgently be protected and whose use must be determined by the resistance of the pathogens and under no circumstances by some industries' potential profits. The medications are non-renewable, and it is therefore imperative that they be used sustainably.

Anything but blockbusters

Three decisive obstacles explain why research and development of new antimicrobial drugs are stagnating:

1. Price: Even major treatment with antibiotics usually costs less than 1,000 euros. Far greater sums of money can be earned from many other medications – one reason for this is that the duration of treatment is usually brief for infectious diseases. In contrast, expenditures for cancer therapy quickly run up to 100,000 euros. And chronic diseases such as high blood pressure or diabetes often require life-long medication.

2. Limited sales: New antibiotics should first be approved specifically for pathogens resistant to traditional medications. The purpose of this approach is to slow down the development of resistance to an antibiotic. At this juncture, the opportunities for generating profits from its use are very limited.

3. Resistance: When resistance spreads, all medications in a class that are based on the same mechanism of action become ineffective. Sometimes several classes of antibiotics suffer the same fate all at once.

Vaccines: progress and new approaches for protection and therapy

'With the exception of safe water, no other modality, not even antibiotics, has had such a major effect on mortality reduction.' The WHO, the World Bank, and UNICEF begin their joint 2009 report on the state of the world's vaccines and immunisation with this quotation. In recent years, vaccinations with blanket coverage have continued to contribute to significantly reducing the incidence of several infectious diseases. The rate of immunisation against the most important paediatric diseases is 80% in most regions today. Yet there have also been minor complications and setbacks.

Sad to say, it has not been possible to take the final step to eradicate polio, for example. The geographical area where polio occurs is now very limited, and basically encompasses Afghanistan and Pakistan. Besides the lack of health care there, this failure is due above all to actions and attacks by aggressive, usually politically motivated opponents of immunisation. The Taliban have obstructed the immunisation campaigns time and again. There was a call to actively fight against polio immunisation, and as a consequence, vaccination workers have been abducted, tortured, and murdered. Vaccination centres have been targeted by suicide attackers.

In 2015, a total of 74 cases of wild-type polio (i.e., the actual polio pathogen) were documented. At the beginning of 2016, it looked like the figures were declining even further. But a new problem came to light in 2015: smaller outbreaks of a mutated vaccine strain. The reason: two polio vaccines are available. An inactivated vaccine with killed pathogens is generally used in areas free of polio. In high-risk areas, however, a live attenuated vaccine is used; it triggers a more robust immune response, thus grant-ing more reliable protection. But under certain circumstances, the attenuated virus in this vaccine can undergo reverse mutation and then cause polio. If the rate of immunisation is high, then the mutated polio virus is unable to spread. But it does have the oppor-tunity to circulate if larger vaccination gaps exist. This is what happened in Ukraine, where only roughly half of all children are immunised. In 2015, two cases of polio caused by mutated vaccine strains were documented, but a further outbreak, which had been feared, did not occur. In Romania as well as Bosnia and Herzego-vina, immunisation coverage of the population is too weak to rule out a polio outbreak with certainty. From 2016 on, the vaccine strains used to date will be recalled and new ones where reverse mutation is largely ruled out will be used. The immunisation pro-gramme to eradicate polio must definitely be continued.

The vaccine alliance GAVI, a public-private partnership provid-ing immunisations free of charge for children in poor countries, is seeing increasing success. The reduction of child mortality by more than half between 1990 and 2015 is due not least to GAVI's work. The German government has fortunately increased its support for GAVI by a significant amount. In early 2015, the GAVI donor conference took place in Berlin under the auspices of Chancellor Angela Merkel, who held out the prospect of funding of an additional 600 million euros through 2020. More than 7.5 billion US dollars were pledged at the conference.

Innovative financing programmes strengthening GAVI's approach are proving beneficial. For example, GAVI used special bulk purchase contracts to make a new vaccine against pneumococci available on a large scale in poor countries a short time after its approval. GAVI assured vaccine manufacturers in advance agreements that it would purchase certain amounts of vaccines over a longer period. In return, the manufacturers guaranteed low prices. The donor countries and the Bill & Melinda Gates Foundation jointly committed to purchasing 200 million doses of the pneumococcal vaccine. The manufacturers pledged to making them available for less than 3.50 US dollars per dose for the next ten years. It is assumed that the GAVI immunisation programmes have contributed to preventing four million deaths between 2011 and 2015.

The WHO's Global Vaccine Action Plan for 2011 to 2020 relies on the value of immunisations. The 194 WHO member states have agreed that the best possible vaccine-induced protection should be made available to all. Licensed vaccines are already available for 25 infectious diseases. They include not only low-cost vaccines whose licenses have expired, but also new ones that have been (too) costly, such as those against pneumonia and cervical cancer. The Action Plan also calls for better support for research and development of new vaccines against the major diseases, newly emerging pathogens, and drug-resistant pathogens.

What is needed?
- **Vaccines against new diseases:** We need a catalogue of pathogens that are likely to make the leap from animals to humans in the near future and entail an increased risk of causing pandemics. We need platforms that coordinate

and guarantee rapid development and then rapid use of vaccines. To promote rapid vaccine development for newly emerging pathogens, a public-private partnership was recently founded with the name CEPI (Coalition for Epidemic Preparedness Innovations). Part of the work has already been completed for some pathogens, or concrete ideas have been developed:

– An Ebola vaccine is in an advanced phase of development, but has not yet been tested sufficiently and approved.

– A dengue vaccine has recently come on the market. Valuable information can be derived from it for developing a vaccine against the Zika virus, which is related to the dengue virus.

– Universal vaccines against influenza are currently under development. They contain conserved antigens carried by all influenza viruses. Such a vaccine could be used both against all the seasonal influenza viruses, which are different every year, and against new influenza viruses with the potential to cause pandemics.

• **Vaccines against old diseases:** We must not give up on developing vaccines against AIDS, TB, malaria, and hepatitis C – even if they pose numerous challenges. First steps have been taken for malaria. A vaccine was approved recently, but its protective effect is only modest. Whether we like it or not, we must settle for the fact that we cannot achieve breakthroughs against the masterful pathogens at one stroke. Instead, we must take one step at a time.

• **Vaccines against (antibiotic-resistant) bad bugs:** The battle against life-threatening pathogens must be intensified, and this must include use of vaccines. In a time of increasing antibiotic resistance, vaccines can open up a new counterstrategy. We need vaccines against superbugs such as MRSA, VRE, CRE, and their relatives, but also against nosocomials such as *Pseudomonas aeruginosa* that are broadly resistant by nature. Vaccines can contribute to breaking the vicious circle of continually new resistances developing. For resistances do not develop under the pressure of vaccines – neither against the antibiotic nor against the vaccine itself. Studies from South Africa and the US show that the share of antibiotic-resistant pneumococci even decreased significantly as a result of immunisation against pneumococci. In the future, we will have to immunise certain risk groups individually. For example, patients can be vaccinated against certain hospital microbes and septicemia pathogens prior to major surgery or a foreseeable weakening of their immune systems (resulting from an organ transplant or chemotherapy, for instance).

- **Therapeutic vaccines:** Passive vaccination, namely targeted administration of antibodies to treat an already existing infection, must be implemented again. Such an immunisation remains effective even if the pathogen has become resistant to a number of drugs. Moreover, it is suitable for treating newly arising pandemics for which we have no medication (for example, the Ebola and Zika viruses). Although a passive vaccine using Ebola antibodies existed at the time of the Ebola crisis, its effectiveness had not yet been ascertained, and only very small amounts of it were available.

- **Host-directed therapy:** While antibodies induced by current vaccines target the pathogen directly, we should increasingly work on a new generation of antibodies – active agents that affect the immune system directly or can restore an immune response that was inhibited by the pathogen. Such procedures have been developed for cancer therapy – for example, treatments that strengthen the body's immune response to the abnormal cells. Such new medications can be a blessing, especially for fighting pathogens that are difficult to treat and that modify the immune response to their own advantage.

Conclusion: initial progress following the wake-up call

When I wrote the book *The New Plagues: Pandemics and Poverty in a Globalised World* in 2008, I developed two scenarios. The best-case scenario envisioned an ideal vision of the future. The worst-case scenario sketched out a gloomy trend. Looking back at the years since then, it is evident (as expected) that neither of the two models has become reality. Reality was somewhere in between. We are far away from the best-case scenario with prospering developing countries establishing functioning health-care systems so that outbreaks can be fought effectively and the risk of pandemics averted. But it is also fortunate that no new outbreak has expanded to a dramatic global pandemic. However, Ebola showed how explosive even a limited outbreak can be and how massively it not only affects individual people, but also the economy of entire regions.

The Ebola crisis in particular set things in motion and triggered first steps in many respects. It was a wake-up call for numerous major economic and financial organisations (World Bank, International Monetary Fund, G7, G20, and others). The Berlin Declaration of the G20 Health Ministers 2017 reflects the increasing political awareness of the threat of plagues impressively. The necessity of effective prevention of epidemics was recognised – not least to secure the functioning of the global economy and to prevent enormous losses. Moreover, Ebola shows vividly how similar some mechanisms are that can contribute to the development of either a global financial crisis or a major pandemic crisis.

Financial philosopher Nassim Nicholas Taleb illustrates this in his theory of the black swan:

- Extremely rare events that are difficult to imagine but have enormous consequences do occur.
- Most experts are blind to such events and consider them unforeseeable.

Although disease outbreaks are not entirely unexpected events, we cannot predict them precisely. Nobody could foresee whether it would be Ebola, bird flu, or an entirely new pathogen such as the MERS virus that would galvanise us into action. That is why optimal preparation for such events is essential. In the short term, a solid health-care system, paired with available diagnostics, therapeutics, and vaccines, as well as effective preventive measures, especially in hot spots, reduce the risk of epidemics progressing into pandemics dramatically. Moreover, it is necessary to invest in research and development in a systematic way and take a long view. In this way, we can obtain deeper insights into the biology of the pathogens and the causes of disease, into the underlying immunology as well as the epidemiology of pandemic diseases. Societal and cultural components that decisively influence epidemic outbreaks must be researched as well. This will enable the development of new intervention measures that protect us from a large number of events.

The theory of the black swan applies to known pandemic diseases only to a limited extent. They are by no means unexpected. Yet our view of these diseases is distorted: they are taken as given, and the positive consequences of potentially containing them is ignored all too often. A change of perspective is required here – less fatalism, more realistic hope and action. We should continue to put all our energy into paving the way that may one day result in our making the decisive breakthrough. On the basis of current knowledge, we cannot predict when a vaccine against AIDS will be available. But it is realistic for research on this issue to continue to make progress.

So much for the theory. What we need in practice is the willingness to move quickly and make decisions. If the economic perspectives on minimising epidemics are not to be ignored as if they were empty warnings, then urgent action must be taken – and in clearly defined steps whose success can be measured continually using established milestones. To date, no easily applicable goals formulated in detail are available for the problem of epidemics.

Although it is true that 194 countries committed to the WHO's international health standards, they have entered into force only exceedingly slowly, if at all. The new United Nations Sustainable Development Goals are not very helpful, either. Their sheer number alone makes them seem overwhelming. They lack clear prioritisation, which in turn would be required for the scheme to be funded. By comparison, the Millennium Development Goals, which were in force until 2015, were much clearer and were outlined more pragmatically, even if they were not particularly ambitious. It is alarming that the different needs of poor and rich countries are not taken into account sufficiently in the new sustainability goals. Only at the last minute was support included for research and development for vaccines and drugs against diseases threatening the poorer countries in particular. Not least under the weight of the Ebola crisis, the rights of poor countries to affordable medications, strengthening of their public health systems, and the establishment of monitoring systems were added. The task will now be to guarantee and distribute the funds for the necessary measures.

Regardless of clearly defined goals, we also need new structures for modern and hard-hitting pandemic prevention. I believe the WHO should continue to play a key role, despite numerous shortcomings. However, this outsized institution must commit to reforming its overly rigid structures. The work of the WHO should be linked more closely with that of the World Organisation for Animal Health. In addition, we need a global centre for health emergencies that can provide vaccines, therapeutics, diagnostics, and hygiene measures to combat outbreaks and prevent pandemics. National, international, and civil-society organisations are called on to improve health care in poorer countries. Finally, an international research organisation should be established whose remit is to develop up-to-date predictions and intervention measures to fight epidemics. It could stimulate research and development in a targeted fashion and ensure that intensive networking develops between public academic institutions and industry.

How should all this be funded? An obvious candidate for funding is the International Monetary Fund, which has a particular interest in preventing crises with systemic consequences. The ball is also in the World Bank's court; it has also recognised the significance of health care in the past. It should establish a financing structure for epidemics. The financial needs total roughly 4.5 billion US dollars. Two to three billion are required for early detection and combating of outbreaks, in particular in hot spots and high-risk countries. One billion US dollars should be earmarked for research and development. An additional 150 million US dollars per year should be budgeted for establishing the structures. The concept may appear expensive at first glance. Yet it costs just a fraction of the amount calculated for epidemics and pandemics, which is estimated at 30 to 60 billion US dollars per year.

Highest priority must be granted to combating new and existing diseases in poor countries as well as containing drug resistance in industrialised, threshold, and poor countries. The consumption of antibiotics by humans and animals must be drastically reduced through better monitoring. New therapeutics and alternative intervention measures must also be developed. I would like to mention two incentive programmes in this context: first the Longitude Prize, with a fund of 10 million British pounds and run by the innovation foundation Nesta, and second the EU's Horizon Prize, which is endowed with one million euros. These kinds of pull programmes should also be established for infectious disease control.

Numerous epidemics and pandemics have made headlines in recent years, providing rich material for discussions in the media, the general public, and the political community. The cost calculations support the firm belief that humanitarian questions and financial considerations are not mutually exclusive – on the contrary, they cannot be separated from one another. International bodies are now massively advocating for active intervention. This is reason to hope that we will slowly be able to get a handle on the threat of pandemics. It would be a sustainable improvement to the prospects of future generations.

Bibliography

Introduction/Conclusion

Commission on a Global Health Risk Framework for the Future (2016), The Neglected Dimension of Global Security: A Framework of Counter Infectious Disease Crises. Washington: National Academies Press

Taleb, N. N. (2007), The Black Swan: The Impact of the Highly Improbable. New York: Random House.

Jonas, O. B. (2013), Pandemic risk, Background Paper for the World Development Report 2014. Washington: The World Bank.

Policy Cures (2015), Measuring Global Health R&D for the Post-2015 Development Agenda. Sydney: Policy Cures.

United Nations (2015), Millennium Development Goals Report 2015. New York: United Nations.

World Economic Forum (2016), The Global Risks Report 2016. 11th Edition, Geneva: World Economic Forum.

Berlin Declaration of the G20 Health Ministers, 19–20 May 2017, Berlin, Germany. http://www.bundesgesundheitsministerium.de/fileadmin/ Dateien/3_Downloads/G/G20-Gesundheitsministertreffen/G20_Health_ Ministers_Declaration_engl.pdf.

Old pandemics
The Price of a Pandemic: Counting the cost of MDR-TB. London: All Party Parliamentary Group on Global Tuberculosis, 2015.
UNAIDS (2015), AIDS by the numbers. Geneva: UNAIDS.
UNAIDS (2015), 2015 Progress Report on the Global Plan: Towards the elimination of new HIV infections among children and keeping their mothers alive. Geneva: UNAIDS.
White House, The (2015), National Action Plan for Combating Multidrug-Resistant Tuberculosis. Washington, DC: The White House.
WHO (2015), Global Tuberculosis Report 2015. 20th Edition, Geneva: WHO Press.
WHO (2015), Accelerating Progress on HIV, Tuberculosis, Malaria, Hepatitis and Neglected Tropical Diseases – A new agenda for 2016–2030. Geneva: WHO.

New pandemics
Paixão, E., Barreto, F., Teixeira Mda, C., Costa Mda, C., Rodrigues, L.C. (2016), History, epidemiology, and clinical manifestations of zika: a systematic review. American Journal of Public Health 106(4), 606–12.
Peck, K.M., Burch, C.L., Heise, M.T., Baric, R.S. (2015), Coronavirus host range expansion and middle east respiratory syndrome coronavirus emergence: Biochemical mechanisms and evolutionary perspectives. Annual Review of Virology 2, 95–117.
Quaglio, G., et al. (2016), Ebola: lessons learned and future challenges for Europe, Lancet Infectious Diseases. 16, 259–263.

Antibiotic resistance
Deutsche Akademie der Naturforscher Leopoldina (2013), Antibiotika-Forschung: Probleme und Perspektiven, Stellungnahme, Akademie der Wissenschaften in Hamburg. Berlin/Boston: Walter de Gruyter Verlag.
Review on Antimicrobial Resistance Chaired by Jim O'Neill (2014), Tackling a crisis for the health and wealth of nations. London: The Review on Antimicrobial Resistance.

Review on Antimicrobial Resistance Chaired by Jim O'Neill (2015), Antibiotics
    in Agriculture and the Environment: Reducing Unnecessary Use and Waste.
    London: The Review on Antimicrobial Resistance.

Review on Antimicrobial Resistance Chaired by Jim O'Neill (2015), Securing
    New Drugs for Future Generations: The Pipeline of Antibiotics. London: The
    Review on Antimicrobial Resistance.

Review on Antimicrobial Resistance Chaired by Jim O'Neill (2015), Tackling a
    Global Health Crisis: Initial Steps. London: The Review on Antimicrobial
    Resistance.

Vaccines

GAVI (2015), The Vaccine Alliance Progress Report 2014. Geneva/Washington:
    GAVI.

Review on Antimicrobial Resistance Chaired by Jim O'Neill (2016), Vaccines
    and Alternative Approaches: Reducing our Dependence on Antimicrobials.
    London: The Review on Antimicrobial Resistance.

Vaccine Confidence Project, The (2015), The State of Vaccine Confidence, The
    Vaccine Confidence Project. London: London School of Hygiene & Tropical
    Medicine.

Sustainable world politics

Harald Müller

What does sustainable world politics entail?

Sustainability means arranging individual and collective human life on planet Earth so that it does not impair the foundations of the livelihoods of future generations. That sounds simple, yet it is difficult in practice even if both the knowledge about the causes of such damage and the knowledge about how to remedy the situation are available. Efforts to efficiently translate this knowledge into action have not yet been successful across the board. The normative systems and the incentive systems in the economy and society in general do not provide sufficient motivation for them to put sustainability into practice.

Setting the course in this way is at its core a political task. It can direct society's actions by laying down rules, and it can change that direction. Studies of economic, agricultural, social, environmental and energy policy, etc. show what has been going wrong in these policy areas. The effect of these policies taken together is that state and private investments, and production and consumption decisions are running counter to sustainability.

This chapter does not discuss these individual policy areas, each of which has a *direct* impact on the degree of sustainability. Instead, it is about the framework that transboundary political processes set for the policies of the individual states. Analyses of world politics seldom turn their attention to the question of how it influences the capability of the ecosphere and its living organisms to survive. If this framework of world affairs is constructed in a misguided way, then it obstructs rationality-driven decision-making favouring sustainability at the level of individual states. Unfortunately, the major players on Earth and their emissaries have great difficulty keeping the public interest goal of survival in mind during their disputes about power, territory, status, and distribution.

The following sections discuss factors of world politics with disruptive effects on sustainability: power rivalries, fragmentation and state collapse, terrorism, nationalism, and right-wing populism weaken the willingness to place controversial political questions of regulation under the primacy of sustainability, which is oriented toward the common good. Since the publication of the book *Building a New World Order: Sustainable Policies for the Future* almost a decade ago, these factors have unfortunately developed in the wrong direction.

First, I would like to sketch out the desirable conditions for a sustainability-friendly framework for world politics: (1) multidimensional justice, (2) tolerance of diversity, and (3) peaceful conflict resolution. Injustice, intolerance, and violent conflicts, in contrast, create detrimental normative and material incentives.

Conditions for sustainability

Justice
Justice is not only most people's pious hope and something philosophers believe to be most desirable from a moral perspective. Instead, the desire for it is hardwired in us. Neuroscientists, psychologists, ethnologists, evolutionary biologists, sociologists, and experimental economists have demonstrated that a sense of fairness is anchored in the structure of our brains, that it influences our behaviour, and that it triggers strong emotions – good ones when we experience justice, negative and aggressive ones when

we feel we have been treated unfairly. On the one hand, it is the foundation of human morality, on the other, it holds the seeds of great disaster. This sense of justice is expressed most strongly when a person's own demands are at stake; when it is about those of our in-group; more weakly, but still measurably, when it is about others'. The ability to feel justice empathetically and altruistically exists, but competes with partiality toward oneself and one's own collective. Our attitude toward the demands of others can change over to hostility if those demands contradict our own ideas: people have different notions of 'justice', and they often have different opinions about how a common principle of justice is to be applied concretely in a particular situation.

There are various dimensions of justice (Nancy Fraser). The first dimension of justice is the sphere of *distribution*. One core element of justice is who gets what, and this is reflected in the primal principle 'to each his own'; it remains controversial who counts in this context and what it is that each individual is due. The second dimension is *participation* (representation), involvement in decisions that affect a person individually or as a member of a group. The third dimension is *recognition*: all individuals/groups seek to receive recognition from their surroundings. If recognition is refused, people feel this is deeply unjust. The three dimensions are closely interconnected: a person who loses out in terms of distribution, who is excluded from participation, will interpret this as alarm signals of a lack of recognition. The psychological consequences: see above!

Little international political research has been conducted on these questions to date. As early as 1993, Canadian scholar David Welch designed a concept of the problem of justice in international relations: actors make demands whose validity they are convinced of. If these claims are fulfilled, they see that justice has been done. If not, they feel they have been treated unfairly and react in a negative way. Justice is invoked time and again in international negotiations and conflicts, often in a highly emotional manner. Its impact is ambivalent. If people succeed in formulating a common understanding of justice, even if by adding seemingly contradictory principles, then lasting conflict resolution becomes possible. If antagonistic demands or principles collide frontally, then violence looms.

Recognition of diversity

Recognition of diversity follows as an imperative from the diversity of the global population and its systems of government. The world's population lives in about 200 states, as roughly 1,300 ethnic groups, and with approximately 6,500 individual languages. Cultural differences exist between the collectives even despite increasing communication and the rise of mixed cultures. Seeking to do away with differences is a recipe for generating violence. It is not without reason that fragmented states are the ones most vulnerable to state collapse and wartime violence over long periods of time.

Dealing with diversity is part of our genetic and cultural heritage, and it is ambivalent, as is justice. Individual and collective identity formation requires people to draw boundaries (I – them, in-group – out-group). It does not necessarily result in enmity. Two models of processes exist:

(1) Positive-integrative process: curiosity – interest – utility – sympathy – friendship – integration
(2) Negative-excluding process: mistrust – fear – rivalry – aggression – enmity –mortal enmity

For example, the 'welcoming culture' toward refugees is contrasted by the 'culture of rejection'. Both processes can stop at any point or even reverse. Insecurity and fear, and thus the wish to draw boundaries internally as well as externally, grow during times of societal and political crisis. That favours the second trajectory.

The path to sustainability begins with the recognition of diversity within and between states. This shows how closely the problem of diversity is linked to the topic of justice: being recognised in one's own identity is a fundamental demand of every individual and collective actor. If this existential desire is refused, the people affected feel they have been treated unjustly *and* they feel threatened, and the problems begin.

This is a burning issue because of the dramatic movements of refugees. Integration begins by recognising the humanity of the migrants and refugees. Any discourse conducted by certain parties only in expressions of disapproval, rejection, and hostility will leave its mark on the new arrivals' attitude toward mainstream society, especially if that discourse is conducted without them. Exclusion arouses young people's potential for aggression. They become alienated from the fabric of society into which they are supposed to become integrated. A culture of rejection toward people, many of whom will remain within the society, lays the fuse for long-term potential for violence. It is not only inhuman, but also irresponsible, high treason against the interest of the state and society in stability.

The situation is similar *between* states. Recognition of diversity takes on various forms here. For one thing, the task is to grant the groups demanding recognition the autonomy of their identity in the appropriate form. Refusal to do so can result in bloody, enduring battles within states (the Kurds in Turkey) or between states (Russia's rejection of Ukraine's autonomy). Occupation with increasing annexation intentions is a special case, as shown in the Israeli-Palestinian relationship, whereby the Palestinians have often missed opportune moments for compromises.

Nonviolence

Justice and the recognition of diversity are two conditions for sustainability because they remove causes of violence and set the course for cooperation. The third condition, nonviolence, seals this course determined by the other two conditions. But this does not happen by itself. 'Conditions' in politics are not reliable 'causes' as in Isaac Newton's physics. Instead, they represent barriers to action and opportunities for action. Yet individual or collective actors can climb across barriers and ignore opportunities. Our two conditions substantially increase the probability that actors will opt for nonviolence and favour cooperation. But a few may remain whose notions of justice and recognition are so monstrous that they remain unfulfillable unless massive injustices for the other actors are brought about. In the Near and Middle East, the Palestinians could achieve a state of their own; the Arab states could recognise Israel; dictatorships and monarchies could grant their nations political participation and reduce poverty and inequality by investing in development, education, health, and social services; Shiites and Sunnis could be reconciled; and effective minority protection could be established – in other words, a utopia of justice and recognition. But the 'Islamic State' (IS) would continue to fight nonetheless. For it is precisely these conditions which the IS hates and opposes: just circumstances fully recognising the right of diversity to exist instead of absolute rule by a (ideologised) religion, combined with the privileging of the 'true believers'. That is why sustainability cannot be attained with the IS: refusal of nonviolence makes resistance to this actor's totalitarian ambitions necessary.

Nonviolence requires actors who pursue their own interests and values, which may be competing and conflict-laden, through nonviolent means: by leading by example, through negotiations, willingness to compromise, reliability in fulfilling agreements, free of inflated pretensions of status (as in the case of Putin or Erdogan), and with tolerance and a high frustration threshold if they do not always accomplish what they desire.

The reality of world politics: disruptive factors

Rivalry of major powers

The danger of violent clashes between major powers – the US, Russia, China, India, Japan, the European Union (EU) – seemed to have disappeared after the end of the East-West conflict; a gradual convergence of interests, perhaps even of values, was considered possible. Francis Fukuyama's *The End of History* was an expression of this utopia.

But things turned out differently. Conflicts of interest orchestrated with military means prevail between Russia and the West. China and the US are confronting each other in East and Southeast Asia, observing one another with mistrust. The tensions between Japan and China are making the US a regional player in the conflict, not least as an ally of Toyko. Border disputes between India and China occasionally erupt in border skirmishes. How was it possible for the rivalry between the great powers to reemerge?

The West and Russia

During the negotiations leading to German unification, Western politicians – above all the American and the German foreign ministers – gave the Soviets verbal assurances that they would not expand NATO eastward. Considering the urgency of the matter of unification and the tensions in Moscow, neither side pressed for this matter to be made the subject of formal negotiations, as this would have overburdened the agenda. In other words, no legal commitment on the part of the West exists, but rather a claim that the Russian leadership considers legitimate. In 1993, and in light of the changes in Europe, the West began discussions, which decided in favour of expansion despite Russia's objections. Russia was offered 'compensations', namely the NATO-Russia Council and the assurance in the NATO-Russia Founding Act (1997) that no combat troops and no nuclear weapons would be stationed in the new member countries. These placebos proved to be little comfort because NATO and the US always acted counter to Russia's declared interests if their interests or values so required: the war against Serbia (without a mandate from the UN Security Council); the US withdrawal from the Anti-Ballistic Missile Treaty; the invasion of Iraq; the development of a NATO missile defence system in Western Europe; the second and third waves of NATO expansion; from 2008 on, the explicit prospects for Georgia and Ukraine to join NATO – all this took place against declared Russian interests.

Russia's internal power relations shifted toward the conservative, nationalist, authoritarian forces that had always distrusted the West. But even Putin made some attempts to maintain a good relationship with its stronger partner: such signals included the Moscow Treaty of 2002 ('New START Treaty'), his sober reaction to the US withdrawal from the ABM Treaty, and his cooperation with the US in its operations in Afghanistan. It was only in 2007 that he held a hostile, Soviet-style talk at the Munich Security Conference.

NATO expansion created problems for 'intermediate Europe', which was shrinking: this is where highly fragmented states such as Ukraine and Georgia had been able to remain stable as long as this intermediate Europe included so many states that Kiev and Tbilisi did not have to decide between the West and Russia. This scope for action shrank and, in the end, a decision seemed inevitable; the inner tensions between sympathisers of the West and sympathisers of Russia erupted. The 2008 war in Georgia was the first consequence, the violent Ukraine crisis the second and more consequential one.

Problems of justice and recognition structured this crisis. Russia felt disappointed in its demands; it did not feel recognised as on an equal footing with the US, but felt treated like a second-class partner and considered itself justified in regaining the status of a world power of equal rank single-handedly. The annexation of a piece of land that Moscow considered to be its property in any case (the Sevastopol naval base in Crimea) appeared to be a suitable step in symbolic and strategic terms. The West for its part protected the rights of the sovereign Eastern European states to freely choose an alliance for their national security, defended the Kosovars' demands for their basic human rights, and insisted on the rights of Georgia and Ukraine to territorial integrity. The increasing auto-cratisation of the Russian system of government made Moscow an inferior partner in the eyes of the West. International law was neglected by both sides, as was empathy for the partner they were dealing with; there was no question of nonviolence. In the end, the relationships lay in ruins, as did parts of Eastern Ukraine.

The consequences for sustainability are visible: collaboration concerning the disposal of hazardous materials in Russia has been stopped, nuclear disarmament is not progressing, cooperation in environmental protection is on hold, and economic and energy relations are limited. The G8, the OSCE, and the NATO-Russia Council, which were designed for sustainable relations, are operating at half speed, if at all. And no change is in sight.

China, Japan, the US, and India

If we feel the confrontation in Eastern Europe to be threatening, the explosive conflict situations in Southeast and East Asia are receiving less attention here. The region is the main arena of the rivalry between China and the US; it is not only about control over the region, but about deciding which country is the global leader. China has territorial claims against no less than eight neighbours and is trying to assert them unilaterally, sporadically using military means. The conflict with India is about two mountain regions. Beijing is trying to enforce its claims of enormous ocean areas in the South China Sea, including some groups of islands, against Malaysia, Brunei, the Philippines, and Vietnam. There have already been minor clashes at sea with Vietnam and the

Philippines. China is dumping sand and concrete onto rocky reefs to develop them for military purposes so that airplanes can land and ships can moor. The disputes with Japan and South Korea are also about islands. Finally, China would like to take over Taiwan. This island had declared independence following the Chinese Revolution and has its own democratically elected government. China considers Taiwan to be Chinese territory and its future incorporation into China an indispensable part of reunification after the imperialist epoch; the Taiwanese are quite happy with the status quo.

In all these cases, the US plays the role of the official (Japan, South Korea, Philippines) or unofficial protective or alliance partner of the weaker side; such a relationship seems to be developing even with India. Thus, a direct confrontation of the global powers US and China is looming especially since the Americans are demonstrating their presence time and again in the ocean areas claimed by China: the region is home to a number of powder kegs.

The arms race

When the major powers argue, the arms industry flourishes – the opposite of sustainable investment. Manufacturing and maintaining weapons devours resources, harms the environment, and induces opportunity costs since the financial means for useful investments are no longer available – not to mention the damage caused by weapons used in wars. The US is continually working on its missile defence programme. The response of China and Russia is to expand their nuclear arsenals. The US is reacting by modernising its own nuclear weapons. India is trying to keep up with China, and Pakistan is catching up. In contrast to the Cold War, it is not two powers competing, but five. We have no idea about the dynamics and the risks of a multipolar arms race. Knowledge about the bipolar nuclear competition from the Cold War is of no help here.

Russia is modernising its conventional forces and 'experimenting' with them in conflicts, for example in Ukraine or Syria. In Europe, the Eastern European states and Germany are on edge; their reaction is to build up their own forces. The trend that defence spending in Europe has been declining since 1990 has been reversed.

In East Asia, there is all-out competition between China and the US with their naval and air forces. Seeking to create superior military options in the Taiwan Strait, China is mass-producing short- and medium-range ballistic missiles, the latter in order to be able to attack American bases on the southern Japanese island of Okinawa and to prevent American naval forces from approaching over a wide area. Anti-satellite weapons and electronic warfare are supposed to neutralise the superior American reconnaissance equipment and command and control resources. The US, in contrast, has strengthened its forces in the Western Pacific to be able to conduct strikes far onto the Chinese mainland, thus thwarting the Chinese options. Both plans require early strikes; an extremely unstable situation is in the making. In the meantime, the states of East and Southeast Asia are strengthening their naval and air forces to develop better capabilities to counter military pressure from China.

Rearmament in the Persian Gulf region is dramatic as well. Saudi Arabia now has the third-largest military expenditure in the world – more than Russia! The other Arab Gulf States are doing the same. Iran is using the end of the embargo to rearm.

Defence spending has increased around the world. In addition, millions of small arms are circulating between battlefields in Africa and Asia while new production is continuing unchecked. The new Arms Trade Treaty, at least a small step forward, is only of limited help. Sustainability is falling by the wayside, and the danger of war is increasing.

Meanwhile the proliferation of weapons of mass destruction is hanging over the globe like the sword of Damocles. However, the situation is better than we had been led to expect from the prophecies of doom we have been hearing for decades. The number of countries with nuclear weapons has even dropped from 12 to 9 since 1991: Ukraine, Belarus, Kazakhstan, and South Africa have given up theirs, and only North Korea with its unpredictable leadership clique has joined the nuclear club. This is the success of the power of existing treaties and the measures legitimised by them to prevent the proliferation of nuclear weapons; yet the danger still exists.

New horrors are looming on the horizon: autonomous drones and new types of battle robots that decide about life and death themselves, with no human being bearing final responsibility; nanotechnology that could make it possible for tennis-ball-sized conventional explosives to reduce an entire neighbourhood to rubble; or 3D printers rapidly spreading the capability to mass-produce weapons around the world. If these developments are not controlled, then new stumbling blocks for sustainable politics will emerge.

Fragmentation and state collapse

Rivalries between the major powers and arms races make states, the vested owners of the organised monopoly on the use of force, seem like second-order actors damaging sustainability. This assessment is put into perspective if we consider the consequences of state *collapse*, as in the Middle East and Africa.

We have already seen in the case of Ukraine what can happen to fragmented states. Most states in the areas where imperialism and colonialism played out in the nineteenth and twentieth centuries have collapsed today, for instance in the hot spots of (civil) wars in Africa and the Arab Middle East. All of these states are fragmented, and populations are divided into various ethnic groups, tribes, religions, denominations, and sects. This places high demands on the political institutions and calls for the leaderships to be tolerant and wise – after all, recognition of diversity is a condition for maintaining the state.

Fragmentation itself is not a reason for the state and society to explode – Switzerland, for example, manages it well. But if poor governance enters the picture, things change. It is not only a matter of the leadership's incompetence, despotism, and corruption. If one of the groups monopolises power, for example the Alawites in Syria, or in Iraq the Sunnis under Saddam Hussein and the Shiites after him, that is more serious, as is the resulting unjust distribution of resources. The state institutions, including a justice system that is not impartial, merely serve to maintain power relations. When the disadvantaged, with no hope of remedy, seek to claim their share using violence, the state breaks apart. Today, fanatic religious forces are interfering in all battles in majority-Muslim states.

Wars of this kind tend to become protracted; objective development on the part of the warring parties are rare because the war cements their images of the enemy and their identification with their own groups. Their motivation to fight intensifies instead of diminishing because of sacrifice and suffering. War entrepreneurs making profits – for example by selling mineral resources, antiques, drugs, or slaves – are not interested in a negotiated peace that would put an end to their business. 'War economies' may emerge in this way, becoming permanent in repeated feedback loops, until one party wins or a (risky) external intervention puts an end to the fighting.

Supraregional conflagrations from Africa's Atlantic coast (Nigeria, Mali) across the entire Maghreb and the neighbouring states to the south (Central Africa), to East Africa (Sudan and Somalia), to the Middle East (Syria, Iraq, Yemen) and all the way to Afghanistan are the consequence. The destruction, the collapse of infrastructures, the weakening of states' capacity to act, and the halting of economic and political development are catastrophic. The people have no other option but to desperately try to survive or to flee. The struggle for survival brings about overexploitation of resources, which can be disastrous in these precarious ecological systems (deforestation for fuel, depletion of groundwater).

The goals of the governments are solely to consolidate their own power and to eliminate the enemy, if possible without buying peace by sharing power and prosperity. There is no room to think about sustainable politics and to devote means to sustainability-related activities; the necessary steps toward ecological stabilisation in increasingly challenging climatic conditions are not taken.

Transnational terrorism

Besides state collapse, non-state violent actors challenge states through terrorism. Terrorism has a history reaching back thousands of years. Developments in weapons and communications technologies have shifted the cost-to-yield ratio in favour of terrorist groups. With the technology available today for making and setting off explosives, and in light of the large numbers of people in urban centres and the vulnerability of modern infrastructures, small groups, even individuals, can now cause far greater damage than in the past (with the exception of Bosnian-Serbian terrorist Princip, whose assassination of the heir to the throne of Austria and his wife in Sarajevo in July 1914 triggered World War I).

Terrorism has taken on a particular form. Al Qaida and the 'Islamic State' (IS), which has outstripped the former as the trend leader, are the most recent versions of a phenomenon present throughout history, namely mass movements creating tight community among their members and claiming absolute truth. They claim an elitism of the 'chosen' and a militant mission, ostensibly in the service of a higher being. Their Manichaean worldview divides the world into good (the true believers) and evil (all nonbelievers, including the heretical Muslim majority). A consequence is the dehumanisation of the 'enemy', which justifies doing away with any inhibitions against killing. The distant goal is the paradisial utopia of the everlasting peaceful kingdom of God, combined with worldly dreams of global domination. For thousands of years, such movements existed in all the major religions, but also within the framework of secular ideologies.

Islam too has repeatedly experienced such surges, framed as 'holy war' (jihad). The IS is the most important manifestation and the most dangerous form of transnational *jihadism* since the nineteenth-century Mahdi movement. It bundles the frustrations of (young) Muslims in poorly governed Muslim-majority societies and in the diaspora and offers them a heroic perspective for their lives. It has resources, combat experience, and a tested leadership. It espouses the most bestial ideology and practice since Hitler: this is attractive to some, but is also a decisive weakness: *too many enemies*. The power relations will bring about its defeat, but that may take some time.

We can differentiate four impacts of the IS. First, it undermines the legitimacy of the poorly governed states from North Africa to Iraq to such an extent that sections of the young population feel attracted by its activities and significantly more people prefer the deadly calm created by the IS to the total insecurity of civil war.

Second, it revolutionises the region's territorial structure and questions the statehood of the established regimes, thus destabilising one of the strategically most important regions of the world. The advantages of sustainable energy policy not based on fossil fuels have never been as apparent as today; the IS could bring about the unintended effect of accelerating the trend away from oil.

Third, it attracts – in a way that can be understood only sociologically and psychoanalytically – young Muslims of both genders from all parts of the world, including from Western democracies, and thus breaks apart the superficially anchored migrant communities and complicates their integration.

Fourth, its practice and its advertising abroad fuel the growth of xenophobic, Islamophobic, right-wing populist, radical rightist, and fascist-violent movements and parties in Europe and the US. In collaboration with its antagonistic twin, radical rightist terrorism, terrorism of Islamist provenance creates chaos that reduces the impact of political rationality and universalist empathy and in the worst case destroys it entirely. Since there can be no policy of sustainability in the absence of political rationality and at least a minimal universal sense of community, the IS is incompatible with such policy. Only marginalisation and ultimate elimination of the IS will create perspectives beneficial for sustainability.

Nationalism and populism

The major states must carry the main responsibility for a political turn toward sustainability. They cause the most environmental damage, and they have the resources to initiate and carry out the transformation. The democratic states have the best means for correcting mistakes, namely a public enjoying the benefits of freedom of speech and freedom of association, independent media, and an autonomous judiciary. Since the end of the East-West conflict, however, a narrow-minded, anti-science, anti-universalist, anti-democratic, reactionary, and nationalist right-wing form of populism has been on the rise. It extends from China via Russia and the eerie competition between unconscionable Republican candidates for President of the US – resulting in the election of the worst choice – to the rise of anti-European and xenophobic parties in Western Europe arguing on the basis of irrational fundamentals; they are threatening to destroy the EU, an incomparable project of peace. It is telling that the German branch of this backward-looking movement (AfD) would like to scrap climate policy entirely.

The anti-universalism of the right-wing populist movements switches off the spotlight on global problems. All that counts is people's most immediate vicinity, their own family, their own nation – as multi-ethnic as it may be, and their own economy – as nonviable as it may be without the global market. Foreigners are viewed with mistrust. If they come too close, this aversion escalates to become fear, panic, hatred, and hostility. Diversity is suspect; justice applies only to one's own tribe. The universalist view of global problems and empathy with other people's hardships are entirely alien to this worldview. Complex problems such as the global climate exceed cognitive and emotional capabilities. The ideology is based on ignorance, blocking things out, and obstinate stupidity. Sustainability requires the exact opposite of all this.

These movements have a catastrophic attitude toward the institutions that are indispensable parts of solutions to problems. In domestic politics, hostility to democracy is expressed in contempt for democratic institutions such as the free press (which is rejected in favour of the disinformation of Putin's Russia, which has long turned lies into raison d'état) as well as parties, which are contrasted with the will of the people being identical to an 'alternative' leadership, as expressed in high-class Nazi ideologue Carl Schmitt's praises of the Führer state. *Völkisch*-national leaders, Putin in Russia, Kaczinsky in Poland, or Orban in Hungary, are eagerly dismantling democracy, especially the troublesome opposition and independent media. Thus, the institutional prerequisites for sustainable politics are disappearing: the instruments for correcting mistakes, which constitute an inestimable quality advantage of democratic systems.

Right-wing populism and nationalism are shaking another cornerstone of sustainability: the international institutions. The remit of the latter to create and enforce global norms and to settle disputes between countries is indispensable if the difficult tasks of changing course in the global economy and world politics are to be overcome and the destructive obstacles to cooperation in international conflicts are to be eliminated. With their narrow-minded focus on their own nation and its supposed interests, right-wing populists are incapable of constructive international collaboration, as it requires a willingness not to constantly be forcing through one's own interests. If these movements gain more power, they will oversee the complete dismantling of international cooperation which was created laboriously and with major efforts as a lesson from two world wars, as can be seen in the US Republicans' malicious attacks on the United Nations (UN) and the crude wishes of European right-wing populists to destroy the EU. Then we will be back at square one – in August 1914, at the beginning of the catastrophes for humanity.

Interim assessment

Dark clouds on the horizon: second-order sustainability requires the willingness of state actors to turn their view to the common tasks and to put the existing conflicts under the control of mutually agreed management or to find a permanent solution. It requires capable institutions in which governments seek to settle matters and are able to take on executive functions to solve problems. It requires the understanding on the part of states that they must relinquish small parts of their sovereignty to such institutions and bind their own action to jointly agreed legal rules. This in particular requires respect for diversity – because they have to make contracts with people whose thinking and political orders they dislike. Concessions in favour of justice are necessary as well: agreements are stable only if everyone involved is somewhat satisfied because sufficient demands have been met.

The world seems to be developing in a different direction. States are again pursuing territorial claims, steeped in purported historical justifications and with an emotional bitterness that makes compromises virtually impossible. Resources are again being poured into armaments instead of reasonable sustainability projects; weapons producers are working on the horror weapons of the future. Sectarian movements are developing among groups neglected by world history, such as the Arab Sunnis, movements that believe that justice can be achieved only by suppressing and – *in extremis* – entirely annihilating all others, as did the German Nazis in their era. Terrorism is running rampant especially in failing states whose disappearance is based on the appalling governance of the ruling elites. As already mentioned, right-wing populist movements are on the rise in the highly developed states, undermining universalist thinking domestically, working on dismantling democracy, and threatening to destroy urgently needed international institutions. Their weaknesses are palpable in any case: the most powerful countries of the world manifest an opportunistic way of dealing with international law: Russia and China in the way they handle territorial questions, the US in applying military force without a basis in international law. The UN are weakened, as is the EU. Overall, things are not looking good for sustainable world politics.

Sustainable world politics in difficult times: two rays of hope

Is sustainable world politics still possible? The barriers are high. Nonetheless, rational world politics is showing signs of life.

The Paris Agreement on Climate Change

Seemingly irreconcilable interests were on opposite sides with regard to climate policy. The industrialised countries – the main cause of CO_2 emissions – demanded that the burden of emissions reduction be shared with emerging economies and oil-producing countries. Their concept of justice: the same burdens without consideration of their own historical emissions. The emerging economies insisted on being categorised in the group of developing countries in order to avoid explicit reduction requirements.

The majority of developing countries rejected reduction requirements, pointing to the past, and demanded financial and technical
support for the energy transition. Both groups of states wanted
the sinners of yore to pay for their transgressions in the interests
of retributive justice. The small island states, whose existence is
threatened by sea level rise, were drivers of the negotiations for
years and demanded strict reduction requirements for all producers of CO_2. After the Kyoto Protocol (2007), this contradictory
constellation had prevented any breakthrough at the following
conferences.

In Paris in December 2015, 196 states negotiated climate policy
under the chairmanship of France. Initially, more than 1,600 pas-
sages in the draft were contentious. During the conference, a new
'high ambition coalition' formed at the initiative of the Marshall
Islands, including the US, the EU, and the emerging economy
Mexico. Canada and Brazil joined just before the end of the conference. Conference president Fabius extended the conference by
one day. He appointed the worst opponents of effective climate
policy as chairs of ten working groups, a smart move forcing them
to show responsibility. Bilateral contacts between national governments took effect behind the scenes. On 12 December, the
conference adopted the agreement unanimously.

It requires *all* signatories to reduce emissions. They must publish
their plans and revise them regularly. The goals and measures may
be made more stringent, but must not be watered down. The industrialised countries acknowledge the damage their emissions cause
in developing countries. Although this does not provide any basis
for legal claims, they will provide 100 billion US dollars per year to
developing countries through 2025. Mechanisms for North-South
technology transfer will be established. The agreement includes
numerous individual measures for managing damage, exchanging
information, capacity-building, determining best practices, and
institutionalisation. A sour note: efforts to enshrine the principle

of 'decarbonisation' did not succeed – instead the softer principle of 'emission neutrality'.

Why were the adversaries able to reach an agreement? First, because of the increasing urgency of the problem: global warming was measurable; the melting of ice was visible; two important 'members of the opposition', China and India, had experienced smog in major cities as a brake on development. The formation of the 'high ambition coalition' created a new centre of power in the negotiations. Obama's policy changed the role of the US from slowing the process down to speeding it up. Brazil's change of course had considerable influence on developing countries. Germany's diplomacy toward India and Brazil in advance of the conference; US actions, whereby Obama even spoke by telephone with Xi Linping during the next-to-last night of the conference; Pope Francis's influence on Nicaragua, which was resistant; the moral pressure exerted by island states and civil society; and conference president Fabius's skill were building blocks for success.

The interests, but above all the 'just demands' of everyone involved, were accommodated artfully: the industrialised countries accept their responsibility to act, but the emerging economies must bear their binding and increasing shares of the burdens. The developing countries receive ample support and bear lighter burdens, but must fulfil their commitments. With this outcome, the island states at least have a hope of survival.

The success of the agreement depends on its implementation by states. From the Republicans in the US with Donald Trump at the top to the AfD in Germany, countries harbour ignorant, anti-science, inhumane forces seeking to torpedo the agreement. Political rationality prevailed in Paris, but the foes of rationality are waiting in the trenches.

The 'Joint Comprehensive Plan of Action' (JCPOA) on Iran's nuclear programme

Iran's nuclear activities had been keeping the world in suspense since 2002. At the time, an opposition group confirmed what the Israeli and US intelligence services had been asserting for a long time: besides its official civil nuclear programme, Iran was engaging in secret nuclear activities whose core was a uranium enrichment facility – highly enriched uranium is one of two requisite materials for the manufacture of the bomb. And the Iranians were also taking the path to production of plutonium, the other indispensable bomb material, by building a large heavy water research reactor and a heavy water factory.

Even the Shah had demanded that his scientists make the option of the bomb a reality: developing the nuclear fuel cycle with uranium enrichment and plutonium extraction, i.e., technology for making the materials for the bomb, but not yet deciding to build the bomb itself. Ayatollah Khomeini stopped the nuclear programme, which he declared un-Islamic. It was revived during the war with Iraq. Iraq had attacked Iran and used chemical weapons several times, yet there were no international sanctions against the aggressor, who had broken international law. On the contrary, East and West provided the dictator with weapons and material (including material for his nuclear and chemical weapons programmes). Attempts by the Iranian navy to disrupt the oil exports of the Arab states allied with Iraq resulted in a conflict with the US Navy. The tragic low point was the downing of an Iranian civil aircraft with 250 passengers on board by an American warship. Iran's original motivation was driven by security, triggered by isolation that threatened the country's existence. The memory of elected president Mossadegh (1953) being ousted with the support of the US was still alive. With the consolidation of the Islamic Republic, concerns increased elsewhere that nuclear weapons could become an instrument of Iran's regional power politics and a threat to Israel. Following the revelations of 2002, Iran refused to collaborate unconditionally with the International Atomic Energy Agency (IAEA). From 2006 on, the Security Council imposed increasingly harsh sanctions which were reinforced by additional US and EU embargoes. As early as 2004, three EU countries undertook diplomatic efforts, and were later joined by the EU with its High Representative for Foreign Affairs, and subsequently also by the US, Russia, and China.

The Bush Administration simultaneously rejected moderate Iranian president Khatami's offer of cooperation – hoping for regime change. Instead, the extremist Ahmadinejad was elected president. In the meantime, Iranian enrichment capacity was growing; the enrichment level had increased to the threshold of militarily relevant 'high enrichment', and the heavy water reactor in Arak, which was ideally suited to produce plutonium, was nearing completion. Iran was inching its way toward weapons capabilities.

Fears were strongest in Israel. Ever since the Islamic Revolution, the Iranian discourse had called Israel 'the Zionist entity' and denied its right to exist. 'Death to Israel' was the slogan at Friday prayers. This was not empty talk: Israel's direct foes, Hizbollah, Hamas, and Islamic Jihad, were receiving weapons (Hizbollah also training) from Iran. Israel was not anticipating a direct nuclear attack by Iran, but instead expecting a policy of constant provocations through political, military, and terrorist pressure, which could bring about a direct military confrontation. Two nuclear powers with medium-range missiles: maximum danger of escalation.

The Gulf States envisioned coercive pressure on their policies and the mobilisation of their Shiite minorities. Egypt and Turkey were troubled by the regional ambitions of Iran as a nuclear-weapon state (NWS). The US were concerned about Iran, in possession of nuclear weapons, controlling the Strait of Hormuz. Instead of stable deterrence, they expected destabilisation of the political and military situation with high risks of escalation.

Besides diplomatic initiatives, there were covert operations: cyber warfare against the enrichment facility and targeted killings of Iranian nuclear scientists. Both the US and Israel repeatedly threatened military strikes against Iranian nuclear facilities. Their chances of success were uncertain, but greater than zero. Yet it was unclear whether all Iranian facilities were known. The Iranian weapons arsenal and Tehran's ability to provide more weapons to its allied terrorist organisations and to 'let them loose' highlighted the risk of retaliation. The Israeli and US governments considered a military strike a disfavoured option as a last resort.

The negotiations linked security interests with demands for justice on both sides: Iran demanded to be treated just as any other non-nuclear-weapon state (NNWS) in accordance with the Nuclear Non-Proliferation Treaty (NPT) and claimed the right to plan its own fuel cycle as a sovereign state, especially a 'right to enrich' – precisely the same position that the Federal Republic of Germany had defended with much emotion from 1968 to the 1990s. From an Iranian perspective, unequal standards, which were in any case enshrined in the NPT with the different rights and duties of states with and without nuclear weapons, were contradictory to a just world order. For this reason, Tehran felt the sanctions to be unfair and demanded that they be lifted without it making any concessions. The West, in contrast, saw Iran as breaking the rules and having a responsibility to make extraordinary concessions in order to regain lost confidence.

Following years of fruitless talks, Iranian delaying tactics, feigned concessions and their retraction, offers put forward by Iran's negotiation partners, which Tehran then reviewed for a long time only to reject them, American threats, and much frustration, Hassan Rouhani became president of Iran in August 2013. His campaign promises included cautiously improving relations with the West and an end to the sanctions. George W. Bush, the neoconservative doctrinarian, was no longer in the White House, prudent Barack Obama, who was willing to compromise, having succeeded him. The negotiations gained new momentum.

In the spring of 2015, Iran and the IAEA agreed on a 'road map' for clarifying the open questions concerning the nuclear programme, especially its military dimension. At the same time, a framework for a final treaty was agreed: significant limitations, but no total ban on Iranian enrichment; unprecedented transparency; and complete lifting of the sanctions. Thorny details were yet to be negotiated.

Finally, in June 2015, the negotiation partners announced their outcome, the JCPOA. It was met with a mostly positive response, but also with criticism, scepticism, and concern by Israeli political circles and angry opposition by the Republicans in the US. The hardliners in Iran criticised the alleged sellout of Iranian interests. Yet the opposition in the US Senate did not succeed in overturning the treaty. The compromise also passed the Iranian Majlis (parliament) after Ali Khamenei, Leader of the Islamic Revolution, declared his support.

Iran has accepted strong limits on its current and future nuclear R&D. It will suspend its work on advanced types of centrifuges for enrichment, refrain from new enrichment technologies (lasers), drastically reduce the number of operating centrifuges, mothball the enrichment facility Fordow, and alter the Arak reactor so that it is no longer suitable for producing weapons-grade plutonium.

The JCPOA has put the toughest-ever verification system in place for a country not defeated in war. The IAEA is monitoring all of Iran's obligations arising from the NPT and the JCPOA. Iranian nuclear scientists can be interrogated. The IAEA can demand access to military bases if necessary. If Iran refuses to grant inspection of bases, the Joint Commission (JC) of the negotiation partners reaches a decision with a simple majority. That gives the West the decision-making power, as the US, France, the UK, Germany, and the EU can outvote Iran, China, and Russia. Iran's nuclear-related imports and exports are dependent on approval by the Procurement Working Group, the 'procurement channel' – each member of the commission has veto power. The sanctions enter into force again if one of the parties to the JC, which is a Permanent Member of the UN Security Council, suspects that Iran has broken the rules.

Some of these special provisions will last for 25 years, and others have no time limitation, for example the unprecedented ban on specific steps toward nuclear weapons research and the right of the IAEA to monitor this ban. Iran's renunciation of nuclear weapons and all types of reactors except light-water reactors and its promise to ship all spent nuclear fuel out of the country are not limited in time.

The amount of information available to the IAEA and the partners to the agreement will increase steadily. Attempts by Iran to break the rules will be recognised early on. The Damocles sword of sanctions will hang over Iran for 10–15 years. The agreement also provides the opportunity to improve relations between Iran and the West and for Iran to become integrated into the global economy. However, Iran is not subject to any limitations on its 'revolutionary foreign policy'.

The language of the JCPOA suggests equal footing, respect, recognition among equals. Iran was granted the recognition and the respect that it wanted and needed for its perception of its status and prestige. It was treated like a state with equal sovereignty. The symbolic concessions made are of great importance to the Iranians. After 10–15 years, Iran will have the same status as a normal NNWS in the NPT, with a few exceptions. It has achieved its coveted status of just recognition.

In substance, however, the agreement is unequal; the burden is on Iran's shoulders; the procedures give the West the decision-making power. The West conceded what could not be prevented: Iran is 'permitted' to enrich to a limited extent and will be rid of the sanctions. Otherwise, the West got what it wanted: retributive justice by means of the singular limitations on Iran's nuclear activities and the IAEA's transparency and verification measures. Thus, the optimum for regional and Western security has been reached.

The significance of the rays of hope

The examples illustrate the opportunities for reasonable, sustainable world politics in two different situations. The Paris Agreement shows that conflicts between states do not necessarily have to prevent agreement in individual areas that are decisive for first-order sustainability. Numerous adversaries were involved: Russia, the US, and the EU – rivals in Eastern Europe; China and the US – adversaries in Southeast and East Asia; India and Pakistan – foes in South Asia; many parties to the battles in Syria and Iraq, etc. Yet the factors mentioned made it possible to bundle interests in this way and to satisfy the various demands for justice.

The Iran conflict was about a second-order sustainability problem: a burning conflict about the most dangerous weapon in the world, which could have wreaked havoc on the entire Middle East and would have made any attempts to create first-order sustainability there futile for decades. Here, too, there were common interests – preventing war and opening up economic opportunities. But what mattered was finding common ground for opposing interests *and* demands for justice. That was accomplished through skilful negotiating and wording and the considerable rationality of the decisive actors, Iran and the US.

Both examples demonstrate that it can work. The prior deliberations warn: it will get more difficult. Analysis of the past ten years shows that of all the bad news, the advancement of political irrationality is the worst development. The Paris Agreement and the JCPOA illustrate that success is impossible in the absence of rational people in leadership. World politics is not an automatic development resulting from structures and interests, but the result of human action. Unfortunately, it seems that both democracies and autocracies are increasingly choosing to be led by individuals and movements hostile to reason.

A wake-up call to mobilise civil society

Klaus Wiegandt

Against the background of my professional experience as a corporate executive, and the intensive dialogue with the scientific community in the context of my work with my foundation Forum für Verantwortung that has followed since 2000, I would like to formulate a wake-up call to mobilise civil society. In the process, I will take a closer look at obstacles that must be overcome, but also perspectives that must be appreciated if the future is to be shaped successfully. Neither have been granted sufficient attention so far.

Sustainability – first and foremost a cultural matter

For decades, most decision-makers in the political and business communities around the world have been convinced that they can solve all the large-scale problems in the field of sustainability by means of dynamic economic growth and technological innovations. The elites in the business and political communities are guided by the notion that, in the end, we will succeed in using efficiency gains to absolutely decouple economic growth on the one hand from resource and energy consumption on the other. Yet this hope is improbable in the long run, as long as the political community refuses to force ecologically true prices for natural resources. For at current price levels, both pent-up demand in emerging markets and developing countries and the rebound effect, caused by the wasteful consumption and lifestyles of the global consumer middle class, eat up most of the efficiency gains.

Sustainability concerns cultural questions first and foremost: we cut down and burn down rainforests, annihilate biodiversity, externalise costs and thus facilitate unscrupulous exploitation of limited resources and sinks, widen the gap between rich and poor both between and within societies, contaminate the oceans, crave short-term profit maximisation, and enjoy wasteful consumption and lifestyles.

All these negative developments first and foremost raise the question as to cultural responsibility. In the area of climate mitigation, technological innovations – for example, the invention of an economical energy storage device as well as dematerialisation of our world of products – can make it significantly easier to reach at least the goal of limiting global warming to two degrees, but they are not absolute prerequisites. We can and must cut 50% of today's energy consumption through changes in behaviour by 2050, for the idea of replacing 80 to 90% of fossil fuels by renewables by the middle of this century will also prove impossible to achieve. Despite the encouraging expansion of the use of renewables in the form of electricity generation through wind power and photovoltaics, their share of global total electricity generation is still less than 1%. This fact should make clear to everyone that if most fossil fuels are to be replaced by wind and solar energy, hydropower, and biofuels in the distant future, this effort would require an enormous amount of resources and have to overcome immense problems of societal acceptance.

It also helps us to understand why all the important developments in the field of sustainability have continued to evolve in the wrong direction since the United Nations' 1987 Brundtland Report, despite all the global efforts and countless environmental summits and conventions. All of humankind is further away from sustainability than ever before. The UN had recognised these interdependencies and declared 2005–2014 to be the decade of 'Education for Sustainable Development' (ESD) under the auspices of UNESCO. Unfortunately, efforts during those ten years were not successful in moving even a single country in the world to mandate integration of ESD in its educational system, including kindergarten, schools, universities, and adult education outside of schools. For me, it has been and still is one of my greatest disappointments of the last decade that I have been unable to convince even a single government of the German federal states of the importance of education for sustainable development, despite all my personal efforts. If ESD had been made obligatory at least in the democracies directly following the major environmental summit in Rio in 1992, then it is highly probable that there would be significantly more understanding today of how to secure sustainability in these societies.

At least the global development at the grassroots of our societies is encouraging. And civil society in many countries – by no means only in the rich ones – is increasingly willing to change its lifestyles and styles of consumption and economic activity to achieve more sustainability. The 'Transition Town' movement has spawned initiatives worldwide, and it is not unusual for them to impact municipal governments; the 'Degrowth' movement is attracting substantial attention in Europe, as have the more than 1,500 companies that have now committed themselves to the *Gemeinwohlökonomie*, the 'economy for the common good'.

Numerous social movements over the course of history have shown that if societal change is to be successful and permanent, it must always come from below, from the civil societies. And it takes staying power to achieve change reaching the level of society's decision-makers.

We urgently need a politically initiated, scientifically supported discourse about sustainability in and with civil society. It is for the citizens of a country to decide the answer: how would we like the world of tomorrow to be?

The growth imperative

Economic growth has become a practically sacrosanct ideology worldwide that dominates all other societal goals. This growth entails well-nigh insatiable resource and energy consumption – with all its consequences for the environment and future generations. Rachel Kyte, former vice president of the World Bank, expressed the business and finance world's elites' frame of mind on this matter in a nutshell: 'To talk about anything other than how to grow is a non-starter.' One of the main drivers of economic growth, short-term profit maximisation, has become increasingly important globally since the end of the competition between the systems of the East and the West in the early 1990s, especially in the area of publicly owned businesses, and has massively undermined long-term perspectives in companies.

Today, nobody seriously disputes the imperative of the emerging markets and developing countries to promote economic growth as a precondition for generating prosperity to satisfy at least the basic needs of their populations. But the development in these countries is following the unsustainable blueprints of the industrialised countries in the areas of both consumption and infrastructure. The wasteful consumption and lifestyles of the so-called consumer middle class, which now encompasses more than a billion people in the emerging markets and developing countries, are no different from those in the industrialised countries.

But the industrialised nations also claim a right to economic growth despite saturated markets, mostly employing arguments that cannot lead to results because the problems are, in the end, of a cultural-ethical nature. For example, is our current national income sufficient to achieve more equitable distribution? Or are the industrialised countries forced to realise higher tax yields through greater economic growth, even though sufficient tax revenues could be achieved even today if the tax system were more just?

What is unacceptable and incompatible with the principles of sustainable development, however, are the methods of the publicly traded businesses for generating growth in saturated markets:

- They make every effort day by day to generate new consumer needs. Most of these needs have no relationship to quality of life. I personally estimate that at least 20% of our gross national product now consists of junk, which represents a pure waste of resources and energy.

- My view is supported by the ballooning of companies' advertising budgets around the globe. After all, these new products cannot be sold without massive amounts of advertising. A US study from the late 1990s illustrates the success of advertising strategies. When asked about the success of their advertising, 80% of the CEOs of major companies responded that they used it to sell products that consumers do not need. And an incredible 51% stated that they sold products that consumers did not want to have. So it is not surprising that global advertising spending now amounts to more than 600 billion US dollars per year.

- Another step toward making sure that growth takes place in saturated markets is the attempt to seduce consumers to live beyond their means. Easy-access consumer loans were developed for this purpose. Two figures illustrate their success in the past and present. Consumers in the US are now roughly 2,500 billion US dollars in debt; in the UK, consumer debt amounts to about 1,500 billion pounds.

- The opportunity to get away with externalising costs also creates room for growth.

- There are clear grounds to believe that obsolescence by design is widespread: as early as the design phase of products, components are identified that are to wear out prematurely.

- Efforts to produce more and more products that cannot be repaired pursue the same goal – discarding products and buying new ones increases sales.
- A final example of creating wasteful sales concerns electronics. Businesses have succeeded in seducing, in particular, younger consumers to consider their mobile phones outmoded after a year or two and to buy new ones. Today, 1.2 billion mobile phones are sold per year.

These examples show the unscrupulous waste of resources and energy on our planet in order to achieve growth in saturated markets year after year.

Whoever emits CO_2 must pay

Climate change has become the greatest sustainability challenge of this century. Valuable years have been allowed to lapse since the Earth Summit in Rio in 1992, and instead of reducing annual CO_2 emissions from 22 billion tons at the time to 21 billion tons in 2012, we are now at over 35 billion tons per year. And an end of increasing resource and energy consumption, and thus of rising CO_2 emissions, is not in sight.

Over the next 20 years, the global population will grow by another 2.5 billion people. Another three billion people in emerging markets and developing countries will rise to join the so-called consumer middle class. And according to Dirk Messner of the German Development Institute, the infrastructure investments in Asia will be on a scale corresponding to 2.5 times the amount of all infrastructure investments in Europe since the year 1800.

Climatologists estimate that there is still a window of

opportunity of 10 to 15 years during which the course toward slower climate change must be set if at least the goal of limiting global warming to two degrees is to be reached. In all probability, it will be too late after that because of the threat of irreversible developments. Against this background, I would like to make a few critical remarks on the Paris Agreement without calling its positive momentum into question.

Apart from the numerous uncertainties concerning countries' commitments and the enhancements of the Agreement every five years, two weaknesses must be emphasised which, if not addressed, make it difficult to imagine how global warming is to be limited to 1.5°C.

First, effective climate mitigation is impossible with the currently planned climate fund of 100 billion US dollars per year. Both a McKinsey report and the Stern Report of 2006/07 demonstrated that successful climate mitigation policy can be realised only if at least 1% of gross world product is spent on it by 2050 – at the time of the reports, this corresponded to roughly 500 billion US dollars, at the time of writing to 750 billion. The authors of both reports agree that if we do not make these investments today, then remediating the damage due to climate change in later decades will cost many times this amount, to the extent that they can be remedied at all.

The greatest weakness of the Climate Agreement is the failure of the 196 states to agree to a global minimum price for CO_2 emissions that is binding for all areas of the economy and accordingly to enshrine a global cap-and-trade system in the agreement. The 'cap' is the upper limit of all that can be emitted in a specified period, and 'trade' is the trade in emission rights. Announcing a constantly increasing minimum price and a stepwise reduction of the cap would create predictability for companies either to invest in reducing emissions or to spend the money on purchasing additional certificates (rights to emit a ton of CO_2).

Of course, consistently putting a price on all CO_2 emissions would mean that products and services with high emissions would over time become drastically more expensive for consumers, too. If we wish to provide effective climate mitigation policy using market-based means, then this is a promising path to significantly reduce particularly unsustainable areas such as coal-fired electricity, air travel for tourism, cruises, or gas guzzlers.

Sale of certificates would be a constantly increasing revenue stream for governments. However, there must be a strict requirement to spend these monies exclusively on climate mitigation policy. These additional revenues could be used, among other things, to design the system of increasing electricity, heating, and mobility costs in a socially acceptable way, to transfer funds from the rich countries to the poorer ones, and to finance the 'forest options', which I shall go into later in more detail.

Whoever emits CO_2 has to pay – the counterproductive revival of coal shows how important this principle is. Contrary to all expectations, we are currently experiencing a global renaissance of coal. New coal-fired power plants begin operation every week and are expected to generate electricity for 40 years. Just prior to the Paris Summit, Ottmar Edenhofer, Chief Economist of the Potsdam Institute for Climate Impact Research, warned repeatedly and urgently against this renaissance: If only one-third of the planned new coal-fired power plants with an output of 1,000 gigawatts were to go on line, then, together with the already existing coal-fired power plants, they would emit so much CO_2 that this alone would cause two degrees of global warming. Besides Hans-Werner Sinn, Edenhofer is one of the strongest and most renowned proponents of a global cap-and-trade system.

In Germany, the share of green electricity has grown to an encouraging 30%. Yet the expected CO_2 reductions have not come about because the percentage of coal-fired electricity has increased at the same time. This development will continue as long as the price of coal remains so low on the world market.

Of course, it is obvious that a binding cap-and-trade system for the entire economy is not politically feasible in the short term – the long, intensive preliminary negotiations to the Paris Agreement made that clear. The difficulty of the situation is highlighted by the breathtaking challenge of leaving 80% of all known coal deposits and 40% of all oil and gas resources in the ground if we are serious about the goal of limiting global warming to 2°C – not to mention 1.5°C. Despite this insight, the 200 largest publicly owned energy companies are investing more than 600 billion US dollars per year in exploration of new oil and gas fields because the value of their stock is still decisively determined by successfully exploiting them.

Forest options as climate mitigation milestones

Radical changes in lifestyle as well as patterns of consumption and wasteful production cannot be achieved short term and would also be irresponsible in relation to social policy. They would cause mass unemployment in many countries and result in social and political upheaval. But the introduction of a global, effective cap-and-trade system would be a mammoth and time-consuming political task, as would be the global introduction of ecologically true prices. Societies need more time for all these challenges in order to guarantee a socially compatible transformation of the global economy toward sustainability and climate mitigation.

Yet in the current circumstances, we do not have this time. According to the findings of climate research, the course toward restricting climate change must be set within the next 10 to 15 years. If this does not come about, then irreversible, dangerous climate change will be likely.

The so-called forest options could open the required window of opportunity. They have been recommended for more than two decades, especially by forestry scientists. The New York Declaration on Forests was adopted and approved by dozens of states, 30 of the world's largest companies, and more than 50 civil-society organisations at the UN Climate Summit in New York in 2014. The declaration explicitly assigns the forest options an extremely important role in limiting global warming to 2°C, especially as they are one of the most comprehensive and cost-effective solutions available today for reducing CO_2 emissions. This is all the more true since the Paris summit favours limiting global warming to 1.5°C.

The Paris Agreement again recognises forest conservation as well as worldwide afforestation as biotic approaches to possible emission reductions or removal of CO_2 from the atmosphere and as important instruments.

The measures

1. Rain forest preservation
If the cutting down and burning down of the rain forests were brought to an end, this would reduce CO_2 emissions by three billion tons per year. At the same time, it would make a major contribution to preserving biodiversity and stopping the irreversible process of destroying the rain forests. According to US scientists' calculations, just under 50 billion US dollars would have to be raised per year to compensate the emerging economies and developing countries for losses of income.

2. A worldwide afforestation programme
A February 2016 study by forest scientists Bernhard Felbermeier, Michael Weber, and Reinhard Mosandl of the Institute of Silviculture, Technical University of Munich, Germany, examines the feasibility of a global afforestation programme in depth. In

summary, the following image emerges: from mid-century on, up to five billion tons of CO_2 could be eliminated from the atmosphere per year. A large part of the afforestation programme could be realised without negative albedo effects on an area of approximately 200 million hectares in the tropics.

Such a global afforestation programme would provide many positive impulses for rural and economic development, especially in the emerging markets and developing countries, for example by creating new jobs and preventing erosion. Major opportunities also result for bioeconomic development.

The authors of the study found that the opportunity exists to eliminate an additional two billion tons of CO_2 from the atmosphere by reforesting degraded forests and managing existing forests sustainably.

Implementation of such a programme, they believe, should take place in a subsidiary fashion because of the heterogeneous local and cultural conditions. Alongside a global afforestation programme, functioning forestry management systems in the partner countries should be supported to ensure long-term success. This might be coordinated by a global 'afforestation agency' – imaginable under the aegis of the UN/FAO.

Financing could be provided in the medium term entirely through global emissions trading, in the short term mostly through tax revenues.

The forest options are recommended in the Paris Agreement, but for the time being, it is up to individual countries to decide when and how to use them. Putting a stop to the cutting and burning down of the rain forests, as well as a worldwide afforestation programme, necessitates rapid and coordinated approaches under the leadership of the UN, not least because of the financial means these programmes require. For this reason, it would be misguided to leave the biotic approach to climate mitigation up to the commitment of individual states and civil-society actors. At present, no comparable programs exist which would secure a limitation of global warming to 1.5°C long term. The price: approximately 150 billion US dollars per year for twenty years for an afforestation programme as well as 50 billion US dollars per year long term to protect the rain forests. Besides the climate mitigation impacts, it would also be a significant contribution to preventing people becoming climate refugees in the coming decades.

In terms of governance, it would be desirable for Germany to take a pioneering role, as with the transformation of the energy system, and to organise the relevant communities of interests (clubs) for the forest options. The EU would have to first place them on its agenda and then promote them in the G20. It should be possible to get China and the US, the two heavyweights and drivers of growth, on board for the biotic solution. In recent decades, China has already forested areas as large as Great Britain.

In summary, the forest options are the only available and practicable means to enable effective emission reductions relatively quickly without causing mass unemployment at the same time. And they would buy time to enable societies to restructure toward effective climate mitigation in a more socially acceptable way, while also making it possible not to miss the window of opportunity for climate mitigation. However, the forest options are not a means for companies, consumers, and the political community to gain absolution. They must be added to the Paris Agreement. And in all likelihood, they would prevent politicians having to resort to radical measures in panic in 10 to 15 years, if it became apparent that we would exceed 2°C global warming as early as 2050 despite the Paris Agreement.

Taking a chance on more democracy

Most sustainability challenges are of a cultural nature. Mastering or solving many problems would in principle not require new technological innovations. The transformation of democratic societies toward sustainability could have taken shape long ago if the potentials of democracy had been used by the civil societies to any extent at all.

For example, only about 1% of the German population is prepared to engage actively in a political party. Yet in democracies, this is one of the most essential and most promising ways to exert influence and design policies according to the needs of broad strata of the population. It can be achieved by founding a new 'party of the progressive forces' or by several hundred thousand active progressive people joining the currently existing parties. After all, less than 30% of current party members can be assumed to be politically active today. In addition, people can approach their elected representatives, confront them with the urgent questions, and demand answers.

A third way to take a chance on more democracy in climate mitigation would be the endeavour to initiate and organise a mass protest movement under the umbrella of climate mitigation, first at the national level and growing beyond it later. In Germany alone, there are several million progressive citizens who are actively working toward a sustainable world of tomorrow in different ways, and many of them are members of relevant organisations such as BUND (Friends of the Earth Germany), NABU (Nature and Biodiversity Conservation Union), or the two major churches. If it becomes manifest to these progressive forces that all individual interests would be sidelined in the event of unchecked climate change, then this would be the opportunity to unify them under the umbrella of climate mitigation. This would be a first spectacular step toward a wake-up call for politicians.

In his book *America the Possible: Manifesto for a New Economy* (2012), James Gustave Speth called for precisely this networking of all progressive forces in the US under the umbrella of climate mitigation and has committed himself to working toward this goal during his retirement. Naomi Klein rightly points out that recognising and proclaiming crises is not limited to politics in her newest book, *This Changes Everything: Capitalism Vs. the Climate* (2014). A 'planetary emergency' can also be placed on the global agenda by a mass protest movement of broad strata of society.

Discouraged after fighting for successful climate mitigation policy for decades, a number of scholars including Dennis Meadows, Jørgen Randers, and Stephen Emmott openly acknowledge that humanity will react only when every individual can feel and see the consequences of climate change – but then it will be too late. They assume that, at the end of this century, the Earth will provide conditions fit for only a few billion human beings.

I do not share this cultural pessimism, yet I too have little hope any more that decisive impulses for climate mitigation will come from the political community. Galvanising civil societies is the probably most promising way to force a change of direction departing from the 'business as usual' on our planet.

However, I am convinced that this can succeed only if people are shown fully and clearly where the current course will likely lead by the end of the century, even for our grandchildren. If this is to happen, then scientists must also give up their posture of being uninvolved analysts, as Hans Joachim Schellnhuber explains in his book: 'For moral reasons, it is imperative that the messages from the sciences enter into the awareness of decision-makers to such an extent that they have a clear understanding of the fact that they must decide between certain options.'[1] This is all the more true for the broad strata of the population.

---

1   Hans Joachim Schellnhuber, *Selbstverbrennung*

Social scientists in particular, however, warn against providing full and clear information to the public at large. They fear that people would then either be in a state of shock and unable to act or would act hedonistically in order to enjoy the world to the full one last time.

I do not share this view. If people really become aware of the likely consequences of 4 to 6°C of global warming and recognise at the same time that it is still in our power today to at least limit global warming to 2°C without throwing society back to the Stone Age, then I believe they would be prepared to finally take on their roles in climate mitigation, both as consumers and as citizens. For in light of all the uncertainty as to what a world with 4 to 6°C global warming would look like at the end of this century, the presumably greatest dangers for the then approximately ten billion people can be derived from the laws of physics alone.

A 1°C increase in global warming results in a 7% increase in evaporation of ocean waters, or 100 trillion more litres of water per day.[2] In the case of 6°C global warming, an additional 600 trillion litres of water per day would have to rain down on parts of our planet. Extreme droughts in other parts of the world would dry out soils completely. In addition, the danger would arise that there would be no monsoon in Asia for several years; it would instead rain down on other regions during this time. Increasing the amounts of water vapour and energy in the atmosphere compared with current levels will cause chaotic processes in the atmosphere, and with a probability bordering on certainty.

The possible consequences of all this for agricultural food production cannot even be imagined. In this respect, the probability that billions of people will have to fight for food and water on a daily basis at the end of this century and that far too many will starve to death is not an entirely unrealistic scenario. But 8°C

---

2   Schellnhuber, *Selbstverbrennung*

global warming cannot be ruled out completely, either. The non-linear physical impacts of such a development are beyond what we can envisage today.

A number of renowned politicians, especially in the US, have often argued that it would be irresponsible to invest trillions of dollars in climate mitigation as long as the scientific community is working with probabilities. Whoever argues in this way fails to recognise that there are not and cannot be absolutely certain statements about future developments. For this reason, we must decide on the basis of current scientific data whether we want to risk the occurrence of tipping points in the climate system in this century, with catastrophic impacts in the case of 4 to 6°C global warming.

Of course, it cannot be ruled out, even if it is very unlikely, that the development for all of humanity will be less dire. But even then, the investment of roughly 1% of gross world product in climate mitigation per year would not be an irresponsible waste, in particular with respect to future generations.

Even setting aside all the impacts of global warming, measures to reduce CO_2 emissions are investments in a sustainable society. The atmosphere's increasing concentration of CO_2 is responsible for ocean acidification, which is putting massive pressure on marine communities. Burning down rainforests is wiping out biodiversity to an unimaginable extent. And our exorbitant consumption of fossil fuels is burning valuable resources, especially oil, that will no longer be available to future generations for much more rational uses. In other words, it would be absolutely inexcusable in ethical and moral terms to permit unchecked climate change.

Yet before the consequences of unchecked climate change pose practically unsolvable problems for all of humanity, climate refugees will endanger political stability in some parts of the world. The population in Africa will grow by another billion people by 2050, and the UN is even expecting it to increase to 4 billion by the end of the century. Progressing global warming with its consequences for agriculture and drinking water are hitting Africa especially hard. Scientists such as Dennis Meadows predict that 200 million Africans will overrun Europe and 300 million Chinese, Siberia, as climate refugees in the next 30 years. If only one-quarter of this were to come about, it would amount to a political earthquake in Europe; after all, two to three million refugees are plunging the European Union into an existential crisis today.

Our grandchildren, who will be facing the strongest impacts, can only hope that their parents and grandparents are not willing to hazard the consequences of unchecked climate change for the planet, but will finally begin to use the opportunities of democracy to force an effective change of direction.

Author biographies

Klaus Hahlbrock, Prof. em. Dr. rer. nat., Max Planck Institute for Plant Breeding Research in Cologne, former Vice President of the Max Planck Society, emeritus since 2002.

Dr. Friedrich Hinterberger has been the Founding President of the Sustainable Europe Research Institute in Vienna since 1999.

Dr. Jill Jäger, internationally active independent consultant, has worked with numerous international research institutes.

Stefan H. E. Kaufmann, Director, Max Planck Institute for Infection Biology, Berlin, and Professor of Immunology and Microbiology, Charité Berlin.

Mojib Latif, Professor at Kiel University, Head of the Research Division: Ocean Circulation and Climate Dynamics, GEOMAR Helmholtz Centre for Ocean Research Kiel.

Wolfram Mauser, Professor of Geography and Remote Sensing at Ludwig-Maximilians-Universität (LMU) München.

Bernd Meyer, Professor of Economics at Osnabrück University (retired) and Director of Research at the Institute for Economic Structures Research (GWS) until 2015; member of the Resources Commission at the German Federal Environment Agency.

Prof. Dr. Harald Müller, former Executive Director of the Peace

Research Institute Frankfurt (PRIF) and Prof. emeritus of International Politics and Peace Research, Goethe University Frankfurt am Main.

Rainer Münz, adviser to the think tank EPSC of the President of the European Commission and teaches at the Central European University in Budapest.

Dr. Ines Omann, senior researcher at the Helmholtz Centre for Environmental Research (Leipzig) and works independently mentoring and moderating transformation processes.

Stefan Rahmstorf, Professor of Physics of the Oceans, Potsdam University, and directs the research domain Earth System Analysis, Potsdam Institute for Climate Impact Research.

Josef H. Reichholf, Dr. rer. nat., until 2010 director of the Vertebrata Department, Bavarian State Collection of Zoology; taught nature conservation at the Technical University of Munich.

Albert F. Reiterer, retired demographer, social scientist, and statistician, currently active in civil society.

Katherine Richardson, Professor of Biological Oceanography, Copenhagen University, directs the Sustainability Science Centre and is a member of the Danish Council on Climate Change.

Friedrich Schmidt-Bleek, nuclear chemist. He formerly co-directed the Wuppertal Institute for Climate, Environment and Energy with Ernst Ulrich von Weizsäcker and is, among other functions, President of the Factor 10 Institute in Carnoules, France.

Dr. Wolfgang Schuchert directs public relations at the Max Planck Institute for Plant Breeding Research in Cologne.

Prof. Dr.-Ing. Hermann-Josef Wagner, Professor for Energy Systems and Energy Economy, Ruhr-Universität Bochum. He is a member of the German National Academy of Sciences Leopoldina.

Klaus Wiegandt, founder and CEO of Forum für Verantwortung. He has published numerous books on the topic of sustainability with Fischer Taschenbuch Verlag.